STOKER

The Life of Hilda Matheson OBE
1888-1940

BY THE SAME AUTHOR

Britain In Pictures: A History and Bibliography
Published by Werner Shaw Ltd,
26 Charing Cross Road, (Suite 34)
London, WC2H 0DH

STOKER

The Life of Hilda Matheson OBE

1888–1940

MICHAEL CARNEY

Published by the Author

Published by Michael Carney
Pencaedu, Llangynog, SY10 0HA, Wales, UK.

First Published 1999

Copyright Michael Carney 1999
The right of Michael Carney to be identified as the author has been asserted in accordance with the Copyright Designs and Patents Act 1988.
All rights reserved
ISBN 0 9536391 0 X
Without limiting the rights under copyright reserved above no part of this publication may be reproduced, stored in or introduced into a retrieval system, or transmitted, in any form or by any means (electronic, mechanical, photocopying, recording or otherwise), without the prior written permission of the copyright owner. This book is sold subject to the condition that it shall not by way of trade or otherwise be lent, re-sold, hired out or otherwise circulated in any form of binding or cover other than that in which it is published without the publisher's prior consent.

Produced by Biddles Limited, Guildford GU1 1DA

Contents

Preface vii

One EarlyLife 1888–1926   1

Two In Love with the BBC 1926–28   23

Three Love Affair with Vita 1928–31   49

Four The End of Both Affairs 1928–31   63

Five An African Survey 1932–38   85

Six Another War 1939–40   109

Main Sources and Page Notes   138

Appendix Authors and Titles of BIP Books   157

Index   161

Preface

The Biography

Hilda Matheson never married and her only sibling, a brother, died childless, so the sort of material collected and preserved by families does not exist. Most of her contemporaries are dead and the few people still alive who met her know more about her working life than her family background. Her public life, however, was well documented, and one important aspect of her private life, her love for Vita Sackville-West, is described in more than 800 pages of letters. While the paucity of information about family life and upbringing might disappoint readers, I hope they will understand that its absence is not due to lack of interest or research on my part.

The Letters

As far as possible I wanted Hilda Matheson to speak for herself and I have quoted from the letters which reveal the intensity of her love and shed light on the rest of her life. In using the letters as an important source for many aspects of her life I have tried to keep a reasonable balance between the love affair, which lasted for only three years, and her very great contributions to the public life of this country over twenty-five years. The letters contain frank and unashamed descriptions of her homosexual feelings and frequent references to difficulties experienced by homosexual men and women. She did not see any need gratuitously to publicise her own sexual preferences, but she hated pretence and avoided lying about her sexuality. I have not tried to censor or bowdlerize the letters, my only reasons for omitting material being relevance, interest or pressure of space.

Quotations from the letters (and other sources) are printed in italic script. Sometimes I have put together within a single quotation sentences from different letters and this should be clear from the notes. I have also corrected misspellings when these were obviously not intended as such and changed some punctuation. She often used dashes instead of full stops or commas and while I have retained some of the dashes - particularly when they illustrate the sort of break-neck speed at which she lived - I have omitted many others. I do not think that any of these minor textual liberties falsifies or misrepresents what she wrote and readers who are keen to check can use the notes. I have not provided a modern glossary for words which have changed their customary usage since she wrote because her meaning is usually obvious from the text, but perhaps I should point out that her use of "queer" means something or someone odd in some way and "gay" means light-hearted, neither means homosexual.

The Notes

The notes contain references to all the sources used and provide supplementary information on some of the people mentioned in the text. When considering whether a note with biographical details was necessary my three criteria have been the importance of the person in Hilda Matheson's life, the need for additional personal information to supplement the incident described, and whether a person is now likely to be familiar or unfamiliar to the general reader. I doubt whether readers would want mini-biographies of people whose details are readily available in reference books.

Acknowledgements

I am especially grateful to three people who knew Hilda Matheson: Mr Nigel Nicolson loaned me the originals of all the letters from her to his mother, Vita Sackville-West, allowing me quote from them, and gave permission to reproduce the photograph by Howard Coster which forms the dust-jacket; Mrs Mary Bennett knew her as a great friend of her parents, Warden and Mrs H A L Fisher, and later worked for her during the Second World War in the Joint Broadcasting Committee; Mrs Sheila Dickinson, then Sheila Shannon, also worked for Hilda Matheson during that war helping to edit the series of books known as "Britain In Pictures". All three went out of their way to help and I thank them.

For permission to use and quote from material for which they are copyright holders I would like to thank Lord Lothian and The National Archives for Scotland in respect of the Lothian papers; Sir John Astor, Sir Edward Ford and Mr Michael Bott, Keeper of Archives and Manuscripts at the University of Reading for the Astor papers; Mr Anthony Richards, Archivist at the Imperial War Museum and Mr T. Hill for the papers of Colonel Kell and others; The BBC and Mrs Jacqueline Kavanagh, Archivist at their Written Archives Centre, Reading for various BBC records; Mrs Clare Brown, Archivist at Rhodes House Library, Oxford for the Oldham, Perham and Pedler papers; the Principal and Fellows of St Anne's College Oxford for papers relating to the Society of Home Students; and Chatto and Windus Publishers for the Hogarth papers. The Master and Fellows of Balliol College Oxford gave me permission to consult the diaries of Harold Nicolson and HarperCollins Publishers gave permission to quote from them. Mr Fred Hunter loaned me his article on Hilda Matheson, Mr Bernard Keeling showed me an extract from his history of St Felix School, Southwold, and Mr and Mrs D K Green, Mrs Jean Furley-Smith and Mr J L F Buist helped me with information about the ministry of Hilda Matheson's father in Putney and Oxford. Alison Layland helped with proof reading

Extracts from my previous book, *Britain In Pictures: A History And Bibliography* have been included by kind permission of the publisher Werner Shaw Ltd.

I am grateful to all of them.

None of these people, of course, or the many others whose help I acknowledge in the notes, are responsible for the views expressed or for errors or omissions, all of which are my own.

MICHAEL CARNEY,
Llangynog, Powys
1999

Chapter One

EARLY LIFE
1888–1926

Introduction to a Forgotten Woman

Hilda Matheson's small, trim figure contained a spirit which soared above her contemporaries. Few men and women could resist for long the dash of her personality or the fluency of her tongue. Her intellect, too, was formidable and her knowledge encyclopaedic, but she was never a bluestocking. Her vivacity and charm accompanied by a sweet gravity in her character bewitched almost everyone she met. Some were intimidated, many more were entranced, and all had to acknowledge a person of exceptional ability.

At a time when few women had a working life outside the home, she had six successful careers. Whether working for MI5 and MI6 in two world wars, or acting as political secretary to the first woman in Parliament, or pioneering the art of broadcasting, or writing a weekly magazine column, or single-handedly organising a great academic survey, she showed the men how a job should be done. Perhaps that was why she did not conquer everyone. To John Reith, determined to stamp the BBC with his singular personality, she was little more than a traitor; to civil servants fighting to protect their departments during the Second World War she was a great nuisance; and Virginia Woolf hated her; but they were exceptions. Vita Sackville-West adored her, at least for a time. Cabinet ministers, writers, artists and poets sought her company. She was "the woman who knew everyone". Yet almost immediately after her death in 1940, at the age of 52, she dropped out of public memory. Now, nobody has heard of her. Why?

War, with its obscuring characteristics, was partly to blame. The blitz accounts for the small number attending her funeral and together with paper rationing probably explains the almost perfunctory obituaries. The fact that much of her work was done behind the scenes of public life, leaving others to take the credit, contributed to her later obscurity. She slaved in the service of ideas and other people, while giving little thought to self-publicity. Sometimes too her successes were achieved only after bitter struggles, and the record became cloaked by the hostility of those she worsted. So a great public servant, a woman who dazzled and delighted or infuriated those who knew her, and who in everything she did soon made herself notable, was forgotten as soon as she died.

To resurrect her fame and tell the story of her life is difficult. The Secret Service remains secretive about her work in both wars. This is not, one suspects, because what she did remains sensitive, but simply because it is the nature of the Service. Even now, nearly a hundred years after her first assignments, many details remain hidden, with no obligation ever to place them on public record.

Her work as Lady Astor's political secretary is almost as well concealed, not through malice, but simply because her contributions were made usually in Lady Astor's name, or through Lady Astor's voice.

The great *African Survey* of 1938 which she edited also appears under another name, that of Lord Hailey, though he was sick for much of the time and the Survey was planned and produced mainly by her. Indeed she became so adept at presenting the final material in Hailey's style that even he was not fully aware of how much of the writing was hers.

She was the first director of talks for BBC radio, but only historians of broadcasting now know her pioneering work. Marmaduke Hussey, shortly after he ended his period as chairman of the BBC governors, confessed that he had never heard of her. Yet during her time with the BBC she made headline news with her uncompromising determination to raise programme standards. She struggled hard to overcome the hostility, timidity and obstruction of politicians and newspaper proprietors towards the new medium of radio. Almost as fierce was her fight inside the BBC against the purveyors of a philosophy of broadcasting based on light entertainment. Her resignation, following a row with John Reith, was an event of high drama. Yet all these battles, together with her important contributions to broadcasting, have been hidden. The BBC did not retain her personal records and there is little of her inflammatory correspondence with Reith on file – it is possible that many of the exchanges between them never reached the official records. While Asa Briggs' *History of British Broadcasting* pays her a high tribute, the latest biography of Reith hardly mentions her at all and the BBC's own history of itself is silent on the subject. Dissidents within the BBC like those in the former USSR sometimes disappear.

One of the most visible records of her work is the wartime series of books "Britain In Pictures", but few people know because her name appears on only ten of the 126 books, those prepared for the printer during 1940, just before she died.

This public life was sufficiently distinguished to justify a biography, despite the paucity of record, but her personal life too was remarkable and, in one respect at least, better documented. While much of it remains obscure – she never married, had no children or sisters, and her only brother died childless, so few family papers have survived – she left behind one important record of her private life in the form of letters to her lover, Vita Sackville-West. Although the letters are primarily love letters in which she pours out her passion for Vita, they also provide an unrestrained commentary on her family and friends, on eminent acquaintances who were writers and politicians, and on Reith and other BBC colleagues with whom she did battle. They give a vivid account of some of the most important years of her life and make up for the lack of other records.

Her public and private lives show an attractive personality, complicated sometimes by conflict between the demands of the powerful positions she earned by her intellect and organising ability and the weaknesses of an unconfident nature at times too ready to surrender to others. She was ferociously energetic in her work and drove herself wildly, whatever her state of health, but was concerned for other people, making excuses for weaker colleagues unable to keep up. There was extraordinary clarity of purpose in everything she did, and she pursued her aims with single-mindedness and courage, yet she had little trust in herself or in her own tastes and abilities. Sometimes she was unscrupulous, but usually more in thought than action. Her powerful intellect was allied to very practical skills and interests, taking pleasure in mundane tasks such as getting things like boilers to start. She could appear totally dominant when working, but was completely submissive when loving. The modest, naive, unworldly, innocent, daughter of the manse delighted in her sexuality, and displayed sometimes an openness and sensual abandon that frightened the more experienced, but very much more prudent, Vita. Vita's pet name for her, Stoker, catches the mixture of cockiness and compliance in her personality as well as her readiness to get stuck into things. At work she powered forward relentlessly the tasks that needed to be done, while at home she cared for and cosseted her women friends to an extent that enslaved her to weak and strong alike. A friend commented that all her geese were swans, and she ended up always being their goose-girl.

Hilda Matheson was not a suffragette and except for any words she might put into the mouth of Lady Astor did not act as an ideologue for the women's movement. Her great contribution to women's rights was to demonstrate in positions usually reserved for men that a woman could be at least as effective. During her lifetime few women achieved high positions in any sphere outside the home, which makes her own success in several different jobs all the more remarkable.

Family and Early Years

Hilda Matheson was born on 7 June 1888 in the manse of the Presbyterian Church in Putney, south London. She was the first child of the minister the Reverend Donald Matheson and his wife Margaret (known as Meta), born in the second year of their marriage. Another child, Donald Macleod, was to be born eight years later. Both her parents were Scottish. The Mathesons, according to Hilda,

> *were foolish Highlanders who squandered money and never kept any very long and loved their own unproductive moors and islands,*

while her mother's family, the Orrs, belonged to the ambitious getting on sort of Scot. Hilda's affections lay with her "sweet and plucky" father, who seems to have been regarded by friends and colleagues as something of a saint. After studying at the universities of Cambridge, Edinburgh and Tubingen, he was called by the Putney congregation to his first job in 1879 when he was twenty-seven years old. Her mother was decent and intelligent and kind, but Hilda just didn't like her and felt that she had to escape. She said that she always felt a perfect brute about her mother, having no affection for her at all so far as she could discover. Meta represented too many of the attitudes Hilda would run miles from. As well as such admirable qualities as intelligence and a sense of duty there was,

> *hardness and ungenerosity and tyranny and intolerance and insensitivity,*

and it was not until Hilda was in her twenties that she freed herself from fear of her mother. In her letters the comments she made about her family showed always the deep affection for her father and strong dislike of her mother, while for her brother, who scarcely figures in them, her feelings appear gentle, but detached.

The Mathesons lived a comfortable middle class style of life. In addition to his stipend of £300 a year (equivalent to about £30,000 today), the Reverend Matheson had a share of his parents' marriage settlement trust fund. The annual income from the fund was sufficient to finance decent schools for his daughter and son, and nearly two years in France and Switzerland for the whole family as he recuperated from a nervous breakdown towards the end of his ministry in Putney. When he moved to Oxford in 1908 his stipend as chaplain to Presbyterian students was £500 a year, and a house was provided rent-free. His estate when he died in 1930 was valued at just over £20,000, an enormous sum at the time. After his death her mother suffered some shocks from falling investments – as did many during the nineteen thirties – but the family seems always to have enjoyed at least a modest sufficiency.

From the age of fourteen she attended St. Felix School, Southwold, founded in 1897 by the daughter of the historian S R Gardiner. Not surprisingly in view of its origin the teaching of history was especially strong and this was to be her main subject later at Oxford. The one time she took part in a sporting event at school was in 1906 when she was in a team of Liberals which played hockey against a team of Conservatives. Whether this was the only form of political activity allowed at St Felix in that historic election year is not known, but it was certainly the only event which the Conservatives won. Away from the hockey field and study she spent her time on stage, keeping the audience constantly amused with her performances of M. Jourdain in the 1905 production of Moliere's *Le Bourgeois Gentilhomme*, and Sir Charles Marlowe in Goldsmith's *She Stoops to Conquer* the following year, her last at school.

In a girls' school someone had to play the male roles, but whether she volunteered or was pushed is not known. She never at any time looked mannish and with her lovers she always took the submissive role, but there must have been something that set her apart from the girls, perhaps the driving energy which later characterised so much of her work and which to the extent she manifested it is not usually regarded as lady-like.

Her school remembers her even today, but in her letters her schooling doesn't figure at all, apart from a passing reference to a close friend. Until her father's breakdown in 1906 when she was eighteen she lived either in Putney, then little more than a village in which she moved from manse to manse as the church grew, or, during school terms, in Southwold. The quiet and ordered life at home would not necessarily have been dull, excitement of an intellectual kind being provided by her scholarly father and a lively church. Regular attenders at the Presbyterian services included the radical and Quaker John Bright of anti-corn law fame, Ramsay MacDonald the future prime minister who opened a church debate on socialism, the future Lord Hailsham who became Lord Chancellor in Baldwin's government of 1934, and Lady Christian Moule one of Queen Victoria's ladies-in-waiting. The Granard Society, a debating club named after the first church and founded in 1883, remained active for many years and Hilda was to speak in a debate there on "Broadcasting and Public Opinion" in 1934.

The distance, sometimes hostility, which she felt towards her mother were balanced by her fondness for her father. His influence was due less to prayer or preaching than to an essential holiness and a sense he gave of being close to God. He provided a calm centre in a household which under an unrestrained Meta could have been unsettled, but we do not know whether it was domestic or pastoral difficulties which caused the deterioration in his health which began at the end of 1903 and developed into a severe nervous breakdown. He was given six months' leave of absence in 1904 and after further periods of illness tendered his resignation in June 1906. He had married quite late in life at the age of thirty-four and his second child was not born until he was forty-four. The combination of a restrained, academic nature, a religious calling, and, perhaps, Meta, could have meant strains within the marriage. Equally, ministering to an expanding Nonconformist congregation would also have been uncomfortable. Day to day administration was not congenial and he did not hide his distaste for the demands made by the inevitable church building fund.

A new church costing over £8,000 was opened in 1897 with £3,000 still to be found, a large burden for a small congregation with scarcely 100 regular attenders on the communion roll. The loan was not paid off until 1919. He showed his repugnance for much of the work in his annual address to the congregation in 1896 when he spoke bleakly of the huge task ahead which would require the dreary labour of raising money and the patient discussion of endless details. Church records of the time, mainly the annual reports, disguise in committee language what must have been an unpleasant battle within the congregation. Once built, the joy of moving into a new church in 1898 was considerably reduced by defects of lighting and heating, which required the attention of the building committee for several years, and by the inability to clear the debt promptly. The over-emphatic way in which the Reverend Matheson attributed his resignation " ... to ill-health and to nothing else" indicates that there must have been some other grounds for leaving which his congregation could speculate about. Her father's breakdown disrupted Hilda's life in Putney and Southwold. She left school a year earlier than normal and joined her parents in France, Italy, Switzerland and Germany where she developed fluent Italian and good French and German.

Oxford

She was twenty when she joined the Society of Home Students in Oxford in the autumn of 1908. (The Society was an offspring of the Association for the Education of Women started in 1878.) At the time Hilda moved to Oxford, Lady Margaret Hall and Somerville Hall were providing teaching and accommodation for women students who wanted to live in, and the Society of Home Students provided similar education and support for women students who studied from home. None of these societies for women were then constituted as part of the university and it was not until 1920 that their students were allowed to graduate. In all other respects, however, they were Oxford colleges and their women students were becoming, slowly, part of university life.

A constant complaint of Hilda's tutors was that she lived far too full a life, and her studies suffered from this. Compared with student activities today, her life outside college walls which so alarmed her tutors seems tame. Hilda Matheson's own memory is that most of her social contacts outside of home centred on the Society and its formidable principal, Mrs B H Johnson, who arranged terminal teas and sometimes charades. Students who lived at home saw very little of those who lived in lodgings or in college. The university seemed to her, as no doubt to other women students who were excluded from full membership, something marvellous and remote. There were many fewer social and athletic societies, at least for women, than there were in 1930 when she recorded her recollections for a history of St. Anne's College. (St Anne's was the successor to the Society of Home Students.)

Nevertheless, as her contribution to the Society's history showed, there *was* a world outside tutorials and the lecture room and she joined it with enthusiasm. At their tiny house in the Turl, in the very heart of the University, she helped her parents entertain the students to whom her father was chaplain. As there was no chaplaincy building at that time, or even a Presbyterian chapel, their social and religious centre was the Matheson home. Like most new students they were often so shy that they never knew how to get themselves away, arriving for tea and staying until well after supper. It seems surprising that Meta was not able to shift them, but perhaps her tolerant husband and sociable daughter prevented her.

These fairly regular afternoons and evenings were fitted around her other activities. She was a keen and reliable hockey player and in her second year captained the team formed from all the women students. It was a year when the hockey club was put on a more secure basis, with fixed subscriptions and, as a result, greater activity and "much keenness" among the players. The annual report which comments on the changes does not say who was responsible, but there was never an activity involving Hilda Matheson which was not put on a more satisfactory footing during her tenure. People would invariably find her leadership a bracing experience, and would emerge considerably gingered up.

She was an ardent member of the Christian Union and sang regularly in the Bach choir, but while she never wavered in her commitment to Bach, becoming later a faithful member of the London choir, not even her father's example could sustain her religious faith which did not survive the First World War. Passions that might have made her a great missionary were transferred elsewhere.

Her expressive voice, allied to a strong literary feeling and a power of losing herself in a part, made her prominent in student dramatic productions. She made an unusually powerful impression on her audiences, many of whom recalled in detail years later the parts she played. There is an intensity about these recollections which goes beyond the normal courtesies of memorial comment, or the sometimes indulgent appreciation of good student acting. They convey something of the impact of her personality on other people, both on and off the stage.

As the young King Eagerheart in a Christmas play performed in a village hall in the Cotswolds, she had to visit the local pub before the performance in order to light her censer at its fire. One of her tutors recalled the effect on a group of awe-struck labourers as this young girl in a white tunic, wearing a circlet on her short golden hair and shrouded in incense, seemed to appear from another world. In another off-stage appearance she captivated a friend when she arrived for supper wearing her kingly robes,

> *her innocent earnest eyes gazing like the young King's on a vision beyond herself.*

These theatrical appearances in pubs and drawing rooms must have had more than a degree of calculation behind them, but the impression left on those who saw her was of a sweet, innocent, eager and earnest young girl. These are the words that appear again and again in the recollections of others about her Oxford days.

More powerful still was the effect she made playing the part of Andromache in a performance of *The Trojan Women*, given with the help and encouragement of Professor Gilbert Murray whose new translation was being used. Andromache is forced to surrender her infant son Astyanax to his murderers, and to do so without expressing resentment or hatred lest she deprive him of the rites of burial. The scene as she bade him farewell,

> Go, die, my best beloved, my cherished one, in fierce men's hands, leaving me here alone,

reduced the house to tears. The only person left unmoved was Astyanax himself, a cherubic looking boy called Pat Wild, who remained sublimely indifferent to his approaching fate and gladly allowed himself to be carried away by Greek soldiers. (Poor Astyanax was later a chaplain in the Dunkirk campaign of the Second World War and came home shell-shocked.) Those friends in the audience who later wrote about it obviously saw her as having in full measure the qualities of gravity, nobility and innocence that the part required her to present. In real life, of course, she would have saved Astyanax: he would live, either because of her passionate, unanswerable advocacy, or because she would die in his place.

Passion and self-sacrifice were the qualities present in all her personal relationships. In her love affairs, she would be the partner who sacrificed herself, putting first the other person and looking for ways to please, to mother and to nurse. Meta always claimed that the fact her daughter never married was not for want of suitors. Hilda was certainly attractive to men. Male friends and colleagues always commented approvingly on her appearance and H G Wells was later to make forceful overtures. This attraction was never, however, reciprocated by her. Whenever she fell in love, which she did several times, the object of her passion was in each case a woman.

There was a close friend at school, who was killed. In Oxford and for a year or two afterwards she was very much absorbed by someone she called "the vamp" and for whom she "would have done anything". She came to realise that this woman, who appeared on the outside to be all softness and helplessness, was fundamentally hard. Men fell in love with the vamp and she encouraged them, very much liking to have them as friends but not as anything else. Nevertheless the vamp married twice, her first husband committing suicide within a year of the marriage. Hilda had come across her during one of the vamp's many crises and felt sorry and protective, continuing to deal with the wreckage until the end of the First World War when the siren found other people to lean on. Her mother hated the creature, " ... which of course made me champion her more". There was never any "amorous dalliance" between them, Hilda being content to provide the tenderness which the woman always managed to elicit. She mattered to Hilda because she was a genius at accepting the help which Hilda was always ready to offer. Hilda's own thoughts or worries mattered very little. Whether the women Hilda Matheson loved were helpless, bringing out her sympathy, or strong, enabling her to lean on them, the relationship was always one of their dominance and her submission.

Her scholastic abilities held out the prospect of a first class degree, but she never had enough time for her work. Reading was done and essays written wildly against time, often in the hours that should have been given to sleep. She worked for the Honours History School, giving special attention to the Italian Renaissance period. Her tutors thought sufficiently well of her work to agree that she should embark on a new venture just introduced into the History syllabus, the presentation of a thesis as part of the work for the Final School. Reflecting her enthusiasm for Italy she chose to write about Savonarola, the puritanical scourge of fifteenth century Florence. His campaigns to rid Italy of corruption and sin, usually associated in his eyes with the arts or anything beautiful or pleasurable, led ultimately to his arrest, torture and execution. The thesis has not survived so we do not know whether her stance towards her subject was critical or approving, but the choice is interesting. She did not share in any way Savonarola's sort of puritanism which disdained art and beauty and sensuality. In poetry and music she loved sensuous qualities as well as precision of language and form: Byron, T S Eliot, Bach and Wagner were all favourites. In writing her thesis she lacked also some of Savonarola's single-mindedness. Because of her other activities the final script was not completed until the dark morning hours of the last day for its submission and had to be left outside her door for a friend to rush to the examiners while she slept off the effects of her all-night writing. In other respects, however, there was always something of Savonarola's earnest intensity in her own character and a good deal of his energy. Her later life amply displayed the single-mindedness also, but at Oxford she spread herself too widely and in the end got a good second.

The First World War and Secret Service

Her tutor in economic theory and history had been Lettice Fisher, wife of the historian H A L Fisher, with both of whom she formed a close friendship. In 1911, when Hilda had completed her course, she became part-time secretary to H A L Fisher who had just taken on the editorship, with Gilbert Murray and another professor, of the newly invented Home University Library. She was fully involved in the planning of this new series, suggesting authors and subjects and assisting with other editorial work.

(Some years later she was to contribute a volume of her own, a small book on broadcasting which reflected her experience with the BBC. When Reith described this as another manifestation of her treachery he was probably not aware of the close relationship between Hilda Matheson and the Fishers, or of her early involvement in the Library. It was entirely natural that she should have been invited to contribute to a series she helped to get started. Later still during the Second World War she was to originate another series of books, "Britain In Pictures" which, notwithstanding its title, was a series of essays written by many of the distinguished writers of the time as part of war-time propaganda.)

Shortly after her work on the Home University Library she was appointed as an assistant in the Ashmolean Museum, but her brief period of work there was soon overtaken by world events. The war of 1914-18 was to be for some people, especially women, a liberation, providing opportunities for work that would not otherwise have become available in their lifetimes. In the first year of the war she remained at the Ashmolean and worked for the relief committee of the Mayor's emergency fund. Later she moved to Wandsworth in south London, where during 1915 she was secretary as part of the Voluntary Aid Detachment at the 3rd General Hospital. The following year she became a clerk in the War Office and then, as described by her in information she supplied to her college magazine, she worked in the Special Intelligence Directorate from August 1916 to July 1919.

Before the war, intelligence matters had been handled by several government departments as well as by the police, postal and customs authorities. In 1909 a secret Bureau was established, independent of all departments, but under the supervision of the Military Operations Directorate in the War office. The Bureau divided its work into two sections, home and foreign, and on the outbreak of war in August 1914 the home section became part of a new directorate of military intelligence. At first it was designated as the Security Intelligence Bureau or MO5 (g) and later became known as MI5, responsible for counter-espionage in Britain and developing counter espionage links with governments within the Empire, under the direction of Captain Vernon Kell. (The foreign section was placed under the director of military intelligence as MI(c) responsible for counter espionage outside the Empire and generally for the collection of intelligence abroad, becoming known as MI6). It was in MI5 that Hilda Matheson worked, first in London and later in Rome where she was seconded to the Military Mission, but it is possible to provide only glimpses of what she did.

Until 1997 all domestic records of the security and intelligence agencies were withheld from the Public Records Office and few researchers were permitted access to any retained in house by the agencies themselves. Those placed on public record for the first time in November 1997 relate to the early work of MI5, including the period when Hilda Matheson worked for them, but while they provide a useful general account of how German spies were tracked down they say little about the contribution of individual members of staff. An incomplete picture of her work can be pieced together from these released records, from her letters and the recollections of her mother, from histories of the period, and from a few other references in public records in the Imperial War Museum.

Captain Kell started his work with just one clerk, but soon built up a large establishment of men and women who referred to him always as "K". By the end of the war MI5 employed 844 staff and at various times during the war no less than 650 women were employed. There were frequent reorganisations, but Section H, the main registry, was the continuing centre,

> the mainspring of the Bureau and the basis of all useful counter-espionage work.

The prime task of the registry was to build up card indexes containing information on people suspected of being German spies. Suspects' mail was intercepted, routinely opened and secured again, without leaving any trace of its examination or the various tests used to check for secret ink. Information obtained from this correspondence would find its way onto index cards. Hilda Matheson worked in the registry, devising and maintaining these record systems.

She never described her work, but one of the clerks who worked with her, a Mrs Line, provided a picture of the registry's work in a paper which she sent to the Imperial War Museum. Mrs Line's hope of studying at university had been thwarted by the war and she was pleased to be invited by a letter out of the blue for an interview at the war office. She discovered that she had been recommended by an acquaintance of an aunt and that everyone she later worked with had been recruited in a similar way by personal recommendation. (Hilda Matheson's sponsor would probably have been a college tutor.) No previous training or secretarial experience was required, the essential qualifications being some further education and the ability to hold one's tongue. Mrs Line was a "search clerk" and she likened the card index stretched around a large room to an enormous snake, which grew daily. The clerks were given bits of information about suspect spies, accomplices and places, and had to relate these to information already stored on cards. Sometimes through a chance reference to a person or a place they would hit on a connection which then led to an exciting trail and the construction of a complete case history. Usually only women aged between twenty and thirty were employed because of the intense nature of the work which required scrupulous attention to detail. The office never closed, staff working in shifts throughout the twenty-four hours and on every day of the year.

Hilda Matheson almost certainly had a senior position in the registry, probably managing one or more groups of searchers. The work would have suited her particular gifts because as well as attention to detail it required a mind which could organise disparate pieces of information into coherent patterns by a combination of analysis and flashes of insight. She helped to compile a special intelligence index for counter-espionage purposes, prepared and maintained a black list of suspects, and processed information destined for both.

In a rare reference to an individual, the released records of MI5 mention her and describe useful work she did to reorganise and improve the indexes. She was also singled out for comment in a satirical revue, "Hush Hush", put on by colleagues in 1919 to celebrate the Armistice. The programme records her as one of four "Lessees and Managers" of the office. There is also a pen and ink caricature of a certain "Hilda Von Schuttledorf" and an obscure reference to books by "Matheson and Moirs". It is unlikely that a junior member of the team would have figured so prominently in a revue put on by juniors to lampoon their bosses.

The revue provides a light-hearted glimpse of MI5 at play, but even at work the office had about it the informal air of a pioneering unit. "K" was ready to adopt unconventional ways of tackling work which itself was unprecedented. The extensive use of women was novel. So was the enlistment of boy scouts as office messengers, but the boys were found to be troublesome, filling their considerable periods of inactivity with mischief of all sorts. Girl guides proved more amenable, their ways of getting into mischief apparently being less distressing to those who had to deal with them than were those of the boys, and eventually replaced them.

A simple description of the registry gives little idea of its importance. Its work was vital, deadly serious in fact. Great reliance was placed on the records because they provided indications and possible early warning of what was widespread German espionage against Britain. Asquith, then still prime minister, on a visit to the MI5 office where he saw a map marking the locations of all the known spies, commented that the work of MI5's staff amounted to a major victory. Using the index as their base, the counter-espionage activities organised by "K" (now Colonel Kell) were highly successful. On the outbreak of war, in addition to many thousands interned as aliens, twenty-one people were arrested as suspect spies. Between 1914 and 1916 numerous other suspects were arrested, tried and given terms of imprisonment. Of these, eleven who had been arrested as active spies and later tried by a military tribunal were shot in the Tower of London. The fact that spies were being tried and executed was public knowledge. At least some parts of the trials were open to the public and brief details of the executions were released to the press. Hilda Matheson would have known of the bloody outcome of the work she and her colleagues carried out for "K".

By 1916 the threat from enemy agents had been overcome and some time in the same year she left for Rome as part of a team to set up something called the Military Control Office. Her mother records the astonishment of Italian officials that such an absurdly young looking girl should be entrusted with such responsibilities, which amounted to establishing an office on similar lines to MI5 in London. It is unlikely, contrary to what her mother proudly implied, that she set up the new office single-handed, but MI5's released records do highlight the work she did in Italy along with a Major Haldane. The fact that she spoke fluent German and Italian no doubt influenced the decision to second her, but many of the women employed by MI5 in London were also well-educated university graduates so her performance at work must have been exceptional for her to have been selected. The work in Italy, as in London, was to design and maintain records to help in counter-espionage, keeping the six other consular offices in Italy informed of suspects travelling through the country.

Her clarity of thought, allied to imagination and a gift for organisation, were just the qualities required for this "passive" side of counter-espionage work. (In this context "passive" is not a pejorative term. The work of MI5 was basically divided between the "passive" work of collecting and analysing information, and "active" espionage operations directed against known or suspect spies.) The work she did in Italy had a profound impact on the later development by MI5 of a comprehensive intelligence index which would include information collected not only by its own staff but also by several other agencies in Europe and elsewhere. On her return to London in 1918 she was put in charge of an important section of the main registry. Later a post in Constantinople was offered, but refused, because she,

didn't want to be a policeman all her life.

Her work in counter-espionage was highly valued by MI5 which recommended her for a war medal for her "work in a theatre of war", namely Italy. The War Office did not accept this recommendation, but she was among those few members of the team awarded a mention in despatches and a listing in the *London Gazette*. Within about three months of leaving MI5 she was recruited by Lady Astor to become her political secretary, a job which at first she refused.

Lady Astor

When Waldorf Astor succeeded his father as Viscount Astor in October 1919, and had to exchange his Commons seat for membership of the House of the Lords, the parliamentary vacancy in Plymouth was offered by the local party to his wife Nancy. She accepted the nomination and on 28 November was declared elected with a majority of just over 5000 votes in a three cornered contest against Labour and Liberal candidates. She entered Parliament on 1 December 1919 and made her maiden speech on 24 February 1920. The Countess Markievicz had refused to take the oath of allegiance following her own victory in 1918 for Sinn Fein after an election campaign conducted from Holloway Gaol, thus she disqualified herself and left open to Nancy Astor the distinction of becoming the first woman to sit as a member of the United Kingdom Parliament. This gave Lady Astor a commanding position of which, with her combative and original personality, she set out to take full advantage.

The exact date and circumstances of when Hilda Matheson became her political secretary are uncertain and there is no record of how they first got to know one another. It is possible that Hilda was introduced by her friend and mentor H A L Fisher some time in 1919 or 1920 when he was still a friend of the Astors. (The Fishers remained close friends of Hilda Matheson until her death, but their friendship with the Astors did not survive the publication in 1926 of H A L Fisher's book *Our New Religion*, which was very critical of Christian Science. Lady Astor had been converted to that religion in 1914 and she never forgave him for the attack.) Another possibility is that Philip Kerr, also a friend of Lady Astor, recommended her; Hilda Matheson had worked as his secretary for a period after the war, probably just after her service with MI5.

Philip Kerr, later Lord Lothian, remained a lifelong friend to both of them. He appears often in Hilda Matheson's life and was to be instrumental in securing another important appointment for her in 1932 as secretary of *An African Survey*. Lady Astor met him first when she became a leading political hostess on the election of her husband for Plymouth in 1910. Like Lord Franks and Lord Goodman in later years, Kerr was a strange but influential figure. Baldwin thought him "a rum cove", but he was taken up by several prime ministers, including Lloyd George, as a stimulating, non-partisan adviser. He played a significant part back-stage during the peace settlement discussions at the end of the First World War, represented the Liberal Party in the National Government of 1931 and was a successful ambassador to Washington at the beginning of the Second World War.

What began as a job soon became a deep friendship, but it was a rocky start: Lady Astor liked people who stood up to her and could be cruel to those who didn't. Her previous secretary, a Miss Benningfield, knew her character well and sometime in 1919 or 1920 wrote to her to remonstrate following a visit she had received from a very depressed and discouraged Hilda Matheson:

> She feels that you have no confidence in her and that until you can trust her a little more she won't be able to give her best or to please you in any way. From what I know of your beloved, bewildering and exasperating character, I think she is right ... she's used to a certain amount of approval and satisfaction for value received ... now she gets no sympathy, or encouragement, or patience, or consideration. Her chief faults are ignorance of your character and bewilderment. She's giving you her very best and is trying hard to learn your ways. You'll have these difficulties with any secretary you take on.

There is no record of what immediately followed this blunt ticking-off, but future comments by Lady Astor and Hilda Matheson register high satisfaction with one another.

Nancy Astor had an opinion on most things, usually expressed with vigour and a total lack of self-control. She devoted her political life to three causes in particular: the rights of women, the health of children and, notwithstanding her own intemperate personality in other respects, the prohibition of alcoholic drink. Confident, assertive and rather bullying, combining outrageous talk with strictly moral behaviour, she was in many ways the perfect boss for Hilda Matheson who liked strong women as well as weak, and needed a challenging environment, provided that it was basically sympathetic. To have significant influence in political life, but without the need to engage in the vulgarities of the hustings, suited Hilda's personality and talents perfectly. She could organise Nancy Astor's days, deal with her correspondence, draft her speeches, and promote and lobby for her ideas.

Lady Astor was nobody's puppet, and if she ran short of ideas of her own she could always turn to her husband Waldorf, who made a quiet but significant contribution to her work and helped sometimes to draft her speeches. So it would be wrong to imagine that when Lady Astor spoke, the words were always those of Hilda Matheson. Nevertheless, the first years in Parliament for Lady Astor were, she wrote later, only made possible by Hilda's unremitting work and service:

> *She was really completely magnificent and we worked as one. I might describe it as my zeal and her brain, with the backing of Mrs Fawcett and all those suffrage pioneers.*

Because of the nature of the job and the discreet conventions of the time, political secretaries were rarely in the limelight and their contribution was usually hidden within the activities of the principal they served. Some idea of what Hilda Matheson did and its importance can be gained indirectly from a record made by Waldorf Astor when he had to act in a similar role during a seven-week visit to the United States in 1922:

> *I sigh daily – nay, hourly for our Secretariat from St James's Square who know my ways. What with helping with speeches, dealing with the press, watching the papers tackling endless correspondence, answering cable invitations [to speak], altering dates of meetings, telephoning, fixing cross-country journeys etc etc it's like being in a maelstrom and in a monsoon in a thunderstorm.*

This is a good description of the variety and whirlwind pace of work done in the private office of any major figure. Superficially it might seem to be the sort of organising and administration performed by a private secretary, but it was far more than that. As political secretary in addition to much of the day to day office work she would be involved in thinking about the social and political issues in which Lady Astor was interested. When drafting a speech or dealing with correspondence she would be Lady Astor in another form and the requirement to brief her on everything would give her considerable influence. Waldorf Astor's account of the work probably understates the pressures involved in assisting the restless force of nature that was Nancy Astor.

The range of subjects on which Hilda Matheson briefed her would have included all those on which the member for Plymouth (Sutton) spoke or wrote, and many more which had to be considered before any decision was taken on whether she should become actively involved as an MP. Lady Astor was a frequent attender of the House of Commons and an assiduous constituency worker. In addition she accepted almost every invitation to speak outside Parliament and would make speaking progresses through all the major cities. She didn't initiate any important legislation, but she influenced much, and in particular brought to the House of Commons new thinking about the rights of women and the care of children.

From 1919 until 1926 when she left Lady Astor for the BBC, Hilda Matheson was involved in issues such as the protection of children from indecent assault, the legal conditions governing Guardianship, the suppression of prostitutes and brothel-keeping, the elimination of venereal disease, the need for more women appointees on official bodies, the raising of the school leaving age from 14 to 18, and the supply of healthy milk generally and of free milk to schools. Voting rights for women remained on the agenda throughout her period of service because the 1918 Act had limited the vote to women aged 30 and it was not until the Act of 1928 that women, like men, were allowed to vote at the age of 21. The other perennial topic was the control of alcoholic liquors, as Lady Astor fought to regulate the pub and brewing trades more strictly on the way towards her goal of total prohibition. Of all these topics the only one towards which Hilda Matheson was likely to have been unsympathetic was prohibition. She did not share Lady Astor's aversion to alcoholic drink, although limited and practical steps such as controlling the sale of liquor to minors would have been easy to support.

In its early days Hilda Matheson acted as secretary of the Consultative Committee of Women's Organisations, established by Lady Astor to improve the position of women, and this brought her into contact with most of the leading suffragettes. At Cliveden and St James's Square she met leaders from all walks of life, especially politics and journalism, and was able to develop her friendship with Philip Kerr who was a frequent visitor to both houses. He was a good friend for her to have, providing a rather more sober model in the handling of business than Lady Astor.

The Astor network of influential contacts was to be invaluable in Hilda Matheson's later work, and Lady Astor's strong, sympathetic and radically minded leadership provided something that she needed in order fully to exercise her talents. Unfortunately there were disadvantages. In particular, Lady Astor's propensity for making a noise when she wanted something done, which was not always sensible even in political life, provided a disastrous example to Hilda on how to get one's way. Her mentor and protector romped her way through political life, always quarrelling, always making up, courageous, pugnacious, boisterous, inconsistent and irresponsible. She could get away with it, partly through force of personality and partly because of her wealth and position. Even with both noise and social advantages she made surprisingly little difference to the conduct of public affairs. Harold Laski's description of her as the Pollyanna of politics contained a grain of truth. Behaviour similar to Lady Astor's outside the rumbustious environment of politics, and by someone without the same advantages of wealth and position was likely to achieve even less, and to be treated less indulgently. The Astor connection had another perverse effect; by providing continuing access to high influence in British political life it gave Hilda Matheson an illusion of security, almost of invulnerability.

In 1926, during one of the activities arranged in support of women's rights, her career was to take a new direction. She had started regular "at – homes" where MPs of all parties and other eminent people could meet women and learn something of what they wanted from Parliament now that they had the vote. On one occasion John Reith, managing director of the British Broadcasting Company, was invited and set out almost immediately to recruit her. At first she did not want to go, her usual reaction to any new job, but Lady Astor insisted, feeling that hers was too good a brain to be kept in her present role. In July 1926 she left and was given a

> *nerve-shattering cheque, sufficient to make me an independent capitalist.*

Her letter of thanks to Lady Astor made clear just how much the last six years had meant to her and she offered still

> *to draft an article, or do you some notes, or help to get out lists for a party.*

They did keep in close touch, but her new work was even more pressurised than the private office and did not allow her to continue with briefings or anything else other than friendship.

(There was one last service which she would have been uniquely qualified to render, but her death in 1940 deprived her of the opportunity. When Lady Astor was persuaded to begin writing her autobiography in 1951 she failed to finish more than a first and very incomplete draft. What she lacked, according to Christopher Sykes one of her biographers, was a good editor prepared to work full time on a gigantic task. Hilda Matheson would have done this admirably, preserving Lady Astor's authentic voice and hiding her own contribution, just as she did when working for her from 1919 to 1926, and as she was to do for others in subsequent work.)

When she left Lady Astor she thought that she had been ruined for any other job and that she would certainly get kicked out of the new one within a month. The estimate of time was unduly pessimistic, but the basic uncertainty turned out to be only too prophetic.

What Sort of Person?

In 1926, as she took a holiday in the mountains of Savoy to recover from her hectic life with Lady Astor and prepare for what was to become an even more frenetic period with the BBC, Hilda Matheson had completed thirty-eight years of her life. The first twenty years seem to have been unremarkable, but the lack of information about her family is tantalising.

At Oxford, she did not show any special promise academically or display brilliance of any kind. A first class brain was detected and her tutors tried to put it to work, but high academic ability never showed itself in results and History always took second place to life. The most significant characteristics noted by her Oxford contemporaries were a certain loftiness of character, a high degree of earnestness and selfless energy in helping others. There were few signs of the organising power allied to imagination and insight and the capacity for quick decisive action which became evident during her later work.

What struck people most about her in the years before the First World War were her looks, her smile, her eagerness and warmth of character, and her trim, almost dainty, style. She was short and slim, always looking younger than she was. Her ash-gold hair, grey eyes and ready smile were noted and commented on. She was never described as beautiful, but her clean-cut, openhearted features had a freshness about them which was echoed by her personality. While her father gave out a sense of holiness to all whom he met, she sparkled and delighted people with the brightness of the natural world. Harold Nicolson in his novel *Public Faces* used Hilda Matheson as the model for his heroine, Jane Campbell, and the characteristics he describes in Jane are confirmed by observations made of Hilda by others who knew her well:

How girlish she looks thought the Secretary of State as he watched Jane walk briskly into the room. How tight, how trim, her skirt around those little thighs...swinging her hips a little with ... her girl-guide gait.

Jane Campbell is alert, intelligent and humorous, but more than that, according to the head of the consular department who had a weakness for the right word, she "shines". For one of her Oxford tutors, years before Jane Campbell had been invented, Hilda Matheson was like the heroine in another novel, John Buchan's *Mr Standfast*, who couldn't scare and couldn't soil. This pristine, scintillating quality, rather like the effect she created through the incense in the Cotswold pub, offset the earnest and energetic seriousness which otherwise might have been forbidding.

Marjorie Maxse, whose work at the Conservative Central Office had accustomed her to the inflated egos which peopled political life, thought that Hilda was preserved from this sort of intensity and self-regard by her humour and detachment, which were

sifted through a screen of light and radiance.

Added to this was a charm which worked as potently on those who had grown up with her as on those who went down under its first impact.

Her war work had been structured and disciplined. She and Lady

Astor had real mutual respect and affection as they zipped through political issues on which they held similar views. At this stage in her career there was no reputation for being difficult, indeed quite the reverse. So it is surprising that in the BBC years which followed it was said that she frightened her staff and could appear sometimes as a bit of a battle-axe. It was her ability to encourage and inspire that was commented on most often in the years before she joined the BBC:

> *I don't think I have ever met anyone who so succeeded in making me feel her superiority without emphasising my inferiority. So often I grudge to others their success, but she just deserved it all.*

This was the sort of judgement echoed by many who did not see any assertiveness or ostentation, but appreciated the quick, precise response that encouraged them and carried all matters easily forward. Lionel Fielden, one of her staff at the BBC, wrote of her immense kindliness and the way in which she drew instant loyalty and support from her subordinates:

> *It was never "I must think it over" ... or "passed to you please" ... or "You've got us into a fine mess" or any variant of censure; it was always "Well now, let's think it out" or "Well now, what are we going to do about it?" and always the decision – your decision– emerged as though we had made it ourselves.*

These differences in perception about her in the job on which she was about to embark are perhaps explained by the fact that at the BBC she was for the first time to work in a man's world in a senior position at a level usually reserved for men. In the battles which were an inevitable feature of that volatile organisation the label of "difficult woman" was an easy way of putting her down. Before she joined the BBC any aggressive or domineering side of her character had not shown itself.

From her Oxford days she displayed a gift for friendship which manifested itself in attachments towards people badly treated by life as well as in close relationships with members of the establishment. Her reputation for knowing everyone was deserved. The Fishers were personal friends for the whole of her life, but they were also very useful to her as the professor climbed the greasy pole of politics into the cabinet, and the even slipperier poles of academic life into the wardenship of Oxford's New College. A short period acting as secretary to David Hogarth at the Ashmolean Museum before the war led to a memorable dinner in London at the end of October 1918 with the Hogarths and T E Lawrence, fresh from his recent triumph in liberating Damascus. Lawrence started the day with a meeting with Lloyd George, went on to an audience with the King when he declined politely the offered honours, and ended it by dining with his good friend David Hogarth and his other guest, Hilda Matheson. Shortly afterwards her job as secretary to Philip Kerr led to the Astor connection and all that followed. During her time with the BBC she must have met most members of the Baldwin and MacDonald cabinets as well as many of the leading writers, artists and intellectuals of the time. Her organising abilities were outstanding, but so were the personal qualities which captivated so many people and turned employers into close friends. Only in the BBC was the magic to fail and even there for a time, Reith too was enthralled.

Her own perceptions of herself were startlingly different from the favourable public impact she made. Some uncertainty about the impression one is making is commonplace, but her disparagement of self was extreme. Beginning with her stuffy, stodgy sort of name, she saw "Hilda" as fair and fat and Teutonic, full of self-distrusting panics and miseries, an ugly little scrub, devastatingly penny plain. Her thick stocky legs were a constant grief and, though serviceable for mountain walks, were of little help when skiing or skating or dancing, when she felt like a small elephant. She did not swim or play tennis or golf and was

> *a social failure, a blot on any festive gathering – odd man out you see.*

An unattractive appearance was only ever commented on by one other person, Virginia Woolf, who had special reasons for disliking her, and is not borne out either by photographs or the comments of other people. The picture of clumsiness is even more grotesquely at odds with the reality and with how other people saw her. One of her outstanding gifts, shared with Jane Campbell, was the ability neatly and skilfully to create an ordered environment around her, whether this was pigeonholing paper or tidying up disordered thinking. Like Jane, she had a liking for india-rubber bands, desk trays, and cardboard boxes marked "answered", "unanswered" and "suspense". When Jane observed that a strip of marquetry upon her writing desk had become unstuck:

> *A shaft of pleasure pierced her gloom. There were few things in life which occasioned greater joy to Jane than the sight of small objects requiring Durofix. For the next ten minutes she was neatly, happily, employed.*

On walking holidays in Savoy, Hilda would produce everything one could possibly want out of a rucksack as a conjuror produces rabbits out of a hat. Her bag was stuffed with little gadgets. She could as easily make a pudding out of apricot jam and snow, or a waste paper basket out of *The Times*, as she could read the maps of the area to avoid getting lost as she and her companions walked the hills. She would, of course, always have with her a complete first-aid outfit, but she would also more romantically plan to use the lids of all her tins to make little Alpine gardens for the bedroom. She could never look on disorder without wanting to put things into their proper place. Just visiting a photographer and observing a welter of negatives entangled in a basement brought out her reorganising instincts and she longed to tell the staff how badly organised they were not to have numbers and an index and filing cabinets.

This liking for order, accompanied by a vivid and generous imagination and remarkable energy, had made her a successful "spy catcher" as well as an effective political secretary. She always had real knowledge of the things she talked about, never wasted time and always made her points clearly. In everything she said her listeners could feel a controlled, realistic, but ardent enthusiasm as she succeeded in bringing her subject to life. These were the qualities too of a great teacher, and as talks director of the BBC she was to be given an opportunity to educate the nation.

Chapter Two

IN LOVE WITH THE BBC
1926–28

Beginnings of a Golden Age

Broadcasting in its first years attracted men and women who believed in it almost as a social and cultural crusade. The British Broadcasting Company (BBCo) was established in 1923 and its more famous successor, the British Broadcasting Corporation (BBC), in January 1927. The announcer Stuart Hibberd sensed in both organisations an all-pervading pioneer spirit where nothing mattered but broadcasting. Every few months, according to Vernon Bartlett another notable broadcaster of the time, the engineers would produce a new type of microphone and Hilda Matheson would produce a new type of talk. There was a high proportion of young people among the staff, mainly men who had served in the war, and who because of some awkward versatility or some form of fastidiousness, idealism or general restlessness, never settled down to any humdrum profession after the war.

Hilda Matheson was 38 when recruited by John Reith in 1926 to one of the most highly paid jobs for a woman in any organisation at that time. As director of talks her salary was £900 a year, more than most men holding senior posts in the civil service and significantly more than most women could earn. Job advertisements of the time offered £50 a year for nurses, £60 for ladies' maids and £100 for schoolteachers. Few women worked in professional jobs. Most employers would not employ married women at all and many, although not always the BBC, would require women already employed to resign on marriage. In other respects, too, the BBC was a notably liberal employer, paying men and women the same salary for similar work, but it employed no women at the most senior levels. It is not surprising that other women regarded Hilda Matheson as a role model, opening up opportunities for women in professional jobs and competing with men on equal terms with no quarter expected or received.

The period 1926-31 when she worked for the BBC nearly matched the time of her love affair with Vita Sackville-West whom she met first in 1928. These two great passions, for the BBC and Vita, flowered and wilted together. She was alternately ecstatic and frustrated about both, but rarely confident that either would last. In some ways both loves were the high point of her life. She went on to perform outstanding service in other areas and to form at least one other close attachment with a woman, but the six years 1926-31 were a golden period in Hilda Matheson's life.

In the life of the country it was one of the most difficult periods of British history. The General Strike of 1926 was followed in 1929 by the crisis in the world economy and consequent slump, leading in Britain to the formation of the National Government in 1931, the rise of Sir Oswald Mosley's National Party, and a decade of high unemployment. In Europe the League of Nations progressively weakened and there was a steady drift towards war. At the same time developments in air and motor transport, in cinema, radio, and the gramophone, and in other popular entertainment such as dancing, all added a fizz to life. After the 1914-18 War there was a feeling that old barriers were breaking down. Social and artistic life in the twenties was dazzling, almost frenetic. Rose Macaulay thought that the twenties were,

> *as decades go, a good decade; gay, decorative, intelligent, extravagant, cultured. There were booms in photography, Sunday film and theatre clubs, surrealism, steel furniture, faintly obscure poetry, Proust, James Joyce, dancing, skating, large paintings on walls of rooms ... The roads were jammed with cars; cocktails and successive negro dances crossed the Atlantic; swinging old rhythms gave place to monotonous jogging. Heavier make-up decorated female faces; skirts shortened for a time to the knees; those who valued easy motion were happy in this, but it did not last ... The next decade was more serious, less cultured, less aesthetic, more political. The slump blew like a cold draught at its birth, war stormed like a forest fire at its close.*

It was to be Hilda Matheson's misfortune that she joined the BBC just when some of the bubbles were beginning to burst and she had to contend with the less confident, more fearful, attitudes of the thirties.

Broadcasting was very much part of the excitement of the age. The wireless, as the receiving equipment was still called, had a powerful impact. People from all walks of life wrote to the BBC about how their lives had been changed by the ready availability of music, news, talks and other features. The medium itself began to have an impact on music and the arts as middle class ideas of "taste" competed with the more rigorous "standards" of the educated and literary minority. The wireless provided in some ways a battleground on which popular and minority cultures fought for dominance. In the newspaper industry, the first of the mass media, the conflict between majority and minority tastes was reconciled by producing different newspapers aimed at different audiences. Competition in broadcasting had been ruled out, at least in the United Kingdom, and because of limitations in technology the BBC could not for some time offer any significant number of alternative programmes. For many years millions of listeners had to be satisfied with a single programme or a very limited choice. This had two important consequences for BBC programming. There was first the pressure to broadcast popular programmes to satisfy the majority of listeners. Although a balance had to be struck between minority and popular preferences, accepting that some listeners would simply switch off some programmes, it was always tempting to go for the largest audience. Secondly, because any broadcast potentially had an audience of millions, usually listening in their own homes, programmes had to conform to conventional standards of good taste, even those programmes directed at a minority with more sophisticated tastes. These conundrums – how many listeners to go for and what to transmit into people's homes – still exist today when there are many different programmes to choose from, because they follow from the nature of the medium itself. For a monopoly broadcaster not yet able to offer any significant choice of programmes the dilemmas were greater. Programme makers were faced with difficult choices and it is not surprising that they sometimes opted for the easy, popular way out. The Corporation began with a certain zest for experimentation which matched the twenties spirit, but gradually adapted to the popular nature of the medium and to the more reactionary values which came to dominate political life.

Hilda Matheson was at the centre of these conflicts. For her, radio should broadcast the best of everything, and the best was judged by the highest intellectual and artistic standards. The fact that the medium entered every home was not for her a reason to avoid experiment or lower standards, but simply a feature of broadcasting that could be dealt with by effective presentation. Difficult subjects could always be presented, in her view, in an entertaining, amusing and stimulating way. A monopoly provider had to play fair with all the listeners, aiming to satisfy as many as possible, but that did not mean ignoring minority tastes or accepting low quality standards for majority programmes.

When she arrived at the BBCo, the news and talks services were amateur, hedged around with restrictions and regarded almost with contempt. There was little interest from senior programmers in developing talks and to have only one talk a week was not unusual. Often broadcasters were not paid for giving a talk, the novelty of the experience being regarded as sufficient reward. By the time Hilda Matheson left the BBC she had transformed both news and talks, establishing the basis of what became Radios 3 and 4, but that was achieved at great personal cost:

> *I can see her now, exhausted and white in those battles, but as firm as a rock in what she thought was right,*

wrote Lady Astor. In the end she felt driven to resign, but her six years as talks director left a distinctive mark on broadcasting.

Broadcasting in 1926

In 1926 the BBCo was reaching the end of its life. Established by the radio manufacturers, it had been licensed by the Post Office in 1923 to broadcast throughout the country. With the customary sensitivity of government towards infant enterprise, the Post Office confiscated up to half the annual licence fee of ten shillings (fifty pence), limited severely the number of hours of broadcasting and forbade any discussion of controversial matters. Between 1921 and 1924 there were no less than seven postmasters-general, but none of them paid much attention to the new medium except to wag an admonishing finger. There was no statutory basis for censoring the content of programmes, but governments made it clear that neither vulgarity nor controversy should contaminate the airwaves. On 24 April 1923 the Postmaster-General, replying to an MPs complaint about a broadcast relating to a building strike, said that he thought it undesirable that the Broadcasting Service should be used for the dissemination of speeches on controversial matters. In that characteristically British form of social control he added that he had called the BBCo's attention to the incident. The PMG could be confident, because he had the sanction of granting or withholding the BBCo's licence, that merely to draw something to their attention would be accepted as an instruction not to repeat the offence.

By the beginning of 1927, when the BBC took over from the BBCo, the broadcasting day was still only seven hours long. Programmes did not begin until 10.15 in the morning when a religious service started the day. After a mid-day concert which lasted for an hour there might be no further programmes until late afternoon. Broadcasting at weekends was not continuous and Sundays were characterised by long silent periods. There were just over two million wireless licences and the *Radio Times* had a circulation of nearly a million. Listeners could receive one programme from the "national" transmitters in London and Daventry or from the network of regional transmitters. (A very limited choice of programmes became available in August 1927.)

The staple broadcasting diet was music, which took up more than sixty per cent of broadcasting time, followed by news and talks with twenty per cent and children's programmes with ten per cent; drama, religion and special features took up the remainder.

Vested interests imposed many restrictions. The Newspaper Proprietors' Association (NPA) prevented the BBCo from directly collecting news or reporting direct from live events. Instead news agencies provided each day a bulletin which the BBCo was permitted to read, but not allowed to edit. No news could be broadcast before 7.00 pm. When the BBCo in 1923 established the *Radio Times* the newspaper proprietors could hardly object, as they had previously refused to carry details of programmes in their newspapers, but the establishment of *The Listener* in 1929 resulted in a battle of epic proportions. A deputation of proprietors demanded to see the Prime Minister. Reith persuaded Baldwin to stay out of the row and after skilful negotiation, which included a lunch-time blitz by Hilda Matheson of the chairman of the proprietors, (see p 63), agreement was reached on a weekly paper to record talks and other material already broadcast. This was to develop under staff such as R S Lambert, Janet Adam Smith and J R Ackerley into a wide-ranging and influential literary magazine.

Theatre owners and managers were as restrictive and unimaginative as newspaper proprietors. They sought to prevent artistes from broadcasting and refused to give permission to the BBCo to broadcast live shows. Radio reviews of plays and other entertainment, especially of course critical reviews, were deeply resented by both managers and actors. There was much debate about the social effect of broadcasting with fears that the wireless would keep people from attending concerts and plays or reading books. The Headmaster of Rugby lamented that instead of solitary thought, people would listen in to what was said to millions of other people, which could not be the best things. There was little appreciation of the way in which radio could expand audiences to the benefit of all media and increase the number of readers.

There was an amateur flavour about the first years which Roger Eckersley, Hilda Matheson's boss, captured very well in his autobiography. He joined the BBCo in 1924 on the recommendation of his brother Peter who was the BBCo's chief engineer. Roger's lack of broadcasting experience was shared by everyone at that time and the only skills he had to offer had been gained from a period managing a golf club followed by an unsuccessful attempt at chicken farming. Despite this unpromising background he found himself reading the news, playing the piano during interludes, and even taking part in variety revues. Everyone had to be ready to do everybody else's job and to come up with ideas for "programme fillers", a useful one being a talent competition. He didn't remember any radio stars being discovered during these amateur events, but his own career flourished. The new medium suited him better than chicken farming and in 1926 he became director of programmes from which position he had to try to manage Hilda Matheson for most of her time at the BBC. Roger Eckersley was not a strong or especially intelligent character. Anyone reading his autobiography would be bound to conclude that he was a nitwit, but he flourished under Reith, the man mainly responsible for establishing the national broadcasting service. The feebleness of Eckersley's management meant that there was no buffer between Matheson and Reith. This was to have disastrous consequences for her.

John Reith was generally recognised as having done a good job at the BBCo. The radio manufacturers who were the main shareholders gave him a free hand. He had a clear view of what he wanted to achieve, a single national organisation with high standards and preferably within the framework of a public, non-profit making corporation. From the start he managed the BBCo as though it was already a public body. There were few objections when the Postmaster-General told the House of Commons on 14 July 1926 that the government proposed to set up by Royal Charter a British Broadcasting Corporation with effect from 1

January 1927. The decision to include in the charter the appointment of John Reith as director-general was also welcomed. When Reith recruited Matheson he had very much in mind his plans to make the BBC a far different animal from the BBCo.

Reith and Matheson

Reith was responsible for nearly 800 people, all of them tightly controlled and organised under a new board of governors and himself as director-general. The role of the governors was to be a source of friction for several years. The first chairman of the governors, Lord Clarendon, described by Lady Astor as the stupidest man she knew and incapable of keeping any idea in his head for an hour even if capable of absorbing it, tried to get involved in detailed management. Mrs Snowden, wife of Philip Snowden the first Labour Chancellor of the Exchequer, on her appointment as a governor began almost immediately to complain about particular broadcasts and to challenge the accuracy of Board minutes. "It is really awful", moaned Reith, and in the safety of his diaries he castigated the interfering ways of Clarendon and "the Red woman" (Mrs Snowden). Such extreme language was not unusual for him, at least in the diaries, which contain frequent references to idiots, rogues, sinners and incompetents. The favourite one day could quickly become an enemy the next. Hilda Matheson, unwisely, was to try and use the governors to get her own way. This was to be regarded as treasonable by Reith who saw them as akin to the Cabinet, with himself as commander-in-chief in the field. With his immediate deputy, (Vice Admiral Sir) Charles Carpendale famous for his quarterdeck manner, he kept the governors at arm's length. It was Reith's broadcasting philosophy and management style which prevailed.

From the beginning of broadcasting in 1923 he had established himself as the sole arbiter of programme standards and of behaviour in the studio and the office. There was an early row with Julian Huxley who made a brief reference to birth control in his broadcast *Is Science Best for the World?* Reith set up an enquiry immediately about this departure from "our" principles and assured readers of *The Times* that the necessary action had been taken to prevent a recurrence. When laying down the law on birth control, he questioned also the propriety of broadcasting on a Sunday the song "Oh No, John". It was pointed out to him that the particular song was a very old English folk song and had been passed on that account. He concluded that it was necessary to be particularly careful with songs, especially on Sundays, and instructed Roger Eckersley to watch it.

The appearance of staff in the office also had to be watched; plus fours and games rig were not be worn except on Saturday mornings while shirt-sleeves were undesirable in the wearers' own offices and were on *no* account to be worn about the corridors. During the evening suitable eveningwear was to be worn in studios. The morals of staff were policed as scrupulously as dress: his chief engineer, Peter

Eckersley, was obliged to resign following involvement with "another woman" and subsequent divorce. Some of Reith's rules seem almost pruriently intrusive, but he was able to tolerate a wide range of conduct, not only in his own private life but in that of others, if he liked the person concerned.

At first Reith and Matheson got on well and she felt free enough to conduct her meetings informally, sitting on the floor of her room with her staff gathered around the gas fire, and she regularly brought her dog into the office. These minor infringements of the house rules raised an occasional eyebrow, but no objections. (The more extreme lack of convention in her private life was not yet obvious.) Her novel ideas for talks and news were also indulged, because she had after all been brought in to liven things up. So to begin with she was a favourite:

Miss Matheson has joined us and is doing well,

Reith wrote in October 1926. After listening to a speech he made at a dinner for government ministers she told him that she was sure he would be a future prime minister. Soon afterwards, when he was offered a knighthood and felt very much inclined to refuse, at least partly because he thought he deserved something better, he asked her advice and she persuaded him to accept. As well as these flattering attentions to one another in the office, they met at social occasions to which she was invited because of her previous contacts. There were frequent dinners attended by people such as Lady Astor, Lord Clarendon, Roger Fry, Prince George of Rumania, the prime minister of the day, and many more, at which Reith, something of a novice then on the social scene, would bump into his director of talks, already an old hand. At this stage he seemed to her to be an admirably strong successor to Lady Astor.

Her relations with colleagues, mainly those directors in charge of other programme areas, were tense from the start. The balance between the main areas of music, entertainment, talks, news and education, had to be fought for at a programme board consisting of her immediate manager Roger Eckersley, who was then assistant controller (programmes), and her director colleagues, together with some independent advisers. This group was the creative heart of the BBC so far as programme output was concerned. It was this forum, of which she was not at first a member, which determined how many of her ideas were translated into broadcasts. One of the independent advisers to this board, and one who had a firm belief in radio as a popular medium, was Filson Young, an ebullient Irish polymath who was to become a constant goad. Roger Eckersley thought that Filson concealed a sentimental heart under an aggressive manner, but Young never toned down his pungent criticisms of talks and their originator. In an organisation full of large egos his was one of the biggest, well illustrated in a contemporary *Who's Who in Broadcasting* in which his biography was the longest, far longer than either Reith's or Matheson's.

For as long as she retained the support of the director-general, Hilda Matheson could get her way, and to begin with Reith and Matheson thought that they shared a vision of broadcasting as an instrument of public improvement. They discovered later that the improvements each looked for were not the same. Unfortunately, they did share formidable gifts of intelligence, energy and will in pursuing their own objectives. When the differences of broadcasting philosophy became apparent a clash was inevitable. Reith was determined to break through the limits imposed on the BBC which prevented it from broadcasting on important issues. In selecting Hilda Matheson as his instrument for achieving the breakthrough he showed great perception, but overlooked the fact that she would not be easy to control.

A young recruit to the BBC, R S Lambert, who was to become editor of *The Listener* in 1929, noted some of the differences between them. He wrote that he would not have joined the BBC had he not met Hilda Matheson at his selection interviews. The impression that she left on him was so favourable that it helped him survive a subsequent interview with the director-general. The exceedingly tall figure of Reith leaning over him as he explored the two key questions,

was Lambert a Christian and had he any defects of character?

remained as an unpleasant memory for a long time. (Reith had a similar effect on Harold Nicolson who after their first meeting described him as a huge thin man of six feet seven with angry brooding eyes, a weak mouth, and a strong jaw, and evidently a highly self-centred and self-conscious person.) Lambert was captivated by the quick, intelligent, sympathetic and idealistic nature of Hilda Matheson. These characteristics, he discovered, were not typical of the BBC and its ways. Her own liberalism was a minority influence, seeking in vain to permeate an organisation orientated by its chief in another direction.

Victoria Glendinning in her biography of Vita Sackville-West draws an attractive picture of Hilda Matheson at this time, describing her as a person of integrity and personal distinction, but perhaps rather an intimidating figure to younger broadcasters. The reservation in this judgement is not entirely unfair. Most staff regarded her with affection, but appreciation was tinged with respect. She recognised rather ruefully that she was sometimes seen as standoffish, and while she felt that reputation was unjust she was aware that she lacked the small change which made for easy acquaintance. Partly this was a matter of shyness, but more important was the reality that she was more interested in other things. Her work with Lady Astor and at the BBC obliged her to pretend that she enjoyed being with other people, but her interest was that of an observer calculating how best to exercise the persuasive wiles which would enable her to get her own way. She did not like parties or crowds and mimicry was beyond her. Human relationships meant for her intense friendships within a very small circle. If she could not identify a soul mate who shared similar feelings and ideas, or someone who needed help, the relationship could be either perfunctory or hostile.

It is not surprising therefore that opinions about her as she began her work with the BBC were sharply divided. Roger Eckersley commented that she lived for her work and did not spare herself, and had real charm which she could deploy most effectively, but he felt she was inclined to spoil a case by overstating it. While some considered her a bore or superior, others were bewitched, in particular those clever young men with whom she seemed able to work most easily. Lionel Fielden and Joe Ackerley, who were to go on to have distinguished careers in the BBC, were the two assistants who worked most closely with her on talks. They were totally sympathetic towards her efforts to raise intellectual standards in broadcasting, sharing also her readiness to experiment, to take risks, and to offend conventional taste. The fact that they too were homosexual might have helped their relationships with her, but was unlikely to have been a significant factor. They liked and admired her because of her ability, energy and all the other personal qualities which could mesmerise.

Differences of personality and policy were all in the future. At first Reith created for her a separate talks section, distinct from news and education. Then parts of other sections began to be transferred to her own, starting with criticism and reviews, government department talks and official bulletins. News, running commentaries and eyewitness accounts were soon under her control and she became responsible for a major broadcasting department. Before she could establish the programmes she wanted there were some general problems that had to be cleared out of the way. In particular she had to counter the obstructions placed by newspaper proprietors in the way of developing BBC news, the refusal of government to allow any broadcasts on controversial issues, and the ambivalence of BBC staff towards serious broadcasts.

Freeing the News from the Newspapers

Restrictions on the broadcasting of news had hindered the creation of an effective news service between 1923-26. During the General Strike of 1926 when newspapers could not be printed, BBCo bulletins demonstrated the potential of news by wireless and Hilda Matheson capitalised on this success. In February 1927 she persuaded newspaper proprietors to agree that the first news bulletin of the evening could take place at 6.30pm instead of 7.00 pm. This seemingly minor change was in fact a significant breakthrough. The proprietors had always been determined that all news should be reported first in the press and the starting time of 7 o'clock had been set by them to protect the novelty value of reports in evening newspapers. Between 1927 and 1930 the proportion of hours devoted to news rose from just over four per cent of all programmes to over nine per cent of national programmes and the same percentage of regional programmes. Gradually she began also to build up the BBC's independence from Reuters and in February 1930 finally secured the broadcast of a news bulletin fully edited by BBC staff. This too was an important breakthrough.

Reuters' bulletins had been prepared for the eye, not the ear, and consequently when read aloud appeared formal and stilted. In her view the technique of broadcasting was quite specific: she saw that it was not mass projection, though it seemed to be so, but an individual, even intimate medium. She insisted that scripts had to be written so that they could be listened to easily by people in the intimacy of their own homes. Before her arrival at the BBC, one or two broadcasters had achieved success with an informal, relaxed presentation. The BBC's chief engineer, Peter Eckersley, proved to be a born entertainer, talking to listeners "as if he lived next door". Another was a civil servant, Leslie Harrison Lambert, better known by his broadcasting name of A J Alan, who became one of the first radio personalities. His relaxed style was achieved as the result of scrupulous preparation. He pasted his script onto cardboard to avoid rustling, marked it with instructions to "cough here", "pause", "sigh", and rehearsed carefully. Such successes were rare and it took some years, and the influence of Hilda Matheson, for broadcasters to understand that they had to adapt their style and method of presentation to the new medium. Like A J Alan she identified what radio required: news bulletins and talks written specifically with the new medium in mind and scrupulously rehearsed so as to produce the effect of an easy intimacy.

Her approach revolutionised the broadcasting of news and talks. Even today the lessons she taught have still to be learned. John Drummond, appointed in 1987 as controller of music and Radio 3, complained about the way broadcasters read their scripts; he said,

I am sick of being read at, I want to be spoken to.

However, unlike him she did not think that the answer was to do away with scripts. An impromptu, spontaneous approach at the microphone would result in hesitation, repetition, verbosity and imprecision, acceptable in everyday conversation perhaps, but not in a broadcast, while a script could be made to sound as though it was not being read. Producing such scripts herself, or persuading writers to revise and rehearse until they produced a listenable talk, were among her great broadcasting skills.

In order to propagate her views she appointed young people with a good knowledge of politics and public affairs allied to a non-partisan outlook. What she definitely did not want was anyone with ordinary journalistic experience as she found that they had difficulty getting into their heads the totally different approach needed in broadcasting. Some journalists however came up to scratch and she commissioned Philip Macer-Wright, an assistant editor of the *Westminster Gazette*, to work in the news department and advise on how it could be improved. His report was received in September 1928 and reflected much of her own thinking, in particular its recommendations that news bulletins must be specially written with listeners in mind.

The BBC news service throughout the thirties was based on the foundations she laid. If she had stayed with the BBC, her restless energy and imagination would not have been content with her own early thoughts. News programmes would have developed more quickly and flexibly under her than in the event they did, and much more attention would have been paid to reporting from overseas. It took another war to shake the BBC out of its insularity. In 1939 it was faced with an urgent need to create European and World services which should have been set up long before. There was another gap in the BBC's news which she would have filled, namely the reporting of events in Germany and Italy which never received the attention they merited under her successors. As a reviewer of radio in 1931 and 1932 she commented on these deficiencies, but to no avail.

Removing the Ban on Controversy

News could sometimes be controversial, but talks were trickier still. Always one of the most contentious features of broadcasting, talks were described by J C Stobart, the education director who was her first boss, as the least popular function of the BBC. They were either too boring, stealing valuable time from music and entertainment, or too controversial. A growing core of listeners enjoyed the opportunity to listen to eminent men and women talking about a wide range of serious and practical, more rarely humorous, subjects, but others listened in almost as monitors or spies. Talks were seen as the outward sign of a BBC attitude or policy, as an attempt to put over a particular point of view. There was an impression, then as now, that the BBC was biased to the Left. Reith would reply wearily that his main object in life was not to promote either Left or Right but only to ensure that broadcasting raised the intellectual and ethical standards of the community. Yet standards could hardly be raised so long as any discussion of interesting ideas was forbidden.

The Postmaster General refused to give permission in 1924 for controversial subjects to be broadcast, even when it was proposed to handle them impartially. In 1925 requests to broadcast an Oxford Union debate and another debate on unemployment were refused on the grounds that the results of the Crawford Committee pronouncement on controversy in broadcasting should be awaited. The Committee reported on 5 March 1926 and as well as its main recommendation that the BBCo should be replaced by a public corporation, it recommended that a moderate amount of controversial matter should be broadcast, provided the material was of high quality and treated with scrupulous fairness.

When the BBC was licensed in 1927 the Government transferred the censorship function from the Post Office to the Corporation itself, but specific prohibitions remained. The secretary of the Post Office reminded Reith of them in January 1927. Under clause 4 of the licence the BBC had to abstain from statements expressing the opinion of the Corporation on matters of public policy, which was reasonable, but also from speeches or lectures containing statements on topics of political, religious or industrial controversy, which ruled out practically everything of interest.

Roger Eckersley remembered talks as being the most vulnerable side of his work, the one that received the most serious criticism from BBC management. Not because the broadcasts were dull, but because of the ethical, political and sometimes moral feelings that they stirred up. His staff was always being accused of political bias, or of recommending indecent books. For that reason talks policy was, to a greater extent than in anything else, dictated from above, by a board that believed in moderation, while below them was a band of eager enthusiasts led by Hilda Matheson who wanted to reform the world and were highly critical of being checked.

The prohibition had to be removed if talks were to develop into something worthwhile, able to compete in interest with music and other entertainment. Hilda Matheson set out systematically to demolish the ban. She enlarged the range of topics and speakers, obtaining some of the most outstanding personalities, thinkers and writers of the time. Often the format used was a debate, so that the broadcast would not be open to the objection that only one side of an issue was being presented. Subjects ranged from important economic and social issues such as road versus rail, the value of the League of Nations, and the basis on which wages should be paid, to vast philosophical questions on the meaning of life. There were some less serious enquiries such as whether broadcasting was a temporary fad, or if there was too much of it. She even secured the reluctant interest of Dean Inge. As Dean of St. Paul's he had made clear his dislike of the present age and that he regarded broadcasting as one of its worst manifestations. Hilda Matheson suggested to him the possibility of a debate in which he trounced the present day as vehemently as he liked, and Bertrand Russell or H G Wells defended it, with somebody big like Lord Balfour in the chair.

Reith agreed only reluctantly to some of her more provocative ideas and even refused permission for a friendly discussion on industrial peace and co-partnership between (Lord) Citrine the TUC secretary and an employer. She responded with a degree of challenging insolence by planning to arrange a debate on the subject *Is Safety First a sound motto*? While she didn't think this could possibly have any political complications or associations, being concerned more with the philosophy of life than with traffic problems, she nevertheless thought she should get his approval before proceeding further. When using broadcasting to disseminate ideas Hilda Matheson rarely put safety first, she was prepared to take risks. She could not understand why people objected to the expression of ideas on the air, especially when there was usually somebody in the studio ready to put forward contrary views. Even Lady Astor, a born controversialist, sometimes found her a little reckless: when asked to speak about Josephine Butler, Lady Astor protested that you couldn't talk about her work to a mixed company at all, let alone broadcast on the subject.

Matters came to a head in January 1928 when Philip Guedella complained in a letter to *The Times* about restrictions placed on one of his talks on the fairly innocuous topic *Should Diaries be Burnt*. He made it clear that he did not blame the BBC, which could hardly help itself so long as free speech on matters of public interest was controlled by the same grudging hand that sold stamps. After more than a year of trying to keep talks within the charter constraints Hilda Matheson's frustration almost overwhelmed her. She wrote furiously to Roger Eckersley in February 1928 pointing out that she had about exhausted the supply of non-controversial subjects and, still more seriously, exhausted the supply of people of any standing who were willing to talk on the present terms. Eckersley and Reith shared her frustration to some extent. Their negative response towards many of her suggestions at this time was not always because they disapproved personally, but because they feared the consequences of any infringement of the terms of the BBC's charter.

She was less restrained and kept up the pressure on government, gradually finding political allies. Churchill, Lloyd George and others called publicly for change and *The Times* weighed in behind them. At last the Prime Minister announced in the House on 5 March 1928 that while the BBC would continue to be prohibited from expressing any view on public policy, the ban on broadcasting controversial matter was being removed. This was on the understanding that the BBC would use responsibly the discretionary power entrusted to it. In his announcement Baldwin made it clear that the relaxation was not likely to lead to the broadcasting of parliamentary debates or to any significant increase in political discussion on radio. This was a challenge that Hilda Matheson was delighted to take up.

Political Broadcasting

Political broadcasting had operated under more constraints even than news and talks. Lloyd George and Winston Churchill recognised its importance, especially at a time when the electorate had been enlarged with women voters, but most politicians were at first reluctant to broadcast at all and successive postmasters-general were obstructive. Political reality however was on the side of the BBC. Constituencies now contained far too many voters to be reached by conventional electioneering and the wireless was an essential medium of political discussion; Churchill even went so far as to recommend a regular daily dose of politics for listeners. Baldwin, although a natural broadcaster, was more cautious, preferring to be led by the sceptical attitudes of the majority of MPs. Attempts by Reith to persuade the parties to agree to rotas for political broadcasts failed.

Hilda Matheson led the negotiations with the political parties and provided graphic accounts of her struggles in letters to Vita Sackville-West. A particular success was to persuade Members of Parliament to broadcast on the government's De-rating Bill. The terms of the Bill, which had been introduced as a roundabout way of subsidising industry and agriculture at the expense of the taxpayer, are not important for this biography. However, it is worth quoting from the letters for the light they throw on Hilda Matheson's persistence and powers of persuasion as well as her chronic lack of confidence as a woman in a man's world. Her account appears in several letters sent during January 1929.

Neville Chamberlain, then Minister of Health with various responsibilities for local government, asked the BBC to agree to him broadcasting on the de-rating proposals. Hilda Matheson suggested that this would provide an ideal occasion for a debate involving all the parties. She came back late from lunch on 4 January:

> to find a frenzied Admiral Carpendale sending himself into fits over politics. So I had to draft an ultimatum to the three parties for him. Rather fun that was ... Politicians are a lot of vain and self-important rabbits, most of them, and all parties seem much the same.

On the following Saturday she was telephoned at home with instructions to ring up the admiral who, in the absence of the director-general, had got cold feet because he thought she had rushed him into unseemly and inaccurate letters to the political parties:

> and I couldn't quite convince him. Darling, he was so accusing and unfair that I got all hot and bothered as I did when Roger retailed all Filson Young's attacks on me. I as near as nothing cried into the telephone! How I despise myself for minding about things in a personal way. It's so difficult to tell if it's just hurt pride disliking criticism, or the reflection on one's intelligence, or anger, or stupidity, or what. Anyway, it's very silly. The DG's secretary, an uppish young woman, with an exaggerated sense of her own importance, seems to have egged the Admiral on to attack me ... In spite of myself I began to worry about the Admiral's criticism. To wonder if perhaps he was right and if I lacked judgement and sense too badly and if my advice had been unsound and whether I was landing the BBC in a mess and whether I was rather too apt to jump to conclusions and write memoranda and force action on insufficient evidence and I did want you so badly to come and comfort me ... I think I'm an awful fool in some ways and I am much too impulsive and hasty ... I ended up [the following day] with a triumphant hour and a half solid dealing with the Admiral till I had him wriggling on a pin and ringing up all the parties like a good boy and telling them what I wrote down and put under his nose. (This is partly swank! – but mostly true and it was a good piece of work though I says it who shouldn't.)

The political parties continued to be difficult. The *Radio Times*, due out on 18 January, had to go to press without listing the proposed debate, but after another day of top pressure, telephoning and manoeuvring agreement was reached between the three parties and the BBC.

Twenty-minute speeches were to be made by each spokesman with a further twenty-minute Government reply. On 22 January she described the broadcast debate to Vita:

> back to calm an agitated DG about the debate tonight and to make final arrangements for everyone who had to be stuffed about the place to listen to it. Parliamentary reporters in one room, press in another (and drinks), Dr Randall, a Governor, in another, speakers in another ... then a scramble home to dress and feed and get back to the BBC and then my discussion ... I think a great success. 70 minutes of it and it honestly wasn't dull. They had all tried awfully hard and taken immense pains with matter and manner and they were all very nervous and rather excited and pretending not to be; and so very sweet in their passionate desire to be strictly honourable about their allotted time. I sat beside them in the little studio and David Tennant and two others brought them up to talk, then away in relays, and I had to do awful sums with minutes and give a warning signal to each five minutes before the end. There may of course be an unfavourable press ... but I think it went well and would interest people and certainly the speakers seemed quite pleased. Common and kind and fat little Sir Kingsley Wood, worthy and commonplace, made me a comic little speech afterwards and drank to my health and more political broadcasts.

The reaction to the broadcast was favourable. Letters of support poured in to the BBC from listeners, many of whom wrote that they hadn't been interested in these things before, but the discussion had made them want to know more. Press comment too was positive. The ice had been broken with the De-rating Bill debate and while some difficulties with politicians continued throughout the thirties, radio became established as an essential political forum.

Few accounts of the period record the part played by Hilda Matheson, probably because the main sources, including his own diaries, tend to emphasise Reith's role. Important as that was, there is no doubt that Hilda Matheson's contribution with its combination of clarity, firmness, persistence and persuasiveness was decisive. She demonstrated how successfully she could handle politicians. Reith tried to dominate them and when he failed was prepared often to submit, whereas she flattered and coaxed them, unwilling to take no for an answer when she could play on their vanity so well. There was another significant difference in the way they approached government. Reith was ready to defer to ministers because in the end he thought like they did and recognised the limits which sound men needed to place on the free play of ideas. She thought more like an academic or journalist, excited by ideas and delighting in debate, and so was less prepared to be understanding when politicians or anyone else tried to restrict what should be broadcast. Had she been in charge of the BBC the risks to its survival might have been greater, but even this is doubtful. One of her great skills was to charm and disarm people, especially when they were critical of particular policies. She was a natural fixer. She was also a great creative broadcaster and administrator, while Reith was merely a great administrator.

Entertainment Versus Education

When the newspaper proprietors and the politicians had been dealt with there remained only the enemy within, the lack of enthusiasm within the BBC itself for talks of a high intellectual standard. One of the members of the board of the old BBCo wrote to Reith complaining that there was:

> too much education, too many lectures and matters of that sort...too many uninteresting items, such as Elizabethan music, newfangled songs, weird quartettes and quintettes, groaning chamber music ... readings from unknown poets ... also talks on subjects which are of no interest to 99 per cent of the listeners.

This aversion to serious broadcasting had its supporters among the public and in the press. Letters to *The Times* complained of talks aimed at the vast army of tired, middle-aged listeners who between the hours of 8 and 10 o'clock were looking for relaxation and entertainment. This audience, it was claimed, did not want its armchairs turned into school forms. There was incredulity at the idea that anybody was really anxious at 10 o'clock at night to listen to a serious discourse on economics, or to be told of the intricacies of insurance on the evening of a bank holiday. One MP, expressing the sort of view that was common during parliamentary questions, begged the PMG to transmit to the BBC the general feeling of the people in this matter of talks. The public, he claimed, liked variety and liked it light, but he found the programmes intolerably didactic and usually highbrow.

Cartoons of the time lampooned the BBC for its elitism and lack of humour. When *The Listener* was launched in 1929, The *Evening Standard* published a montage of cartoons poking fun at the high-minded tone of an organisation that so obviously regarded itself as "a boon to mankind". Talks were satirised by inventing such "characteristic" subjects as *Travels in Central Oompom* and *The Home Life of the Artichoke*. Even Sir Thomas Beecham, not famous for being anybody's creature, was caricatured being conducted from behind by the BBC. Rosita Forbes, a formidable *Daily Mail* journalist, who according to Hilda Matheson always looked as though she had come straight out of an up-to-date harem and had unholy influence, wrote about talks directors who were out of touch with what people want.

Suspicion of the BBC's improving tendency was not confined to the popular press. Leonard Woolf confessed his inability to sit and listen to radio lectures or recitations and felt he was not competent to give an opinion on the BBC's programme of talks, discussions, lectures and poetry readings because usually he switched them off. There was also scepticism as to whether the wireless could ever treat serious subjects properly. Aldous Huxley thought that as the broadcaster had to broadcast to the whole population and not to a special public, most listeners would find the subject matter of literature to be too controversial and unpleasant because "people don't like reality". He thought also that listeners had too limited an attention span; the ideal length for a broadcast story was about twenty minutes or three to four thousand words, whereas most books were much longer. A broadcast story also suffered from the necessity for a reader, something he found as a writer unpleasantly intrusive.

Within the BBC the populist view of broadcasting was put most strongly by Filson Young, the FY who appears so often in her letters accompanied by a curse. He argued that as radio went into nearly every home its mass audience was quite unlike audiences which chose to attend, say, a theatre or concert hall. An item which might be regarded as agreeable to people seeking it outside, could be offensive to subscribers receiving a national service at home who expected programmes to be generally acceptable. The BBC was catering to the needs of thousands, and those dozens with more specialised tastes knew where to go to satisfy them.

This was a formidable array of opponents and always with the added uncertainty about whom the director-general would support. Hilda Matheson did not share the doubts of Filson Young or the journalists. As well as broadcasting the best in literature, music and scientific and philosophical thought, radio for her had a special role in breaking down the isolation of people, especially women, whether this was the physical isolation of living in the country or the mental isolation of those who lacked education. In her view, broadcasting could offer quite special services to everyone whose life was in any way circumscribed by seclusion, ill health, age, and lack of leisure or lack of means. For the majority of women whose active lives centred in their own homes, broadcasting could be used not only as a means of practical help with everyday problems, but also as a link with outside interests such as politics, books, travel, and ideas of all sorts.

She took an early opportunity to publicise her own thinking on the subject. On 14 January 1927, only days after the BBC had come into existence, an anonymous article appeared in the *Radio Times* on the subject of *Lectures by Wireless*. The sentiments and language indicate that she was the author. Its main theme was the growing demand for talks that were more definitely educational, covering modern science, literature and philosophy. These demands, it was asserted, were coming from:

> the many thoughtful men and women who have grown up without a chance of knowing some of the fundamental truths about the world we live in, and about the laws that govern our minds and our bodies, and the arts of music, poetry and painting.

Following up her ideas she encouraged organisations engaged in adult education, such as working men's clubs, tutorial classes and the young men and young women's Christian associations to form groups of their members to listen to and discuss the talks. Notes were provided for the use of group leaders. She initiated the collection of information on listener reaction which indicated that the minority that listened to talks was a substantial one. Size of audience, of course, could never be a decisive argument, because while the audience for talks was sometimes large, that for entertainment was always bigger. Nevertheless numbers could not be ignored and she was always seeking ways of measuring audiences and their reactions.

The response from listeners demonstrated that she was indeed feeding a hunger for information, ideas and good literature. The *Radio Times* often carried retrospects of the previous year's broadcasts in which listeners expressed their views:

> This last year has proved [wrote one in 1931 about a series explaining the crisis] that broadcasting is turning politics into something more personal ... the listener can judge at first hand. During the last month or two I have managed to learn something more about the mess which the world has got itself into and what we are doing about it. The gold standard is beginning to mean something more than a form of words.

Ellen Wilkinson MP commented that at meetings with Women's Institutes she was struck by the informed interest in international affairs which had been created by radio broadcasts. She thought that women got more out of the wireless talks than men did, because they were prepared to sit and listen.

Hilda Matheson's enthusiasm for educating people and widening their appreciation of good writing and their knowledge of domestic and international politics was balanced by a degree of realism. She knew that except for news, only a minority of listeners heard most of her programmes. By careful scripting, rehearsal and presentation, however, she hoped that the interest of increasing numbers of listeners could be captured and the minority swelled to a reasonable size. Her aim was always to increase the audience for talks. In an interview with the *Daily News* in 1928 after a broadcast talk about philosophy she claimed that Sussex farm-workers read and enjoyed Plato's *Republic*. Every village in Warwickshire had been "combed out" in an almost house-to-house enquiry as to the results of educational talks and the evidence obtained in this way conclusively proved their value. The BBC kept in touch with libraries all over the country, so that they could order in advance stocks of books on subjects which were going to be broadcast because there was always an increase in demand for books following a broadcast talk. This was not mere wishful thinking; typical of many letters at the time was one from a librarian who had probed the reasons for increasing demand for books of a more serious character and discovered that the interest of borrowers had been stimulated by a broadcast talk. Another librarian described listening to a talk in the series *A Hundred Years of*

Working Class Progress in company with several Post Office workers, a train driver, an accountant and a typist:

> Every member of the group is enthusiastic about the experiment, and we all felt that we were in at the beginning of great things.

Over 150 discussion groups were formed in the autumn of 1928 to listen to talks by Sydney Webb on *How to Study Social Questions* and by Professor Crofts of Bristol University on *The Adventure of Poetry*. Roger Eckersley confessed that he was sceptical about the likely response from listeners and resented having to give up his Saturday morning golf to attend an adult education council set up by the BBC, but the number of groups that came into being surprised him. So did the interest of uneducated men and women: tired gardeners, he noted, would mount their bicycles after a long day's work and ride some five miles to attend such groups, and there was no lack of group leaders.

Starting a Tradition

The *Radio Times* began to boast of the new and exciting approach to talks, lectures and debates. There were now three sessions each year, to match college terms, and a printed syllabus was published in advance. Sales of the syllabus increased from 20,000 to 70,000 per session. A regular pattern of five or six talks was broadcast nationally each day. Additional talks were broadcast locally from regional transmitters. The range of talks was impressive and the framework she established survived for years, long after she resigned. Some series continue even today and many programmes can be traced back to series she started.

The Week in Westminster was one of her many creations and the roots of *From Our Own Correspondent* lie in a weekly talk on international affairs, *The Way of the World* by Vernon Bartlett whom she introduced to broadcasting. On the spot reports of world events, such as debates at the League of Nations, were started by her as she drove the engineers to overcome all the difficulties of reporting back through the infant European telecommunications system. These novel extensions of the news together with general talks and reviews of poetry, literature, painting and theatre were all initiated by her. Even such programmes as those for farmers which started the broadcasting day, the evening stock-market reports, and the poetic rhythms and resonances of the shipping forecast were her idea. Under her direction the spoken word became part of the staple fare of radio.

- Do It Yourself

The first talk of the day, usually at 10.45 am, would be on a practical household subject such as cooking or bringing up children. On Saturdays, when the men were at home, it would deal with odd jobs around the house. These morning talks, which were at first derided as ridiculous, stimulated thousands of letters from working people, many of them struggling to survive on thirty shillings a week or less. There were requests for cooking recipes, so she brought in the "pudding lady" for a regular series. When the Empire Marketing Board printed a number of broadcast recipes they had 3,500 requests almost immediately: "not a bad indicator", she thought, especially as the details had been given out only from a regional station, not London. The series *The Day's Work* was very popular, in which jobs such as Covent Garden porter, steeplejack and postman were described by the people who did them. During the rest of the morning and in the afternoons the spoken word was confined mainly to programmes designed for schools. Talks for grown-ups began again at 6.00 or 6.30 pm with perhaps a talk for motorists, a gardening programme or a topic of general interest such as saving the countryside.

- *Poetry Readings*

The early evening was also the time for poetry readings. From the beginning of broadcasting there had been readings of poetry, and from the start they proved to be difficult. Roger Eckersley sighed over the endless controversy about how poetry should be read; there was never unanimity on the subject. One commentator writing in the *Radio Times* thought that poetry broadcasts tended to run against the grain of the general listener because of the affectation of readers who always seemed to lapse into a rhetorical style. Using poets themselves was no guarantee of success as they were not always natural readers, and certainly not natural broadcasters. Readers of *The Times* agreed, complaining of the dirge-like, monotonous, expressionless tones adopted by some modern poets. They also disliked the singsong voices of elocutionists. Hilda Matheson always attached importance to the right sort of voice for the subject of the broadcast. It was fatal, for example, for people with £10,000 a year voices to talk on how to live on £3 a week. In the same way there was a poetry voice that led people immediately to switch off:

> I have just been voice testing Fabia Drake. Nice and intelligent ... but like other actresses, however intelligent, she recites. I believe one ought to tell them to read as if they were reading to themselves, not performing ... I rehearsed a woman called Lilian Harris reading De La Mare yesterday and she made me sick. She has a good voice – the trained professional – but this damned sloppy, sentimental, coy, bright way of reading fills me with loathing. She ruins the metre and the scansion and overloads the words with emotion. I toned her down and levelled her down as far as I could and shall have to hope for the best, but oh for the non-professional ... [I put a reader] through it for an hour, till she was in shreds, poor thing. I imitated her and parodied her and bullied all the coyness and brightness I possibly could out of her and all her damnable elocutionist tricks. Poor little thing, I did feel a brute. She came today a little defiantly to show me two appreciative letters, both from elocutionists of many years standing!

Even the most eminent of her speakers were bullied into rehearsing and pruning their material. Virginia Woolf complained of the constant repetition required before a broadcast and tried to resist making alterations to her script about Beau Brummell, but in the end,

> Hilda Matheson ... made me castrate [him].

Keep things simple was the basic rule, whether it was poetry or a talk or a discussion. She would search for the simple word, the simple expression of a truth, sitting on the floor in front of the gas fire at Savoy Hill in defiance of all Reith's rules about appropriate office behaviour. Her natural informality towards everything suited the new medium. The declamatory tone was always wrong for radio; what was needed was the note of intimacy as in conversation with a friend.

Because of her interest in poetry readings and her criticism of those previously broadcast she was, in true services fashion, made responsible for all readings. Gradually she began to allocate more time to poetry, first with readings in concert intervals, then at the end of evening programmes and then on Sunday afternoons. By early 1929 there were often four readings a week. Inevitably, once in charge, she began to experiment. There were chronological series, illustrating the development of English poetry, poems on single subjects such as trees or flowers or people in towns, and combinations of poems and music. A particular success was a series of talks and readings by Vita Sackville-West on modern poetry. The *Radio Times* published these in full, including one on T S Eliot and his "difficult" new poem *The Waste Land*, an adventurous approach for a listings magazine. (One cannot imagine similar literary experiments in today's version, described recently by one reviewer as a tawdry cookery-cum-gossip magazine that should be rechristened *The People's Piffle*.)

In 1929 she persuaded the BBC to publish an anthology of the poetry that had been broadcast. Called *Foundations of English Poetry* it gave examples of poetry from the earliest times down to the Victorians and was a commercial success. In 1931 another BBC anthology, this time of modern poets, was published by the Hogarth Press. When writing later about the BBC she contrasted the ample time given to music with the few grudging hours allowed to poetry. Her own efforts to redress the balance did not survive her, and she regarded this failure of British broadcasting towards one of the arts in which Britain excelled as a standing reproach to the BBC.

- *Reviews*

The 7 o'clock spot was often used for cinema, theatre, music or book reviews. Since May 1927 books had been reviewed by Mary Hamilton, a journalist and budding politician who was finally elected as a Labour member in 1929, and in 1933 was appointed as a BBC governor. Her position and influence did not save her from the new broom. Hilda Matheson was determined

> to get rid of [her] because she is so bad.

As good broadcasters were difficult to find this adverse assessment was probably objective, but there were other motives too:

> I would awfully like to know...whether you could contemplate a fortnightly review of new novels, [she wrote to Vita]. Oh darling do go on thinking favourably about it – it would be so perfect from my point of view – excuse for you coming to my office, benefit untold to my listeners, prestige of the most exalted kind for the BBC – oh please do.

There is no doubt that Vita was a skilful and popular broadcaster and that the pressure to broadcast came from Hilda, not herself, but Vita certainly received favoured nation treatment. Hilda reassured her that reviewing novels would involve reading only about four or five books a fortnight and glancing at one or two others; she could just ask for the books she wanted and not bother with the ones she didn't want. There would be a payment of ten guineas for each talk and another three to four guineas for subsequent publication. This would produce about £300 a year for Vita if she reviewed regularly (about £10,000 today). The plot was outlined by Hilda in a letter which shows a calculating and unscrupulous side of her character:

> We should have to work it via Desmond [MacCarthy] I think. FY's horrid nose would smell a rat if it came from me. The next step ... is for me to write to Desmond and see if he is...prepared to suggest it and back it. There will undoubtedly be a battle with FY, but I don't feel prepared to be beaten. I think I can secure Roger and probably Murray, the publications man. Stobart isn't worth considering. I have got the evidence of all the people who say you have got the only decent voice on the wireless of any woman. My own young men I'm not sure of; they will perhaps be amused! I think I can get away with it quite easily ... people like Garvin and Henderson ... would back me every time ... what happens is that I put up a draft programme for the summer to Roger and his absurd little programme board of G Grossmith, FY etc. I shall probably be sent for and have to defend it piece by piece for a matter of three hours – trying to keep my patience – it's the hardest thing I have to do. Then it goes to the Director General and sometimes the Governors and then it comes back to me, usually of course untouched, but after much waste of time and (on my part) temper.

On this occasion her temper was not tried too hard and she won, confirming the prominent role in broadcasting she secured not just for poetry but for Vita. Soon *The Manchester Guardian* was writing about the dangers of monopoly in broadcasting, suggesting politely that perhaps Vita was given too much time on air.

- *The Heavyweights*

The poetry spot and the 7 o'clock review would be followed by a language class or a talk on a scientific or historical subject starting at 7.30 pm and going on for fifteen or twenty minutes. At 9.15 pm or thereabouts came the most important talk of the day by one of her heavyweight speakers: J M Keynes, Dean Inge, George Bernard Shaw, H G Wells, and Harold Nicolson. Each of these stars would often have a series dealing with a single theme such as *Finance in the Modern World, The English Character, Can Democracy Survive? The Modern Novel*. A series of six talks became almost a standard pattern and she was constantly casting about for new subjects and speakers. How about a Bloomsbury symposium on the novel, she asked Vita?

> *Unfortunately Rebecca West was a devil to deal with, had such a temper and didn't really write good novels, but was very amusing; Aldous Huxley just won't broadcast, but might in this series; Clemence Dane had a nice voice, unlike Margaret Kennedy whose voice and manner were annoying.*

The universities were trawled for speakers and while Oxford and Cambridge provided many, so did the universities of London, Birmingham, Manchester, Bristol, Liverpool, Sheffield and Exeter. Roger Eckersley wrote later that it was largely owing to Hilda Matheson's powers of persuasion that so many eminent academics and outstanding personalities were brought to the microphone.

Dangerous Eminence

She began to be acclaimed as the woman who took over talks when they were at a deplorably low ebb, deservedly unpopular with both highbrow and lowbrow, and raised them to a position where they were acclaimed in the kitchen and the university common room. H G Wells recalled first meeting her when she was director of talks. He admired her efforts to make broadcasting a medium for bringing the most stimulating ideas into the home. She made, in his view, a valiant and almost single-handed attempt to save the new medium from the raucous vulgarity, piety and ill-advised propaganda that it was prone to, and to which it had succumbed by 1940, the year in which he wrote his tribute to her. Wells' opinion has to be treated with some caution. His jaundiced view of the BBC was probably influenced by what he felt to have been his unfair exclusion from broadcasting during most of the thirties. His eye for a pretty woman might also have affected his favourable assessment of Hilda Matheson. She described to Vita a squalid and unpleasant approach he made to her in his flat at the very top of the St. Ermin's building near St James's Park:

> *no shouts would have been heard anywhere. So I had to do the best I could ... I had enough sense to realize that to seem frightened and to make a*

scene, or to resist very agitatedly would probably have been sheer folly, not to say fatal. But I took it with the utmost lightness and laughed at him ... and by the end he had become ruefully avuncular.

Other outstanding commentators, perhaps more detached in their views than H G Wells, were no less approving. Harold Laski found it difficult not to praise the syllabus for a forthcoming session. In its varied programme there were few palates whose tastes had not been considered. The selection of subjects and speakers was admirable and confirmed his view that talks now played a vital part in the development of the national culture. He thought that the BBC was still too timid about broadcasting controversial matters and he regretted such omissions as the failure to allow a communist talk on unemployment, but his overall assessment was favourable.

Even the technical wireless press, usually not all that interested in the programmes, recognised that:

through sheer personality Miss Matheson has transformed the whole situation, until now she ranks among those who most nearly approach the status of indispensable ... It is known that the Governors hold Miss Matheson in the highest regard, and there are not wanting signs that she is marked out for high preferment.

Commentators began referring to a University of the Air and Charles Trevelyan MP wrote an article with that title in the *Radio Times*. Another educationist referred to the impact of broadcasting on people living in the country and described talks as the foundation of a rural university. Early in 1927 the BBC and the British Institute of Adult Education jointly established a committee under Sir Henry Hadow to inquire into the potential for using the wireless in the field of adult education. As secretary of the committee, Hilda Matheson organised its agenda, wrote many of its papers and drafted the final report. There is no doubt that the report was an expression of her own views about broadcasting and the mission of the BBC to educate and inform. Her hope was that broadcasting could revive learning as the printing press helped the Renaissance in an earlier age. It could bring knowledge and interest to those who had passed their period of formal training, but retained a desire for wider knowledge. *The Times* welcomed the report when it was published in April 1928, seeing it as evidence that the wireless was in safe hands and expressing the hope that when technology permitted, a whole wavelength might be devoted to adult education.

The *Radio Times* began to publish "striking and witty points from outstanding talks" and then to run full page articles reproducing talks which readers had asked to see printed. Towards the end of 1928 she felt confident enough to put out her manifesto in a signed article in the *Radio Times* under the challenging, if wordy, headline, *The Broadcast Talk is No Longer, As of Old, the Cinderella of Programmes*. The tone of the article was bold and unapologetic, pointing out that it was the people who seldom or never listen to broadcast programmes who still made jokes about talks on white ants. The main difficulty was in choosing from the huge range of subjects in which listeners had expressed an interest. She outlined the programme for the autumn, which was to include many of the most brilliant talkers of the day on subjects on which they were acknowledged authorities. In a final flourish, characteristic of her own style if not that of the BBC, she wrote:

> Someone is supposed to have said that the shortest way out of Manchester was to get drunk. That is really rather a slow and expensive method. An idea, or an effort of the imagination, can take us out of ourselves in the twinkling of an eye; and this is what broadcast talks can sometimes help us to do.

By the end of 1928 Hilda Matheson had completed just over two successful years at the BBC and enhanced her reputation and that of the Corporation. The quality of her programmes, and the decisive way in which she had swept out of the way most of the problems which obstructed effective broadcasting of the spoken word, made her a commanding figure. She was now poised to develop talks and news without the constraints which had previously been imposed. The deal which the BBC struck when being granted these greater freedoms was that it would act responsibly and police itself. Hilda Matheson was to find out that this self-regulation could be at least as irksome as government prohibitions, but all that lay ahead. In the summer of 1928 she was riding high, and it was then that she met and fell in love with Vita Sackville-West. This was to have a profound effect both on her personal life and on her work for the BBC.

Getting to Know Vita

Vita Sackville-West made her first broadcast on 18 April 1928. She must have met Hilda Matheson then, but the friendship did not begin until two months later. Hilda wrote first, congratulating her on a recent broadcast reading from *The Land*. Vita replied, hardly more than an acknowledgement, on 7 June, Hilda's birthday. Later that month the actor Robert Harris read Keats' *Ode to a Nightingale*, Shelley's *Ode to the West Wind* and part of *Adonais*:

> I sat with tears pouring down my face. Oh Hadji, what poetry,

wrote Vita to her husband Harold Nicolson. He urged her to write and congratulate the producer, which she did. Whereupon Hilda invited her to visit the BBC to discuss the broadcasting of poetry. In July, accompanied by Virginia Woolf, Vita visited Hilda at the BBC. In turn Hilda was invited to Long Barn for the second weekend in July.

The contacts continued with a mixture of business meetings about poetry readings and invitations to spend weekends at Long Barn. Many of the autumn invitations could not be accepted because of other commitments, including one when Hilda felt obliged to take part in a ghastly staff play in order to dispel her reputation for haughty standoffishness. By now Vita was describing Hilda to Harold as an angel of unselfishness who had become a real friend. Harold Nicolson recognised the familiar signs of a serious liaison and wrote that he was becoming rather worried about Miss Matheson. It was not until the weekend of 8-9 December that the affair really began to take off when Hilda was invited to Long Barn together with the novelist Hugh Walpole, who was to take part in a broadcast debate with Vita the following Monday. During the weekend they visited Penns in the Rocks, a Georgian house near Groombridge recently bought by Dorothy Wellesley. Hugh Walpole recorded in his journal that they talked all the afternoon in a manner to give any worthy magistrate a fit!

They talked also about the broadcast on *The Modern Woman*, which Hilda had arranged. On the Monday evening after the broadcast, which was described by Vita in a letter to her husband which has been published, Vita stayed the night at Hilda's flat in Sumner Place, South Kensington. Hilda did not go to the office on Tuesday, claiming she was sick. On Wednesday 12 December 1928 she arrived at the office just in time to hear:

> *one of the most charming of our intelligent young men making the most moving speech about my enforced absence through illness.*

Later in the day she wrote the first of her love letters. Her passionate nature was now to be divided between the BBC and Vita, and Hilda could see no end to the bliss that lay ahead. Virginia Woolf, still in love with Vita despite having been supplanted earlier, was more realistic:

> *And now you're off in the bitter black night with female unknown; fresh, or stale and scented rather, from the arms, to put it euphemistically, of Mary – God! What a succession of flea bites and bug bites the life of respectable hard working woman is!*

Chapter Three

LOVE AFFAIR WITH VITA
1928–1931

The Letters

Darling, I love you more than I can ever tell you ... it's the most completely comprehensive sweep I ever dreamed of, all of me, in every sort of different way. I bless you and Heaven and creatures generally for having made it possible for this to happen; and you in particular, not the others, for being so perfect and so good to me, and most of all for loving me ... Here is a sober statement of a giddy fact. You are the most beautiful person that's ever swept across my horizon ... Oh Heavens, you've gone to my head like your Spanish wine tonight. I keep going into my bedroom to look at [your photograph] and to take pleasure in seeing you there and to gloat over your perfection and to swell with happiness and pride that you should love an ugly little scrub like me. Darling it must worry you that I am so devastatingly plain. I wish to God that I weren't for your sake ... Don't fall in love with anybody else just yet. Darling don't, however attractive, alluring, really admirable or charming. I couldn't bear it, I just couldn't.

Most of Hilda's letters to Vita, of which there are more than a hundred, were written during the last days of December 1928 and the first two months of 1929. They had just fallen in love, then almost immediately had to separate when Vita joined her husband in the British Embassy in Berlin, to which he had been posted by the Foreign Office.

There must have been a similar number of letters from Vita to Hilda who recorded in January the fiftieth she had received, but none have survived. It is possible that Hilda destroyed them herself, but unlikely. She described the letters as the most precious possession she had:

I keep them in a bundle ... It is a heavenly occupation to read them through from the beginning.

When the affair ended she kept Vita's friendship, and would have wanted to keep the letters too. Had she survived to enjoy a normal span of life she might well have sorted out her papers and destroyed the most personal, but she died relatively young during an operation which was expected to give her a new lease of life. It was not an occasion for a bonfire of the only remaining record of her great love. If the letters had been among her papers when she died, the likelihood is that her mother got rid of them. Meta might have recalled the curious instructions in her husband's will ten years previously that all her letters to him before and since their marriage should be destroyed, the former at least unread. Even without that stimulus she would almost certainly have followed the polite conventions of the time. In her own will, made on 23 July 1930 about nine months before her love affair with Vita ended, Hilda Matheson does not refer to any letters, and apart from small legacies for some friends, who did not include Vita, she left all her estate to her brother. If her estate included the letters then Donald would almost certainly have found them among her effects and whether read or not destruction would have followed very quickly.

Hilda's letters, however, were kept by Vita, each preserved in its original envelope. As the letters usually give only the day and time of writing the sequence sometimes can be confusing, but the retention of the envelopes with their clear postmarks stamped in both London and Berlin enables them to be dated exactly. (The postmarks, together with comments in the letters themselves noting when Vita received them, bear out the assurance given to Hilda by her local post office that if she posted them by six in the evening they would arrive in Berlin by lunch time the following day.)

The output of letters was prodigious, sometimes three a day. In this activity as in all others Hilda Matheson was driven by her frantic demons. There are more than eight hundred pages and she wrote them on every possible occasion, in all sorts of places. She scribbled away at Long Barn (the Nicolson home loaned to her for weekends while they were in Germany), at her parents' home in Peaslake, Surrey, at Cliveden when staying with the Astors, in the office, on station platforms and trains, or in bed after midnight at the end of an exhausting day's work. One she wrote in the

> *pompous oak-panelled Council Chamber [of County Hall] ... while they all blethered ... but I hadn't counted on an inquisitive neighbour and I had to stop.*

Another was written in full view of all the reporters and the audience in University College Hall while a rabbit-faced young man discoursed about the League of Nations. Like Mlle Vinteuil's lover, who enjoyed the desecration of making love to her in front of a photograph of her father, Hilda Matheson got a thrill from expressing her love for Vita in front of those who would abhor it:

> *By Jove what a shock all these good people would have if they could see what thoughts and longings are filling my head.*

Perhaps it was with similar, almost sacrilegious, feelings that she made extensive use of BBC stationery. Many of her letters were written on the bright orange slips used to record administrative details of talks, or on memo sheets which contained BBC injunctions such as "Do not use this side", which she would score through with the statement "Shall!". These mischievous, covert rebellions against convention and respectability have an adolescent ring about them, perhaps because women in that society, like adolescents at any time, could not expect to be taken seriously. Her frustration at not being able to declare her love openly is a constant theme, and her perkily mutinous gestures might have provided a substitute for more violent actions, the equivalent of spitting in Lord Reith's eye. The letters were not great literary works, as she frankly acknowledged to Vita:

> *I must try to pull myself together and write you a proper letter. This is a rotten specimen. I think I just go on saying the same thing over and over again, till you must be sick of it. It is terribly difficult not to because it is what goes on echoing through me night and day, but as you justly remark it will cloy. I ought to model myself on Dorothy Osborne (I wish I could write her lovely English) and discourse to you gravely about things of importance.*

The letters *are* repetitive and sometimes gushing, but they do discuss matters of importance in addition to her love for Vita, in particular her ruminations about homosexual love and descriptions of her work at the BBC. (See chapters two and four for BBC references.) The style reflects the haste with which most of them were written, giving an impression of someone always running to make the last post, but they are clear, often funny, always acute in their observations of other people, and obviously sincere. They are above all spontaneous, passionate, almost desperate love letters to a person whom she scarcely knew. They had had scarcely ten days together in any intimate sense:

> *Yet here we are writing to each other every day, without any apparent barriers or obstacles or reserve ... I have this incredible feeling of naturalness and absence of shyness or reserve or* anything *towards you – complete and utter shamelessness if it comes to that ... It's perfectly true what you said in your Sunday letter...that all these seventy odd letters we may be writing to each other before we meet will influence our relationship. It will be a longer interchange of thoughts and feelings than we have behind us.*

Stoker

Devotion was the main characteristic of her love, reflected in Vita's pet name for her, "Stoker". Hilda would sign off many of her letters as "your devoted Stoker". Sometimes Stoker appears to be a furry animal, but usually is literally the person in the engine room stoking the boilers:

It is *so odd, so gloriously odd, to love a stoker, it's so seldom done. Stokers grub away in their trousers, down in murky holds shovelling coal and getting awfully horny-handed. They suffer from the limitations of most sons of toil; they are rude and uncultivated, of limited imagination and few wits. Now being in love with Orlando, that's a very different matter. Darling, darling. I did blow down the speaking tube to the engine room and am still blushing hotly and furiously at what the stokers told me ... Do you know I found a beautiful picture in a newspaper ... of dozens and dozens of stokers' trousers all hanging up to dry on a battleship, which I meant to send you. Such a nice picture, how silly to lose it. I feel absolutely tied and bound to you by links of incredible strength ... you possess me and own me utterly. You great big bully, coming it over a poor little stoker like that. Absolutely defenceless he was and how could he know he was letting himself in for this complete extinction of himself as a sober, self-contained individual.*

The lowly, humble, hard working stoker, little more than a slave, provides a clever, telling, almost spiteful image of their love life and Hilda's character. The nickname picks up so many aspects of her character. Her submissiveness offset by a jaunty independence, her busyness and practicality, her delight in making things work, and the relentless, single-minded, selfless way in which she applied herself to tasks and punished herself in the service of others. Hilda was always stoking hard in the various holds she occupied, while the more glamorous captains enjoyed themselves on the bridge. There must have been a particular occasion which gave rise to the nickname. One can speculate wildly, even salaciously given the overtones the word can be given. The likelihood is that it was a mundane event, perhaps ingeniously applying adhesive to seal a leaking pipe, or getting the boiler to work at Long Barn, but she doesn't identify it in her letters.

Sharing Her Love for Vita

Writing to Harold Nicolson in 1912, the year before their marriage, Vita discussed the subservient attitude of her then lover, Rosamund Grosvenor:

> *It is a pity and rather tiresome. But doesn't everyone want one subservient person in their life? I've got mine in her. Who is yours? Certainly not me.*

Now, in Hilda Matheson, Vita's desire for subservience was met again, leaving her free to fulfil her needs for other loves as well. On the same day in December 1928 when Hilda was writing passionately to Vita about living in a queer intoxicated atmosphere of ecstasy and misery, Vita was writing to Harold that he was much more important to her than anything or anyone else. She could never, never cure herself of loving him, Vita wrote. He was dearer to her than anybody ever had been or could be and if he died she would kill herself. Vita's capacity as a serial lover has been well documented in the biography written by Victoria Glendinning and in the various editions of her letters to Harold Nicolson and Virginia Woolf. The details of her liaisons do not need to be repeated, but the facts of at least those attachments concurrent with this latest affair have to be considered for the light they throw on Hilda Matheson, who does not seem to have been upset by the competition:

> Of course I understand about H[arold] and the way you must feel about him. I should never expect you to feel otherwise. He seems to be so entirely the right sort of person for you to be married to ... and so blessedly understanding about what is and what is not possible for you and that you would be bound to hate leaving him in that damned Berlin and all by himself.

In April 1929 when she met Harold at a party and tried to conceal her shyness by her usual "ghastly sprightliness" he was very sweet to her:

> What I thought most charming was the way he talked to me about you as if I had a sort of right to know and love you.

His diaries, which record many meetings with Hilda Matheson, make it clear that he was not just being polite. He held her in high regard and valued her judgement. When he was considering the possibility of leaving the Foreign Service for a job as a journalist, it was Hilda Matheson whom he urged Vita to consult. She became almost one of the Nicolson family, planning treats for Ben and Nigel, the two sons, on their return from Germany and generally acting, and being treated by them, as an affectionate, honorary aunt.

The relationship which included Virginia Woolf was more complicated, less friendly, at least on Mrs Woolf's part. Looking forward to Virginia's visit to Berlin, Vita was counting the 482,000 seconds to her arrival, the moment she was living for. On the same day on which she recorded those feelings she received a love letter from Hilda with a remarkably accepting tone:

> Oh my dearest I am so glad your Virginia thinks me all right ... I should have minded if she hadn't liked me at all.

Hilda recognised the continuing affection between Vita and Virginia and was concerned that her own love for Vita might hurt Virginia. Mrs Woolf never reciprocated this sensitivity:

> My God what friends you have! If I had Hilda, I should not want medicine; but then of course you will say I am jealous. No. It's only that our taste differs. She affects me as a strong purge, as a hair shirt, as a foggy day, as a cold in the head.

When Hilda and Vita went on a walking tour in Savoy, Virginia was furious:

> *She never told me she was going abroad for a fortnight, didn't dare; till the last moment, when she said it was a sudden plan ... these Hilda's are a chronic case; and as this one won't disappear and is unattached, she may be permanent. And like the damned intellectual snob I am, I hate to be linked, even by an arm, with Hilda. Her earnest aspiring competent wooden face appears before me, seeking guidance in the grave question of who's to broadcast. A queer trait in Vita – her passion for the earnest middle-class intellectual, however drab and dreary.*

Virginia Woolf was still expressing her dislike on Hilda's death ten years later, but Hilda was always concerned that her rivals should never be hurt. She showed the same sensitivity towards Dorothy Wellesley:

> *I feel also that Dottie stands for something that has been and is still important to you, though not easy to fit into your present life and that this makes another problem. Darling, I suppose the truth is life can't be simple for a person who has many sides and many gifts like you which attract, very forcibly, so many people ... Oh how queer it is when I see you all mixed up with other people, particularly when the air is as heavily charged as it is when Dottie is about ... I am sorry about Dottie, really sorry I mean, I hate it that a happiness for me should mean an unhappiness for her.*

Being one of four people loved by Vita seems a curious, even bizarre, arrangement when looked at from outside, and surely unsatisfactory. Certainly Virginia Woolf and Dorothy Wellesley found it frustrating. Vita herself was sometimes perplexed and distressed by her own driving need to replenish relationships and about the quality of the liaisons that resulted, the falsity and difficulty of relations with people. On reading the two volumes of Miss Payne's life of Byron she saw something of herself as she read first one letter by the poet and then another, both written the same day to two different people and flatly contradicting each other. One of Vita's most attractive characteristics was that she never deceived herself and was usually frank with her current lover, although Evelyn Irons who succeeded Hilda wrote that Vita was apt to keep her friends in separate compartments. Hilda at least knew about some of her predecessors and the conflicts of loyalty that remained, but it didn't matter, she was ready to excuse anything:

> *If you were to tell me you had murdered your grandmother, deceived your husband, beaten your children, embezzled from your bank ... or broken every commandment in the decalogue, I might regret it, I might even deplore it, but I should love you just as much and perhaps more. It's something much further inside you that I love. Your actual flame. I should know that you'd done these slightly unusual things because of reasons or impulses which ... I would understand. So I should love you just the same. An almost greater test: I should love you just the same if I found you had tricks of habit or speech that would infuriate me in anyone else; or if you were smitten with the most repulsive disease and I had to look after you (as*

I jolly well should by jove). So now you know. And if you want to shake me off or extinguish my love, Heaven help you my poor dear.

Passion and the fear of losing Vita would explain something of her readiness to share, but there was more to it than that. Virginia Woolf's love manifested itself in jealousy viciously expressed, but something in Hilda's character always made her put other people first. She could see that her own relationship with Vita was only one of several that Vita needed, and she was prepared to take her place in the crowd:

> *Whatever happens our relationship must never complicate or get in the way of those other ones if it can possibly be avoided. What I mean is that I ... try not to be an encumbrance – all right my sweet don't be cross – I mean a sort of problem to be coped with. Even before your letter came about Ben's long leave I had been wondering a little what for instance you would do about Dottie if I came down that first weekend, or Virginia supposing she wanted to come down for the day. And from that I began wondering whether you would rather – no – whether it would be easier for you (do you see how conceited I have grown?) if I left the way clear for you to see other people and come down to you the weekend after ... The main thing is that it is you who must decide about what we do because you have got other claims on you that I haven't, so it is you who really matters. You know I am the sort of person to whom you can always say without any kind of compunction – please keep away from Long Barn, or please after all don't come tomorrow, or next weekend, or whatever it is. This ought not to need saying really, because it is all involved in loving you, naturally.*

This remarkable tolerance was extended even towards Vita's "scrapes", the Nicolson word for lesser infatuations. Vita would tease Hilda with accounts of other women falling in love with her, and sometimes succeeded in provoking an angry reaction:

> *No I do not want you to have an affair with a red headed photographer who makes you feel you must disinfect yourself after you've seen her. Darling you wouldn't really like her ... I suppose ... she wants to photograph you without any clothes. A glorious thought if it wasn't she.*

Usually however, the reaction was solicitous. Vita's needs were paramount and Hilda encouraged her to write about her affairs, which were excused and dismissed in an almost light-hearted way:

> *People of your complexity of make-up and your strength of feeling have got to have outlets, and if they haven't got ones they want and like, they have to make believe with shadows or substitutes or ersatz articles of some sort or other. Isn't that what happens? It seems to me quite natural. I expect they don't wear very well and may be very unsatisfactory, but they may be more tolerable than a vacuum. Are the charmers and sirens all finding you curiously unresponsive my sweet? How glad I am. Oh how glad. Yet, having a kind heart, how sad for the poor sirens.*

"How do I Love Thee?..."

Vita was curious about Hilda's own love affairs, often asking for descriptions of the women and the situations, but there had not been many. Hilda wrote that she had been terribly fond of people, going "all out" to provide the affection and support that they needed. The close friend at school who was killed and the "vamp" she was very much absorbed by at Oxford have been referred to. Then there was Kate Walsh,

> *who picked me up after the war, has cared and has done things for me, and does still. I owe her more than anybody else before because she freed me from the fear of my mother. But she has got a jealous husband and two babies and can't care in detail so to speak. Anyway it is and always has been of a different kind, a community of interest at one stage in our careers, and a community of tastes about mountains and country, and a real affection of the "school friend" kind which goes on even though we have diverged quite a lot in some ways. [Then came a wild flare up with Marjorie Maxse three years ago] which was quite unlike anything I'd ever known before. I still don't understand it. It was partly a physical attraction, partly a tremendous liking and it made us both very happy for about a year. I don't quite know what happened to it. M, I think, had a tremendous revulsion of feeling on the physical side and it affected everything. I was awfully unhappy and perplexed and I expect very stupid. But things had got pretty well straightened up by the end of the summer. I had realised that the most that was left was a rather decent kind of understanding and loyalty, but no intimacy of any kind on any plane.*

The quality of romantic innocence which shows through these accounts of her own previous attachments infused also her love for Vita, with an accompanying total lack of realism. Knowing Vita's history, having read it in Vita's letters to her, she still could not contemplate the inevitable termination of their own affair:

> *Our love for each other, yours and mine, is so perfect and lovely and secure and certain and for keeps ... and I don't believe it's exactly like anybody else's love. No two loves ever are, surely, and we've made it and we're going to go on making it, and it's going to grow.*

At work she was critical, forceful, analytical, but in her love for Vita she abandoned objectivity; it was all acceptance, passion and romance. To be in love with one of the most famous writers of the time and to have poems written especially for you was intoxicating:

> *I shall say the musician one in my bath tonight ... I like it terribly and I love it that you should have written it for me ... I think the Donne is a very good joke my dear one. I chuckled and enjoyed it and rolled it on my tongue ... Can't you see the critics and editors hundreds of years hence,*

> busy on a new edition of your less-known poems, writing learned footnotes to explain obscure references to dragon's tongues and reversing calendars, super Freudian explanations or whatever may be the equivalent fashion of the moment.

"... Let Me Count the Ways."

Hilda's tolerance of the competition was probably encouraged by the fact that she had now what none of the others had, Vita's "actual flame"; the single-minded, passionate, physical love that Vita from time to time gave to one person. The physical attraction of Vita's tall, androgynous figure, was overpowering:

> *Virginia Woolf is right. Those eyes and eyebrows and forehead destroy one utterly. All of you does in its own way. I'm observant anyway you know and of you I notice every line and curve ... but your eyes and your eyebrows and your forehead make all my pulses run away with me ... I think I should love to dance with you. I have always thought your long slim limbs were made for dancing, but not for being guided by some stupid man who was probably scared of your height. I should be just the right height for you shouldn't I my sweet ... I want you to love me – to have me – to possess me utterly – I want to give myself to you ... my body is yours as my heart is yours ... sometimes I want you so terribly physically that I can hardly bear it. I can't feel ashamed of that. I can't feel it's anything but part and parcel of the way I love your mind – your poetry – your whole self. I have to be honest with you, you see. You say "I get awful attacks of wanting you ... physically too, I mean, I'm afraid". Do you feel regretful or apologetic or anything? I wasn't sure what "I'm afraid" meant.*

The delights of love included the memory, and anticipation, of bathing one another, sleeping together, and even the vicarious pleasures of Vita's wardrobe, enjoyed when Hilda used Long Barn at weekends while Vita was in Germany:

> *And then I went through your own room to mine and my feelings got queerer and queerer. Sweetheart, I'm ashamed to tell you how foolish I became – you'd think I was silly. You must think of me rather like Jane [one of Vita's dogs] in her most demonstrative moments running round nuzzling things and playing with your shoe or your rug or your cushions. I became quite daft. I had to touch everything – your bed, your furniture, your pictures; yes, and just like Jane, your country shoes all neatly in a row – they gave me a special lump in my throat.*

One cannot imagine Vita getting much satisfaction from lining up Hilda's shoes. Even as a child Vita had engaged in sadistic games, on one occasion tying four young visitors to trees and thrashing their legs with nettles. Hilda would not have enjoyed torture. Her submission was of a more romantic sort, like the uncritical attachment of a child to its mother, the crush of a junior for the Head Prefect, the feeling of a pet towards a kind master, or of a stoker towards the captain:

> *It is a queer thing being managed! I am terribly unused to it. Years, as you say, of glorious, or shall we say lonely, independence. You never know, I might love my chains and hug my fetters. I love my jailer, I know that. And I will be good, just like Queen Victoria, or no, I think I'd rather be like a good dog with a lump of sugar.*

The verbal fencing in this reply, with the change from an image of physical restraint to one of softer, dog-like devotion, shows that there were limits to Hilda's submissiveness even in love.

Discretion and Defiance

Although Vita's affairs were many she was discreet, and disliked the idea that other people might know of them. The First World War had shifted many taboos, but attitudes generally towards homosexuality were hostile. It was a love which still could not be named. A *Sunday Express* review in 1928 of Radclyffe Hall's novel, *The Well of Loneliness*, demanded that it be withdrawn from circulation, the reviewer asserting that he would rather put a phial of prussic acid in the hands of a healthy girl or boy than this book. In November that year following prosecution for obscenity it was banned, not to be re-published until 1949. The work which caused such outrage was described by Vita as a serious attempt to write a frank and completely unpornographic book about lesbianism. Yet the hysteria of the time was such that she felt it necessary even in a private letter to use her codeword "b.s.ness" instead of "lesbianism". In a later letter to Harold about the possible publication of some of her own poems she wrote:

> *It is not on the score of their goodness or badness that I am worried ... but you see they are love poems ... and it has since occurred to me that people will think them Lesbian. I should not like this, either for my own sake or for yours.*

Vita was always careful to avoid any public identification of herself as lesbian. Hilda and Virginia were less reserved, and sometimes they could be bold:

> *I told Vanessa the story of our passion in a chemists shop the other day [recorded Virginia Woolf], but do you really like going to bed with women she said – taking her change. And how d' you do it? And so she bought her pills to take abroad, talking as loud as a parrot.*

Hilda too had little use for subterfuge:

Look here – this business of privacy and prudence – what can one do? I never was any good at acting ... my Sumner Place family are too well aware that my affections are engaged ... Marjorie is the soul of secrecy ... Dorothy ... is loyal and all that to the last degree. Roger, Lionel, Joe, Mrs Barry, the commissionaires, must all know my affections are to some extent engaged. Kate knows the same – Mary Somerville and all that lot. It seems to me therefore worse than useless to pretend complete indifference and I've therefore taken the offensive. Told several of them what fun it has been getting to know you and how much I like you. They'd be far more suspicious if I was ineffectively secretive.

Hilda resented the need for discretion. She never felt that her love was something to be ashamed of, but she knew that the public disapproved. Agonising about how far she could confide in her friends, she feared their likely reaction. Although nobody then spoke in those terms, she would very much have liked to "come out". Sometimes she seemed to be on the brink of making public her feelings, as though seeking a martyr's crown. Time and again she returns in the letters to the paradox of a love which seems to her to be honest and good, but towards which most people reacted with disgust. Yet there are no signs of self-hatred or self-disgust. Usually unconfident about her appearance and many of her tastes and attitudes, she accepted her homosexual feelings and regretted only that they had to be hidden. Her angry frustration at not being able to make public her love for Vita, together with her fear of the consequences if she did, are palpable in the following selections from her letters:

I suppose there would be nothing too bad for my office to say about me if they knew. But you know if there's one thing more than another I feel every day surer of, it is that what we feel for each other is all good. That as far as I am concerned I know it is part and parcel of anything decent in me, of the best parts of me, not at all of the worst. That it makes more of me, not less. Makes me nicer to other people even, more understanding. I cannot feel one shred of shame or remorse or regret or anything dimly approaching it. And you do feel the same too don't you my sweetheart. I loathe the need for furtiveness and secrecy. I find it incomprehensibly absurd. I have to keep reminding myself that it is considered anti-social and immoral and it makes me fairly blaspheme. There – that's a good explosion ... Love, all you've given to me, all the physical side of it too, seems to me to be life in its very highest expression. It's mixed up for me with any decent thinking or feeling I've got or ever had. With everything in fact that is true and beautiful and of good report. And yet I suppose some people would regard it as shameful and vicious. Darling, I can't understand it. One does somehow recognise truth when one sees it by a kind of click and so I haven't a shred of doubt that what I feel is true. But is the world all wrong? At lunch the other day Rosita Forbes (who doesn't impress me at all as being true or beautiful or of good report – how catty I am) told a sniggering story about Tallulah Bankhead and her lady friends and they all laughed. I felt hot under the collar and angry. Sensuality and promiscuity seem to me much of a muchness wherever they are – all part of the less pleasant side of human beings – and love that's worth anything equally so, equally good ... isn't it quality that matters not the sex? ... I was rather cheered last night when I was talking to Rachel Crowdy and Katharine Furse ... they were both saying very much what you say, that prejudice and narrow mindeness or meanness were far worse vices and more destructive than half the forms of sexual immorality so-called and that quality was *what matters really. But I see you're right and that homosexual love is more difficult in itself and takes a lot of intelligence and sensitiveness. Perhaps that's why it usually seems to work badly with men. Perhaps they're less sensitive on those things. There's one thing I would go to the stake for and that is that what I feel for you and you for me is right not wrong, good not bad, good to the nth degree. It feels not only natural and inevitable to love you as I do in every way, but as if it would be wrong if I didn't. I never had one second of doubt or hesitation on that score once I'd found you ... Janet Vaughan ... came to dinner tonight. She's nice and terribly intelligent both with her mind and her imagination. She's fond of me in a detached way ... I gather from her that not only is Bloomsbury talking about you and me – which they would do bless them – but also the BBC. I don't care. Lionel or Joe I suspect, with quite friendly intent. Filson Young and Mr Goldsmith ... with quite other intent. The DG's Presbyterian principles made him demand the resignation of one member of staff who was divorced [P P Eckersley]. Query: will he give ear to gossip and demand mine? Answer: most unlikely. My friends I* think *outnumber my enemies. I hope so ... Janet talked to me for hours about homosexuality, of which she approves...and told me incredible things about how Katharine Furse has been side-tracked because the powers-that-be have dubbed her homosexual because of her friendship with Rachel Crowdy, which may possibly be true ... Have I been stupid not to be furtive about us and not to conceal the fact that we were friends? It seemed to me so much more natural and possible to make no secret of the fact that we knew each other and were friends and it still seems to me to be so. I wish I knew what Roger felt about these things. It might be interesting to talk to him, but I gather people may go off the deep end more completely on this subject than on any other in the world, and most unexpectedly. Besides, I don't think he can be relied on not to talk. It is hard for him not to exchange confidences with whoever he's with, without meaning it, being of a sympathetic nature. Here's rather a pretty problem in ethics ... if I was cross questioned would they deserve to be told a lie, as I think people who ask impertinent questions often do deserve? Or should a gallant stoker strike a blow for liberty, speak the truth, walk out with his colours flying, his head bloody but unbowed? Although it's my own private problem in a sense I'd rather like to know what you think about this. On the whole I'm not sure ... what they deserve is not bluff and blandness making no bones about being friends and treating the rumours of more with lifted eyebrows and contemptuous scorn and pursuing my course unmoved, making you broadcast...but refraining from advertising my visits to Long Barn...it makes me* boil *that the world spies out evil which doesn't exist – if two people love each other as we do – and turns a blind or indifferent eye on vile and beastly injustices and cruelties.* I suppose a few more people are beginning to see the light, but there can't be many I suppose. *I left Janet in the dark about us by the way, said she becoming suddenly wary and cautious. Damn, what a nuisance people are.*

The subject was clearly troubling her as pressures at the BBC increased with the success of her talks. She was becoming a powerful force within the organisation and a well-known figure outside. As always with a rising star, and especially a female star in a professional world where women were not expected to shine, the tittle-tattle of gossip could be marshalled to devastating effect. She had cause to be worried as she agonised to Vita:

I have been having some anguished moments thinking I may have hurt you quite hatefully by retailing all that silly gossip ... and malice. It's my damned thin skinnedness that makes me feel sick and bewildered when I meet it and like a rabbit in a snare in a cruel world I can't bear the vestige of a threat to our happiness and I can't bear *that people should try to smudge It ... we must carry on much as at present, only I will* try *for your sake, at least as much as my own, to behave with even greater discretion and not be found kneeling at your feet ... I think the whole thing is probably Lionel ... who quite thoughtlessly and unintentionally has probably joked about it and no doubt discussed it with Mary Somerville. They cut* no *ice and are too fond of me to want to do any harm. Roger I am convinced is too loyal and too tolerant ... In any case, I think my position in the BBC and yours in the great world are both far too strong for anyone to do anything to us.*

Chapter Four

THE END OF BOTH AFFAIRS 1928–31

Cooling Off at the BBC

At the beginning of 1929 the world outside the BBC was acknowledging the way in which Hilda Matheson had established talks as an equal to music and entertainment. Yet at the end of 1929 Reith recorded in his diary fears of trouble in the programme branch, with Miss Matheson in particular. Wells saw it as a fight between a man, Reith, who was inspired by loyalty to influences above him, and a courageous and indefatigable woman, Matheson, passionate for liberal thought and free expression, but unfortunately not thick-skinned enough for that sort of struggle. Reith played a key role in her resignation, but it was never simply a personal fight between the two of them. Other people and other influences were involved. In particular there were genuine differences of opinion about broadcasting and the role of talks. There was a growing conflict inside the BBC in the period 1929-31 that mirrored the political and economic battles of the time.

Reith wasn't sure what to do. Hilda Matheson had brought some much needed excitement into talks and earned for the BBC the approval of literate and influential people. With her range of contacts and her winning tongue she was invaluable also in helping him to overcome the hostility of the press and other interest groups. The skills he valued in her were demonstrated to good effect in the help she gave him during *The Listener* row. When that magazine was first published in January 1929 with the primary function of satisfying demands for the text of broadcast talks, there was a well stage-managed hue and cry from the press. Garvin, editor of *The Observer*, had "a wild leader" about it and Lady Astor invited Hilda Matheson to Cliveden to meet him. At first she refused, but was then persuaded by Reith to attend in order to defend the BBC:

> *So I accepted. Had an interview with the advertising world Napoleon on a possible debate, settled two internal rows and fled to Paddington. Alighted*

from the tube train one *minute before Taplow train due out, ran with my best sprint up to the upper world, seized a platform ticket, got into the train as it was moving, my onyx necklace snapped by the violence of my speed and scattered all over the platform beyond recall. In the train I had to read all the cuttings and all the replies and think out my plan of campaign. At the house I had a useful half hour with Lord Astor before lunch, who was rather unsound and who had been a bit shaken by his Trade Union, the Newspaper Proprietors' Association. At lunch Lady A played up, as she does, put Garvin between us and whenever his speeches became too oratorical or prolonged she shut him up and made me take my innings. That was so encouraging that I was able to keep my end up and I left him with not a leg to stand on and, for him, comparatively penitent. At any rate I think we've stopped any further rant.*

The Listener quickly established itself, and even a deputation of forty-five newspaper proprietors to see the Prime Minister had no effect. Reith valued her assistance on such occasions, but he was becoming increasingly nervous of her ambition. He could see no limit to her efforts to push out the boundaries of talks.

Fury, Frenzy and Frustration

Her life at the BBC became frantic and embattled. She found it exhilarating and amusing in a way, but it left no time for peace, or reading, or even thinking, and a meeting like that with Garvin,

> *when one is a bit screwed up to win or lose*

was exhausting. It always seemed to be "win or lose". As in most organisations policies became mixed up with personalities. In some ways the mixture of the two in the BBC was especially volatile, perhaps because its culture had a lot in common with the diffuse aims, individualism and passionate enthusiasms of the voluntary sector. The sheer pressures also of working in a rapidly expanding new medium with its voracious appetite for novelty made worse an already explosive atmosphere. There were perennial tensions between programme directors as each fought for a bigger share of air time. Conflicts had to be resolved either directly, face to face, or through the management hierarchy. Hilda Matheson found it easier to handle outside negotiations with politicians and academics than the internal politics of the BBC.

Regular programme boards, when she had to sit opposite arch-enemy Filson Young "... fat and red and fleshy – ugh", were a constant trial. She tried to be friendly, with an occasional smile, a Christmas present for his son, and invitations to lunch, but the benefit of these peace offerings would be wiped out when she responded to his requests to broadcast by telling him that he was no good: she could never dissemble when it came to the quality of programmes. Placating the Mammon of unrighteousness, Commander V H Goldsmith the assistant controller, was difficult because she really did dislike him. Occasionally she would beg his wise advice and take him to dinner and once even arranged a party for him, but he remained one of the enemy. There was never any effort to avoid battles with George Grossmith of light entertainment

> who has the wits of a mentally deficient hen.

Her fury had been aroused when he launched another of his periodic attacks on talks, especially on the reviewers:

> All these attacks ... give me a sinking feeling and make everything seem very insecure.

Her days were packed with meetings, often acrimonious, discussions with broadcasters, consideration and re-drafting of scripts, rehearsals of talks and discussions, plans for future programmes, briefing the director-general, drafting his replies to VIPs on tricky subjects and receiving distinguished visitors. At the same time there were management duties, maintaining discipline and morale among her highly individualistic staff. Her letters to Vita show the variety, pace and intensity of her working life at the BBC:

> A meeting of my department for an hour this morning and it is so cold that we shall probably all sit on the floor round my fire which shocks the great who may come in terribly ... It's not been a bad day, on the whole. A Turkish programme was suddenly thrust on me when everybody else had failed. Something was required in twenty-four hours. Such researches as I could make led me to think that there is no genuine Turkish music or literature, that it's all derivative, except possibly some Anatolian folk music ... and that the people who know anything about Turkey are all either anti-Turk or too Turkophile to be suitable. Several telegrams have drawn blank so tonight at Roger's I threw myself at an FO man ... who is going to try to produce some names tomorrow. I dictated three bitter memoranda that I shall probably regret tomorrow and I sketched out a scheme of poetry readings for four months and have adopted a Mussolini attitude about them to the surprise of my staff ... A nice man who runs the Royal Horticultural Society came to discuss gardening and gardening advice for listeners. Then an hour's rehearsal of four of London's best Bridge players (and dreariest human beings) going through the first of a series of broadcast Bridge games. That was awful and they had to be bullied ... Then lunch with KW [Kate Walsh] and we discussed the queer ways of jealousy. Then an interview with a voice test of an Afghan, an intelligent fellow and nice, I thought, followed by a similar process with a charming docker called Bill, a great find, followed by an hour's discussion with Lionel and a man I have found in the music department who knows as much about poetry as about music. He's going to help us to experiment with some special programmes that begin and end with some music and have poetry in the middle. He wants to collaborate in an Edward Thomas half-hour

and he longs to do something about the L ["The Land" Vita's long poem]. He thinks we can do a lot to set the key by the right sort of music beforehand and after and he is so sensible a fellow that he may be right. I am reserving judgement ... Things are a bit too much of a good thing at the office and I suppose one ought to do something about it because it is so stupid, but what I don't quite know. Another assistant I expect, but Roger has implored me not to ask for one ... The Listener has added about 50% to the work because it means more bother about getting in material early and negotiating with people and all sorts of things. Lionel is away with flu this week, too, and that makes a lot of difference ... You see this is the kind of thing that happens. At one o'clock today I was asked for a report on the month's work for the Governors by 2.30. I had a Manchester woman assistant coming to talk business at lunch, so I had to see her and do the report and make a sandwich ... Lady Bailey came with a perfectly hopeless MS for tomorrow, charming and sensible, but unable to put two words together or to read them. I had to cope with her for an hour and bring the results home to put together tonight after my theatre. I think I want a frightfully intelligent young woman of robust constitution and excellent judgement. But of course what it always comes to is that there are some things one can't delegate. My efforts to educate the Governors for example. And none of the young men will take on the poetry job because they say they don't know modern poetry well enough, which is absurd because I am not much better, only I know what I want ... But why tell you all this? ... because writing to you really does save me and quietens me down (in one sense!) At 3.30 a visit from ... the most engaging Chinaman you ever saw. Mr T Z Koo, in a long blue brocade frock and a long blue furlined coat, and a little round face, most intelligent. He is going to talk about China for me and after we had had a short trial trip in the studio he suddenly asked me if I liked the flute. I said I did and he trotted off to his car ... and returned with a very long bamboo flute on which he played me an enchanting fishermen's story. I can't tell you how charming it was. I could hardly bear to say goodbye to him and I am going to try and arrange a programme for him. At 4 o'clock he was followed by a real contrast – Elizabeth Ponsonby and her father to rehearse a rather amusing conversation they are doing for me. I had to leave them to Joe and go off to a dreadful board meeting about studio design and decoration, where I was put into the dock and bully ragged by Peter Eckersley for nearly an hour, a process I find most exhausting. At 5.30 a film magnate, a foreign Jew of sorts, came to rehearse an impassioned defence of British films – a bad, bad talk. He depressed me. He is not unintelligent himself, but he believes in playing down to the least intelligent public. Darling I do think the BBC are just a little better than the film magnates ... I believe this work is always bound to be a scramble, especially mine perhaps, because I get so many things shot at me for draft replies. The High Commissioner of Australia has written to complain of an emergency talk last night which referred to Australia and that *required a soothing reply and an explanation in writing for the DG. The Government hospitality people, at their wits end to amuse the Sultan of Zanzibar, wrote about a possible broad-*

cast and I had to telephone to Newcastle and make plans about that ... Darling they give him a little book with every moment of his whole visit planned in it – weeks and weeks – where he lunches, what he sees and down one column they tell him what clothes to wear for each occasion! Then the Homing Pigeons became truculent and demanded to be heard on the ether. Then "Aunt Diana" from the New Zealand BBC comes with an introduction from the High Commissioner. Then Sir Oliver Lodge writes to the DG about Osbert Sitwell and Epstein and art in general and your Stoker has to draft a long, polite, persuasive reply. Then Lord Clarendon [BBC chairman] returns to the attack about the Poetry Society and Lady Maud Warrender. And lots more like that. And telephones ceaselessly and interviews ceaselessly and in odd moments the complete autumn programme to map out ... I held an inquisition into the misdeeds of David Tennant who hurriedly announced a speaker and dashed away without telling the poor devil to begin. Poor worthy Mr Hobbs, a farmer talking about manure, or some such subject after your own heart, sat and waited for instruction and after four minutes of agony pressed the little bell, innocently thinking, bless his heart, that it might summon an attendant. All it did of course was to signal to the Control Room to cut off, which they did, bewildered. Finally the careless David was found and an infuriated and completely unnerved Mr Hobbs started off on manure seven minutes late. Later in the evening David appears to have set John Duckworth off reading his new poems, with instructions to go on until stopped, and then left him and forgot to go back and collect him. I am told that he went on until half past eleven!

When fully stretched at the office she could still find time to do more, especially if it involved helping someone in a crisis. When a wartime acquaintance arrived unannounced at the BBC office she asked her to return later that day when she found her looking ill and half-starved. Despite the fact that the woman was very difficult to help, because she had by then so thoroughly messed up her life, Hilda saw her frequently, gave her money and tried to get her a job. The woman began to turn up at the studios with frantic messages demanding instant access and immediate loans. Hilda remained supportive, and ultimately found her a place in a hospital for people with nervous breakdowns.

Even with this huge energy, however, she was beginning to find the pace of work almost impossible. Having worked for Lady Astor she thought there was nothing that could surprise her about the elasticity of the ordinary human capacity for work, "but that was an idle life in comparison." Her idea of bliss was to leave the office every day at five, have tea at home at five-fifteen, lie on a sofa and read for two hours and then have a bath before dinner:

I adore the time between tea and dinner. I love bread and butter and honey and tea by the fire. I love the nice relaxed feeling one can have there after a day's work, it makes one quite ready to do anything in the evening, work and play.

Such bliss was rare. She had never in her life worked at an ordinary pace and a regular nine-to-five job, however idyllic in theory, was never sought or experienced.

Confidence Begins to Slip

By spring 1929 all the signs were that talks had become so well established that they were challenging other programmes. Hilda Matheson always regarded listeners' letters as a "... stupid and unreliable index", but she took a good deal of pleasure from the fact that the number of appreciations for talks was knocking the variety and music people into cocked hats:

> One of today's sheets (we get two or three a day) [shows] variety appreciations 10, talks 72, and such nice letters are coming from regular cottage women about my morning talks; and they do like the best ones best. One very nice one from a working man's wife who hates household work and longs for time to read books and go out to things and who can't and she said her ironing and cleaning were polished off with much less crossness because of being able to listen to a sensible woman talking about events of the week. Cheering for a Talks Director who gets so many kicks and so few ha'pence.

A few days later she commented on astounding figures which showed the extent of the growing appreciation of talks, readings and discussions:

> week after week, all through 1928,[letters about talks] are a steady 2-3 times as many as all the variety, revue and vaudeville shows, although the former represents a much smaller proportion of programme space ... and the public that likes them is not the sort that likes writing to papers and corporations.

In February she sent the director-general a chart with figures showing how people liked talks much more than variety. Despite a lack of sympathy for some of her ideas, often giving an impression that talks were something that had to be apologised for, Reith and her immediate boss, Roger Eckersley, had given her a fairly free hand so far. She acknowledged that she hadn't yet had much to complain about, but she always felt that they were afraid and ashamed of ideas which might be called intelligent or highbrow. Now that the listening figures were so good she thought that that view could be changed, but she was wrong. The political climate had changed: the effervescence and optimism of the twenties was being replaced by the pessimistic reaction of the thirties. BBC management, always sensitive to the signs of the times, became even more timid about talks perceived as controversial. Many of the subjects chosen for talks were vulnerable to the sort of caricature in which the *Evening Standard* had delighted. Newspaper articles fostered the image of a priggishly highbrow organisation, and there were increasing pressures on her to "lighten" talks or to push them after 11 o'clock at night or before 5 in the evening. She had successfully resisted these pressures previously, partly through force of personality and partly because of the genuine if grudging feeling in the BBC that talks were in the nature of a public service commitment. Now the DG became obstinate and unusually antagonistic. Threats were flying around and she was told she couldn't have an assistant and must just do the work less well or be less ambitious. The director-general's renewed interest was so hostile that she became fearful that he was trying to stop all her talks and she began to compose defiant memoranda and "dignified but crushing" letters of resignation. Common sense prevailed and she sent only the firm but polite memos, to be rewarded by a removal of the ban and a promise to review the whole question in April.

A Difficult Woman

By late April 1929 she began to feel squeezed out again as papers which would normally come to her were sent to Roger's assistant. There were rumours in the wireless press about the talks department being reorganised or abolished. Lady Astor was called on for help and said she would try and secure Mrs Snowden's goodwill – an unwise and tactless move given the antagonism between Reith and Mrs Snowden at the time. By June the argument was becoming one about free speech. The DG expressed concern about some of the talks in the *Points of View* series and recorded in his diary that trouble was brewing with Miss Matheson. Things came to a head later that month. At the end of a frantic Friday, which began with her "daily" giving notice and continued with a full day of irritations in the office, she was asked to a meeting with Reith and Roger "... for an hour and a half's arguments – hammer and tongs" about controversial subjects and their treatment and the future development of talks:

> It was all awfully difficult, partly because it was two to one – that seems to be the usual proportion in which one fights at the BBC – partly because the DG, though trying to be nice and friendly and full of compliments, made it difficult for me to keep my end up, by regarding every difference of opinion as a sign of truculence and by finding it impossible to realise his own hopelessly illogical and inconsiderate and ill-informed point of view. He tends to regard as controversial and partisan, and therefore inadmissible, a talk about which any of his business magnates complain or disagree; e. g. Osbert Sitwell, because his views on art were objectionable and because all modern art is objectionable and therefore can only be discussed if there is also somebody to put the case for the Victorians or the Classics. The fact that all talks on art hitherto have been given by spokesmen of the old school and that Osbert, however tiresome, was therefore evening things up, wasn't regarded as relevant ... The DG is obsessed

by the idea that all forms of thought, and all subjects, can be discussed in terms of yes and no. That they are all *in the category of vivisection or capital punishment. But what it really amounts to is this – that he only classes or admits as controversial subjects on which he and his friends have views e. g. Epstein, politics, personalities, business and financial. I pointed out ... all our sermons are controversial, but the DG won't admit it because he agrees with them. Desmond's talks, yours, Agate's, are all in a sense controversial, if by that the DG means that they express individual opinions and preferences in literature and drama which some people may not hold. Only the DG reads very little and probably seldom if ever listens to the talks ... Darling I did keep cool and not get fierce and joked about things, but they didn't really like one to have a view of one's own. They then plunged into discussing talks in general and said that all my talks had been getting more and more "educational" and that they were supposed to be topical and that talks on current ideas and current topics of speculation or discussion were* not *topical, only talks on* events *... The discussion had to end because I had an hour's rehearsal waiting to be done, but it is to be resumed next week. I see what is going to be suggested – that I should be shifted off my own talks, that Siepmann's talks and the relics of mine should be coalesced into a short space in the day, and that News and running commentaries and accounts of things that happen and the appearance of temporary celebrities at the microphone should be developed into another department ... I suppose I must pull myself together and really try and look at it with an open mind and no prejudice ... They are all so damned ready to say to* any **woman** *who disagrees with them that it is unreasonable and shows a lack of balance – I do honestly think that. Darling I did keep good, behaved all right, though afterwards when Roger began to say (a) that they highly valued my work but (b) that I was getting a name for unreasonable truculence I ... got a choke in my throat, which made me so angry and humiliated that I couldn't bear it*

At the resumed discussion the DG and Roger were terribly friendly and "man-to-man" and Hilda Matheson was terribly reasonable until they began to circle around the question of reorganising talks when she decided to say quite clearly what she thought and they listened "in complete silence". She dug her heels in and refused to countenance any "monkeying about with my talks", though she was ready to give up news as a compromise. Gradually, after hours of argument, she began to weaken and to see some of the advantages of amalgamation, but she continued to intrigue with Lady Astor hoping to persuade Ramsay Macdonald, now Prime Minister, to appoint another woman governor favourable to them. Reith observed his chairman visiting Hilda Matheson in her office without any other more senior person present. As he was at this time battling fiercely on other matters with both the chairman and Mrs Snowden his resentment was not unreasonable. By the end of 1929 an accommodation of sorts was reached when the Matheson and Siepmann empires were merged. To his embarrassment Reith received from her at Christmas the present of a picture.

The cracks began to show almost as soon as the new arrangement came into operation. Harold Nicolson described a dinner at the Savoy Grill in February 1930 with Reith and other BBC staff after which they all retired to Savoy Hill to listen to one of Harold Nicolson's broadcasts in the series *People and Things*: the DG listened grimly and evidently loathed the whole thing. Miss Somerville told him that Hilda would be sacked.

By December 1930 Hilda Matheson was getting more and more upset and Reith more exasperated. At the control board the director of programmes, Roger Eckersley, outlined the results of a meeting he had had with the director-general. There was to be another fundamental review of talks. Within a month the full implications were spelled out. Talks were to be split again, with Hilda Matheson as director of general talks and Charles Siepmann as director of adult education, but the significant change was that both departments were to be placed under another person as talks executive. All her objections were brushed aside. It was made clear to her that the previous amalgamation had not worked for reasons of personality and individualism. The number of talks was to be reduced.

As though to confirm that the real problem was less the personality of Hilda Matheson than the nature of talks themselves and the anxieties of the director-general, difficulties now began to arise with Siepmann. He told Reith that the talks department generally thought that Reith disliked them and their work and he demanded as a test of good faith towards the new arrangements that he should be free to initiate a vast educational programme to cover recent changes in the national outlook upon religion, politics, science and economics. As part of the programme Harold Nicolson was invited to talk about modern trends in literature, an invitation which was to prove decisive for Hilda Matheson's career with the BBC.

Crisis Point

The new series turned out to be everything that Reith feared and disliked about the way talks had developed: Harold Nicolson was liberal minded, adventurous, and dangerously inclined to recommend books that no decent minded person would wish to read. The two men clearly disliked one another and it would be difficult to think of anything more guaranteed to cause trouble between them than talks about modern literature. Their respective diaries record a lunch to discuss the impending series and their different perceptions of the same occasion are comical. Reith wanted more good effect from the series than seemed likely from the synopsis he had seen and told Harold Nicolson so. He left the lunch convinced that "Nicolson ... was glad to be told this". Harold Nicolson's record of the same occasion was caustic:

> The man's head is made entirely of bone and it is impossible to talk to him as to an intelligent being. He believes firmly in the eternal mission of the

BBC and tries to induce me to modify my talks in such a way as to induce the illiterate members of the population to read Milton instead of going on bicycle excursions. I tell him that as my talk series centres upon literature of the last ten years it would be a little difficult to say anything about Milton. He misses this argument and remains wistfully hopeful that I will be able to introduce a Miltonic flavour into my reference to D H Lawrence.

Reith began to pine again for the powerful spoken word director whom hitherto he had not been able to find. He ordered a consignment of books "... in order that I could understand myself the kind of stuff that Nicolson was recommending." In the same month the control board asked the assistant director of programmes to see that the traditional school of thought, including some Conservative peers of the old school, was represented among speakers. The battle inside the BBC began to leak out into the press as Hilda Matheson mobilised support.

The conflict between the old and newer schools was joined over references in Harold Nicolson's talks to the writers James Joyce and D H Lawrence, and in particular to those of their books such as *Ulysses* and *Lady Chatterley's Lover* which had been banned from publication in Britain. Legally it would have been very difficult for the BBC, even under the most liberal dispensation, to refer to books that had been banned by law. Whatever the views of staff and speakers on censorship, the BBC certainly could not allow anyone to recommend listeners to read books not legally obtainable in Britain. Getting over that legal hurdle, however, was not difficult. Harold Nicolson recognised the problem and could accommodate it easily enough without imperilling either his liberal conscience or the legal integrity of the BBC. What became a problem was the attempt by Reith to go further and to restrict him from even mentioning these and other unmentionable writers and their works.

Little of this row is documented in the BBC archives or in Reith's diaries, but Harold Nicolson's diaries tell the story in detail and include much of the correspondence which passed between him and Roger Eckersley who was obliged to handle the negotiations. The row continued into August and grew to encompass other authors. The chairman of the BBC governors, John Whitley, was horrified at the list of recommended books. He asked for Evelyn Waugh's *Decline and Fall* to be cut out, together with all references to Lawrence and Joyce. Harold Nicolson pointed out that his terms of reference were to explain what *changes* had taken place in English literature since 1910. He could hardly do that without putting in the forefront the two most important innovators – Joyce and Lawrence. If he was not allowed to mention these people he said he would refuse to deliver the course.

By the autumn of 1931 matters had still not been resolved. Harold Nicolson told Hilda Matheson that Whitley had told him that all mention of novels on the wireless was to be suppressed and that political views of speakers were to be examined so as to exclude all left wing thoughts.

Hilda Matheson gave notice in October that she was resigning, although her resignation was not announced officially until December. The two final straws had been the pressure on Harold Nicolson to change his talks and indications of yet another reorganisation. Reith had decided that general and educational talks were to be merged yet again, but this time there would be a powerful new director of the spoken word, a job for which Hilda Matheson would not be considered, implying that Siepmann was a contender.

The *Morning Post* picked up the new atmosphere on 5 November with an item about BBC censorship:

> It is understood that the BBC is tightening the Censorship on all broadcast talks. It has been known for some time that, following the Morning Post's criticism of the left wing tendency of the Russian talk, the Director General himself has exercised far more direct control over the Talks Department than previously. It is also known that Mr Whitley, the Chairman, has also exercised his authority over the nature of some of the criticisms of books that have been broadcast. A recent talk of this nature, it is understood, has again brought this matter into the foreground, and a far more stringent censorship of what is broadcast may be expected in the future. This will, in all probability, relate to theatre and film criticism as well as books. It will probably be found that the criticism of novels will figure less prominently than before.

In the same vein *The Week-End Review*, in an article suggesting that the board of governors was about to be packed with government sycophants, said that anyone who had to follow the currents of British opinion knew that during the past four months deep changes had been going on in the BBC.

During the second half of 1931 the BBC does seem to have gone through a sort of frenzy which matched the political and economic turbulence in the country. In August 1931 after months of crisis the Labour Government fell, and the October election resulted in a landslide victory for National Government candidates, most of them Conservatives. Despite its unifying title, the new government's economic measures revived the spirit of class war as public salaries and benefits were cut. This was not a time for liberal attitudes or experimentation, whether in economics or the arts, and the BBC's obsession with propriety reflected this embattled spirit. The attitudes of both director-general and governors became mean and petty, far removed from the more liberal spirit of the 'twenties.

The argument with Harold Nicolson, which had continued after Hilda Matheson made clear her intention to leave the BBC, was reduced finally to the banal demand that he should say, not that *Ulysses* was banned in this country, but that it was "difficult to procure". In a splendid attack on this example of unnecessary and unacceptable censorship Harold Nicolson ended a letter to the BBC:

> *I should have thought it cowardly and untruthful to have evaded the word "banned". I should have thought also that from your point of view it would have been better frankly to have stated that Ulysses was an obscene publication within the meaning of the act. Such a statement would have warned people who are squeamish about such things that Ulysses was not a book which would give them pleasure. The substitution of words such as "difficult to procure" for the word "banned" is a perfect instance of the verbal humbug which I was attacking.*

On the day of the talk the BBC chairman refused to allow it to be broadcast, at which Harold Nicolson refused to continue the series. In the end a compromise was reached under which Harold Nicolson agreed not to mention *Ulysses*, provided he could say what he liked about Joyce in other respects and that he could state quite clearly that he was not permitted by the BBC to mention the name of Mr Joyce's most important work. Somewhat to his surprise they accepted this humiliating condition and the talk was delivered on 8 December 1931. A few days later James Joyce wrote to say he had listened to the talk in his home in Paris and that it had given him great pleasure. He offered a copy of the French *Ulysses* and hoped that as a result of his courageous persistence Harold Nicolson would not now be victimised by the BBC. Four days before the talk was broadcast the BBC announced officially that their prime victim, Hilda Matheson, had resigned.

Newspaper Reaction

Roger Eckersley, in a phrase so typical of the way in which the BBC dealt with personnel crises, said it was "... her health and other circumstances which led to her resignation". The *News Chronicle* was less mealy-mouthed and on 3 December 1931 reported on the struggle of a woman against a management of men. It suggested she had pressed her views from a feminine standpoint in the face of overpowering masculine opposition. *The Manchester Guardian* referred to the air of mystery surrounding the resignation, all information on the reasons having been refused by the BBC. In fairness to the Corporation it has to be pointed out that they were not being especially mysterious about Hilda Matheson; silence was their standard policy whenever anyone resigned or was sacked. The *Daily Telegraph* described it as a sensation, and speculated whether Hilda Matheson, who must have interviewed more famous people than any other living woman, would now enter politics. The *Evening News* expressed real regret, not only because Hilda Matheson was one of the most charming people in the BBC, but also because as director of talks she had made the best of one of the most difficult jobs at Savoy Hill. The newspaper concluded its eulogy:

> *From the first she had a hard course to steer between the jibes of those to whom all broadcast talks seem to be dreary and trivial, and those who were so dreadfully afraid of offending somebody that all speech on contro-*

versial subjects was reduced to the most harmless proportions possible. Whether talks were on the habits of earthworms or the Soviet Five-Year Plan, somebody was always blaming the BBC.

For five years Miss Matheson, fair haired, very well dressed and looking the exact opposite of a panjandrum, has carried on, noting with concealed dismay, that every broadcast talk has been too dull for somebody and too controversial for somebody else. It was a hard life.

The *Daily Herald* was the only newspaper to welcome her resignation, and picked up the most important issue that lay behind it: the change was an opportunity to make talks a section of general entertainment, well away from the "professional uplifters" like Hilda Matheson who were in the *Herald's* view the real menace to British broadcasting. Today such an approach would be described as "dumbing down" and the *Herald's* readers were not to be disappointed. The talks department relapsed into the sort of mesmerised state in which she had found it, terrified into immobility by fear of giving offence like the proverbial rabbit in front of a stoat.

Her Reasons and Their Defence

In a draft of a letter to Reith, the final version of which might not have been sent, Hilda Matheson regretted some of the misleading rumours about her resignation. She welcomed, she wrote, an opportunity to refute suggestions that as a woman she had not had fair play at the BBC:

> On the contrary I can never forget that it was your own enthusiasm that decided me to join the Corporation and I should like to place it on record that I have met with the utmost friendliness and consideration from my colleagues. As I tried to explain to the Chairman and yourself, I could not loyally administer a policy which seemed to be turning into a reversal, to some extent, of what I had been instrumental, with your permission, in doing.

She went on to identify the two policies available to a monopolistic broadcasting service. One was to take the middle, traditional, orthodox view on most things with a minimum of latitude on either side of that line. The other was to express all the most important currents of thought on both sides, preserving a carefully balanced diversity. This second approach was, in her view, the right one, and the only one with any hope of bringing the public into touch with the important formative influences of the past and today. She recognised that those who maintained the opposite view did so from a sense of responsibility and the wish to protect listeners who might be pained by the expression of unfamiliar points of view. There was no difference of opinion about the need for difficult subjects to be handled carefully, because of the infinitely mixed audience of the wireless, but her experience had shown that, given speakers with tolerance, imagination and sympathetic personalities, controversial subjects could be, and had been, discussed from many angles with profit and without giving any offence. However, in fairness to the BBC, she felt obliged to resign and to make way for someone who could wholeheartedly carry out the new policy and accept the new methods.

The programme of talks for January to April 1932 sent out by Roger Eckersley to BBC staff seemed not very different from previous months, but there were some significant changes, which indicated that the BBC was now determined to play safe. These new proposals were defended in just the sort of pusillanimous language which Harold Nicolson had complained of, pretending that nothing had changed:

> Rumours respecting changes in policy with regard to talks are without foundation. The range of programme material is kept as wide as is compatible with the particular and, in fact, unique circumstances of the service. Experiments are frequent and such changes as are now made are of method and not of policy. Mr Desmond MacCarthy and Miss Sackville-West are to continue their weekly talks on books old and new, their time being extended from twenty to thirty minutes. Criticism of novels is to be suspended for the time being. Mr James Agate and Mr Francis Bissell, the theatre and film critics, are to speak monthly instead of fortnightly, also for thirty minutes instead of twenty as hitherto, and have been asked to deal with their subjects more generally but in no way to slacken the fight for better films and plays. They have been informed that, while there is no embargo on the mention of any particular film or play, there is no need for them to cover every first night or release.

Goebbels could not have put it better. The denial of a change in policy is untrue. The memorandum slides over the ban on reviews of novels as though it was of no significance. Harold Nicolson's contract was not renewed and he described the "... oily, unctuous coating of compromise" which descended on the BBC's presentation of the more difficult items. Invitations to Vita to broadcast began to diminish. Humphrey Carpenter notes that in the early thirties anything that was not comfortably middlebrow tended to be offered rather apologetically.

Health and Other Circumstances

When Hilda Matheson left in January 1931, to everyone's relief according to Reith, he was obliged to present her with a gift from the staff. The Board gave her six months' pay on Reith's recommendation, somewhat unwillingly made because he felt she had been abominably disloyal and had tried to stir up trouble. In an effort to understand the fall of his protege he interviewed Mary Somerville who explained the resignation to him by attributing it either to a pathological change of personality or to the influence of her new friends. Whatever the cause, she said that for the past year she had not been able to recognise the

Miss Matheson she used to know. The new friends in question were almost certainly Vita Sackville-West, Harold Nicolson and Dorothy Wellesley.

Mary Somerville is not a reliable witness. After the Second World War, when she was appointed controller of talks, she claimed to have been the very first talks producer in the late twenties and early thirties, and the one who had scandalised distinguished speakers by editing their scripts to make them sound more like spoken speech. In this confused memory she had transformed herself into Hilda Matheson. Was her recollection in 1931 of recent events any more accurate than her later fantasy?

The Somerville thesis cannot be dismissed entirely. The months before Hilda Matheson's resignation had been a time of exceptional stress. Her father, whom she adored, had died in September 1930. Within a short time of that bereavement she also lost the love, although not the friendship, of Vita. Their love affair came to an end sometime between December 1930 and March 1931 when difficulties with the BBC were at their height. Vita had a new partner, Evelyn Irons, editor of the women's page of the *Daily Mail*. Hilda had detected some cooling off much earlier:

> Being there in Dottie's house ... I felt a kind of upstart and intruder ... and then when you did not come I was all torn between wanting you frightfully and wanting to eliminate myself because of Dottie and ... I thought ... you were beginning to have second thoughts about me ... and then I felt hideously forlorn when you drove off ... I couldn't go to sleep because I was full of muddly feelings ... and so I was all of a dither when you came today and that is why I was stupid ... I have recurrent terrors of becoming a bore for you, of loving you more than you can do with, of disappointing you. Do you understand? Yes of course you understand everything.

As pressure increased at work the change in her relationship with Vita would have been especially hard to bear. At a critical time she lost one of the most important ways in which she coped with her frustrations at the BBC:

> I get into awful states you know about the work and get awfully discouraged because the powers that be aren't much interested in my part of the work, or are definitely bored or hostile. And I get depressed because I feel I don't do all the things I ought to do, like go to the BBC staff socials, or entertain colleagues and their dreary wives...or make friends with more people at the BBC, or call on Lady Reith and see her baby!!! All so awfully silly and just the very things one curses women for. How superior men are, one says, see how calm they keep. I do sometimes wonder though whether it wouldn't make a difference if one had a person at home with different interests, but who was fond of one and who would be nice to one when one got back. Heavens, how natural and how easy it must be for men to get to feel the way they do. That their wife's job is to make things

pleasant for them. As a matter of fact it is quite amazing with what speed I regain my equilibrium and get on my feet again now, however tired I may be, just because you love me and I love you. The assaults of the devil himself couldn't hurt me because I know you wouldn't let them.

When she lost that vital love and support at the time she needed it most, her judgement, resilience and will to fight must have been severely weakened. Having been unable to hang on to Vita, why bother to cling to the BBC? There was in her character always a willingness to surrender in personal matters. She could fight fiercely for ideas and other people, but not for herself.

These blows to her confidence, together with an over-active thyroid gland which plagued and later killed her, could have produced a significant change of personality. She suffered from Graves disease, an autoimmune disease which causes excessive production of thyroid hormones. In a healthy person these hormones are released in amounts sufficient to govern the body's activity rate, but Graves disease upsets this natural regulation and speeds up the body's metabolism. This results in a number of unpleasant physical symptoms, such as palpitations and loss of weight, and there can also be psychological effects as thyroid hormones enter the brain and impair normal intellectual functions. Depression, extreme lethargy and tiredness are usual, while boundless energy, undoubtedly one of Hilda Matheson's characteristics, is also a symptom but apparently less common. How far the disease had advanced in 1931 is not known, but her remarkable energy, noticed during her university days and a subject of awed comment throughout her time with Lady Astor, had quickened at the BBC.

The events in her private life in 1930-31, distressing enough to test anyone's balance and peace of mind, together with an acceleration of Graves disease, would have made a difficult situation worse. Yet her later success in journalism and in the mammoth enterprise of *An African Survey* demonstrate that she had lost neither her administrative skills nor her power to charm. There were many people able to work happily with her during the next ten years, so the suggestion that she was a "difficult woman" is not a sufficient explanation for her expulsion in 1931. Nor are suggestions of ill health convincing; it was nearly ten years before she needed an operation to remove part of her thyroid gland. The fact is that she left the BBC because of fundamental differences with Reith about policy which were exacerbated by prejudice against women in employment.

Prejudice

Beginning with the prejudice, the *News Chronicle* was right: men ran the BBC and the chief officers of the corporation gave women a hard time. In her diplomatic letter to Reith she denied any unfairness during her time with the BBC, but her other correspondence tells a different story. Whenever there was a clash of views about policies and programmes, her defence of her own position would be treated as the unreasonable reaction of a difficult woman. Every objective difficulty at work contained within it this further subjective difficulty, for men at least, of her sex. The energy, dynamism and aggression which were regarded as strengths when she was establishing the talks department became weaknesses when she challenged the conventional views of Eckersley, Reith and Whitley. Characteristics common to successful executives in most organisations were labelled as those of a difficult, strong-willed, abrasive woman who intimidated her staff.

Men, too, resigned or were dismissed from the BBC, but differences of view between men about work, or clashes of personality, were handled usually in other ways, sometimes by transfers or promotions, more often by management turning a blind eye. Difficult men could survive longer than difficult women could. Male rows about programmes would not degenerate into impatience with a "difficult" man, whereas any assertiveness on the part of Hilda Matheson was considered as one of the defects of her sex. Charles Siepmann, Filson Young, Lionel Fielden and Joe Ackerley were at least as difficult, and some of them were decidedly more eccentric, but all survived within the corporation. An organisation run by men simply found it too difficult to work with a woman in a management position who behaved as though she was their equal.

BBC executives could work comfortably with Mary Somerville, then safely tucked away looking after schools, but they could not work alongside an assertive woman manager. So the experiment was discontinued and it was to be many years before a woman achieved anything like the position Hilda Matheson had held. Had she not resigned it is possible that a way round the difficulties might have been found, even when the conflict of philosophy was so acute, but few efforts were made to persuade her to stay. Reith was glad to see this woman go.

Policy

The prejudice was triggered by the fundamental difference of policy. Her views on broadcasting had become incompatible with those held by Reith. By 1931, as he steered the corporation through the years of slump and national government, his views hardened. Roger Eckersley conveyed some idea of the atmosphere when he described his six-year watching brief over talks during Hilda Matheson's directorship as the most nerve wracking work he had ever done. He did not know from day to day whether something was about to be said on the air that might cause trouble for him and the BBC. Lionel Fielden, one of her supporters, later wrote that while some had blamed Reith, he fancied that:

> both you and he were victims of circumstance. Voices whispered to him, of course, that he was being RUN by a gang of REDS; he made dictatorial gestures; you took up a cudgel; he became domineering, you wild; until at

last there was nothing for it but your resignation ... The blimps were on the warpath, and you and your kind were doomed.

For a time Fielden acted as the sort of buffer state which should have been provided by Roger Eckersley, trying to persuade Reith that Hilda Matheson was invaluable to the BBC, and trying to stop Hilda from writing offensive memoranda, but to no avail. Their differences about broadcasting were too clear and definite to permit easy compromise.

Asa Briggs in his *History of British Broadcasting* acknowledges her significant contribution to broadcasting, but attributes her resignation more to personality than to policy, suggesting that as she lost her monopoly of the spoken word she became testy and difficult with a good deal of bad temper and jealousy. In fact policy was far more important than personality. For as long as her dynamism and vivacity were used in the cause of the BBC, persuading everyone that the corporation was right, Reith was content to put up with her personality. When those persuasive powers began to be directed towards him, they became symptoms of a disordered mind. His interview with Mary Somerville is breathtaking in its assumption that his own personality, his own style of management, and his own policies could not be to blame. Reith's sense of duty and morality was Cromwellian in its strength, but he never shared Cromwell's modest view that in some things he might be mistaken.

It was sad that Matheson and Reith could not co-exist within the BBC. In so many ways they saw eye to eye, both of them recognising the need to set and maintain high standards without losing contact with the general public. They acknowledged always that the BBC could not successfully frame programmes too far ahead of general taste and enjoyment, that it had to play fair with all those who paid the licence fee, but they approached this basic perception in different ways. Hilda Matheson recognised the chronic public undercurrent of irritation against a superior attitude, the resistance of listeners towards being elevated and their resentment against being bored. Without compromising her high standards she tried to meet these feelings by appropriate presentation and by developing the art of broadcasting. Reith was less sensitive and also less interested in disseminating ideas as such; it depended very much on the ideas. Where religion or his favourite music or writings were concerned he was ruthless, and listeners just had to put up with what he thought was good for them. He drew the line at provoking them with unfamiliar or unpopular ideas only when he himself disapproved of the ideas or the people presenting them. Reith's own high vision of broadcasting, as presenting what was best in music, thought and entertainment, was more limited than hers was. He *knew* what was best, which was what he liked, and insisted that listeners must hear it, whereas she preferred listeners to make up their own minds after being presented with different ideas of what was best. Reith genuinely admired creative power, but his own certitude and tendency to moralise crippled his appreciation. He made his own best comment on his standards when he suggested to Harold Nicolson that perhaps Galsworthy merited more attention than Joyce did.

Creativity and Control

Reith was faced as director-general with the perennial conflict between creativity and control, a dilemma which was particularly acute in the nineteen-thirties. There are many examples of the courageous way in which he defended the independence of the BBC. His judgements that some subjects were too controversial for radio were never the result of cowardice. The fact is that he was prepared to swim along with many of the reactionary currents of the thirties because in the main he shared them. With Hilda Matheson at the helm the BBC would have been more adventurous, less timid. Her intelligence and powers of persuasion, evidenced by a successful record of negotiation with politicians of all parties, would have enabled her to steer the BBC clear of the rocks. In the end she was the genuine creative spirit, an administrator and programme maker of genius who had a particular gift for presenting serious programmes in an entertaining way. Reith was essentially middlebrow, content that broadcasting should reflect a conventional, lower-middle-class view of what was best.

It was her concern for creativity and the art of broadcasting which produced later one of her most splendid reviews as radio correspondent of *The Week-End Review*, a job she held during 1932 and 1933. In June 1933, no doubt responding to the spirit of the age, the BBC appointed a professional soldier as controller of all broadcast programmes. Hilda Matheson was aghast. Her column that week concentrated on the business of making programmes and the inventive, imaginative, intelligent and fresh approach required of the programmers:

> Their work demands conditions which must be considerably more elastic than those of the civil service, and which differ in many respects from those of a business organisation. The creative worker needs stimulus and quiet, incentive without slave-driving, freedom from irrelevant detail and red tape, time to go about in search of ideas and to keep his contacts with ordinary people fresh. A delicate adjustment is therefore called for between the claims of administration and creation. To the rigid administrator the behaviour of the programme man may, at moments, seem another name for idling. To the programme man the administrator may easily seem a boot-faced bully. One of the main tasks in broadcasting is to find the right relation between these various functions and the right frame to contain them. From time to time – and this is one of those times – the policy of two parallel staffs holds the field, one administrative, one creative. However much may be said for this on paper, in practice it is almost bound to lead to friction, and so to inefficiency. The creative man may well find himself asked to work to requirements fixed by an unsympathetic administrator who understands nothing of the conditions of his work. This accentuates the pull between the two functions and the introduction of conflicting loyalties.

It is apt to mean, also, the side-tracking of those who supply the actual stuff of programmes into a permanent collection of *non-descript geniuses, while responsibility and authority go increasingly to a hierarchy of red-hats. In contrast to this policy stands the view that broadcasting offers peculiar scope to men and women of first class ability who possess something of the gifts and experience for both functions, and who can appreciate the problems from both angles. The BBC is not devoid of such persons, and for this, if for no other reason, it seems a pity not to follow the good general principle of promotion from within ... To appoint as Controller of Output (the newly coined term for programmes) however distinguished a member of the fighting services has a regrettably disciplinary and mechanical air which seems more appropriate to a munition factory than to the most influential cultural agency in the country.*

(Her views might well find echoes today among broadcasting staff as the BBC struggles with the balance between efficiency, economy and creativity and programme makers complain of increasing administrative bureaucracy. The appointment of a military man in 1933 reflected increasing pressures on the BBC to play safe. In the 1990's the policies of the director-general, John Birt, responding to increasing costs, technological change and severe competition from other broadcasting organisations have produced similar tensions. Ironically the resignation of Sally Feldman, the distinguished editor of *Woman's Hour*, in January 1998 contains echoes of that of Hilda Matheson nearly sixty years earlier. Both women were colourful and unorthodox figures within the BBC, lively, interesting and uncontainable, and both reached the "glass ceiling" which seems to contain the careers of such women broadcasters. Commenting on the changes introduced by John Birt, many of which she supported, Sally Feldman pinpointed their fundamental weakness as the failure to combine a system of accountability with the nurturing of talent. Identifying like Hilda Matheson the basic need to combine administration and creativity, she laments the lack of creative managers capable of operating the new systems and the starvation of the programme makers who actually deliver the programmes. It is depressing that the lessons taught by Hilda Matheson have still not been learned and that talents like hers find it necessary still to resign.)

The golden age over which Hilda Matheson presided was not unlike the television renaissance which followed the ending of the BBC's monopoly. When independent television was given its franchise the BBC was at first left floundering, but it soon produced an effective response with programmes such as *Tonight, That Was The Week That Was* and the series of Wednesday plays. Under the stimulating direction of Sydney Newman, plays like *Culloden, Cathy Come Home* and *The War Game* demonstrated his gift of presenting tough problems in an entertaining, amusing and stimulating way. This was precisely Hilda Matheson's great broadcasting gift also, to devise programmes that were serious, but were also a bridge between the cottage and the common room. Both of them produced broadcasting for everyone, not just for toffs, whilst maintaining rigorous standards. It is fascinating that these efforts to raise standards in the 'sixties produced much the same outrage as hers in the 'thirties. There was one significant difference: Newman's director-general was Sir Hugh Greene whose enterprise and courage were both rather greater than Reith's. More recently the efforts of James Boyle, controller of Radio 4, to change established programmes and raise standards have echoes of Hilda Matheson's innovations. The sort of controversy he aroused was endured by Hilda Matheson throughout her brief tenure in the job. Almost at the birth of broadcasting, she had pointed the way towards an adventurous and stimulating public service. She was the pioneer of most that was worthwhile in the years that followed and pioneered also the appropriate punishment.

Future of Talks

The later history of talks was not glorious. The new "supremo" turned out to be her colleague Charles Siepmann, an odd appointment in many ways. Roger Eckersley thought of him as an individualist, a firebrand, unlikely to stay the course in an organisation where opinions had to be somewhat pruned to marry with policy. If Reith could not live with Matheson, how could he put up with Siepmann? Yet it was Siepmann who was appointed, albeit with many misgivings, and all the separate departments of general talks, adult education, schools and news were recombined once more. Reith's diary entry for December 1931 is baffling. He had just interviewed Siepmann and agreed to his elevation, yet recorded that he was "most unhappy" about it. Some years later he annotated the entry with the words "and how well justified I was".

A review committee in 1934 reduced educational talks from five to three a week to include a regular Sunday talk on matters of national or international importance "... though they shouldn't inspire acute or drastic controversy". Shortly afterwards news and topicality were detached from talks and put under a Professor Coatman. Soon there were difficulties between him and Siepmann, office gossip recalling the days of Miss Matheson. The resolution was handled differently; in June 1935 Siepmann was removed from talks to a post of director of regional relations. Later on, when Reith had gone, Siepmann became director of programmes for the whole of the BBC. Humphrey Carpenter in his recent history of the Third Programme confirms the change in BBC programming. He suggests that the demands of the majority gradually began to swamp more intellectually ambitious programmes. By the end of the decade, he asserts, most intellectuals regarded the wireless with scorn.

Postscript to Both Affairs

The ending of her two great love affairs must have been especially bitter for someone who had thrown herself with such energy and enthusiasm into both, and also puzzling. The proper course for the BBC to take seemed so obvious, yet she could not persuade them to stick to it. The love she felt for Vita was genuine and had seemed to be mutual, but Vita could not sustain it. Years later, in 1938, Vita published a poem *"Solitude"* about cheap and easy loves in which she took another's heart, while leaving her own intact. Hilda Matheson had read some of it in manuscript some years before, but was obviously hurt by the published version:

> *I am puzzled by your attitude to love – cheap and easy, a charlatan, the stifling tendrils of ivy – do these epithets apply to your own past attitude to love, or to love itself and all human relationships? If not, what differentiates love of that quality from love which liberates the heart and opens the mind?*

Hilda Matheson's philosophy of love was the same as her philosophy of broadcasting, both should liberate the heart and open the mind. That last sentence of her letter stands as a suitable epitaph for the ending of both affairs.

Chapter Five

AN AFRICAN SURVEY
1932–1938

Searching for Work and Love

When Hilda Matheson left the BBC at the end of 1931 she did not know what to do. Resigning from a well-paid job with no other work in prospect was a brave decision, reckless even, at the beginning of the Great Depression. There was no family fortune to cushion her. The estate left by her father after his death in 1930 should have produced an income more than sufficient for her mother, but the 1929 stock market crash in the USA and the subsequent crisis in Britain produced some rude investment shocks for Meta. Hilda's brother could not help because he was in danger of losing his own job. As a single woman earning £900 a year for the past five years she should have had some savings, but it was not in her nature to build up a nest egg. She was bored by money and never saw the sense of saving much of it, sentiments she expressed often to Vita:

> It isn't worth scrimping now for the sake of a few more pennies when one is old, better to live on a pea and a bean from, say, 70 onwards, in a garret, provided there's just enough to ensure that and to prevent one from being a burden to other people, and spend money while one can enjoy going to places and doing things and seeing people and buying things.

Her idea of a major economy drive was to stop using taxis, one of many resolutions about money never kept for long. Clothes and travel were particular extravagances, and her dog, too, was indulged as she booked him first class on his introduction to London's underground. A well-paid job was necessary. More important, a testing, interesting job was essential to make proper use of her talents and absorb some of that driving, restless energy.

It was at this time that Harold Nicolson wrote her into his novel *Public Faces*, recording his first thoughts in April 1932:

> *I think it should be a dramatic, even a romantic novel. Dealing with diplomacy and character. A central figure, intense as Charles Siepmann ... A Secretary of State such as Joynson Hicks – unctuous, evangelical, insincere. A woman Under-Secretary of the type of Hilda Matheson.*

The novel was published in the summer. Harold Nicolson had first got to know Hilda professionally through his own broadcasts and those of his wife. When she became Vita's lover, and afterwards remained a family friend, he came to know her very well indeed. His admiration for her character as well as her professional abilities was unqualified, and his portrait of her as Jane Campbell, the heroine of the novel, was almost entirely flattering. Some parts of that portrait have already been described (chapter one p 18-20), but it is worth revisiting to consider two characteristics: as well as being intelligent, energetic and deft, with a particular gift for putting things in order, Jane Campbell is described as very ambitious and having a good deal of feminine charm, she:

> *liked being female: she displayed this liking in every curve of her trim body ... she also liked, and exceedingly, being Under-Secretary of State.*

Now, Hilda Matheson's own femininity and ambition had been dealt severe blows, rejected by both her lover and her employer. This twin rebuff was hard to bear, but resilient as ever she set about repairing the damage.

Dorothy Wellesley

Some relief in her personal life was provided by a growing relationship with Dorothy Wellesley, at least during its early stages. When Hilda fell in love with Vita she got to know two of her predecessors, Virginia Woolf and Dorothy Wellesley. Hilda's attitude towards Virginia Woolf, which has already been sketched, was concerned and friendly. She invited her to broadcast and in letters to Vita wrote about Virginia kindly, without the malice or triumphalism that a rising star might show towards a rival. They were poles apart; the sensitive Mrs Woolf found it impossible to warm to the brisk, aspiring Miss Matheson. While she kept the worst of her bile for her diary, in letters to friends, including Vita, Virginia Woolf displayed her intense dislike of the upstart now enjoying Vita's love.

Dorothy Wellesley was more generous and more open. She could not hide how painfully she felt the loss of Vita's love, but this did not poison her feelings towards her successor. For her part, Hilda hated the idea that happiness for her might mean unhappiness for Dorothy. In February 1929 she responded generously to a sad letter in which Dorothy said she had been plunged into melancholy since Vita's departure for Berlin. They met for dinner and according to Hilda talked naturally and straightforwardly about Vita, and about life and death and love and relationships and gardens and books and poetry, taking it for granted that she was now Vita's lover. Hilda was invited to Penns in the Rocks, Dorothy Wellesley's home in Sussex, and asked to call her "Dots", because "Dottie" was impossible and "... I've a theory that a child grows like its name". Dorothy Violet Wellesley was the wife of Lord Gerald Wellesley. They married in 1914 and had two children. Now she was living apart from her husband, alone in Penns, where she delighted in entertaining her friends, most of them connected with the arts. Vita described Dorothy as a natural rebel, a fiery spirit with a passionate love of beauty in all its forms. Her childhood, although privileged in material terms, had not been happy; her father died when she was seven, her only brother when he was twenty, and her mother was a remote, rejecting figure. Sir George Goldie, a great friend whose biography Dorothy Wellesley wrote in 1934, told her at the age of eleven after examining her scalp that she had the three bumps of temper, pride and combativeness more developed than anyone he had ever known. She was a born romantic but, according to Vita, the bad fairy at her christening had decreed that her intellectual power should never equal her gifts of the imagination. Consequently her poems, which she dashed off as fast as she could write them down, never received the revision they demanded; grammar and syntax bored her and she rejected impatiently the counsel of her friends.

A Troubled Relationship

In 1929 Dorothy Wellesley was 40 years old, a year younger than Hilda Matheson, and their friendship grew as Hilda responded, inevitably, to the lonely, tired, depressed and rather pitiful figure who talked of a difficult upbringing and problems in relationships with men and women, but who was capable also of listening sympathetically to Hilda's own woes, especially her accounts of battles at the BBC. Soon Dorothy was telling Hilda that she was like a cat, and dreadfully feminine, and that she had nearly fallen in love with her; and Hilda was assuring Vita that Dots didn't raise one flicker of physical attraction in her. The friendship continued like this for three years, in parallel with Hilda's love for Vita, and it is not surprising that Hilda and Dorothy should turn to one another to lament the lost love they had in common. In the autumn of 1932 Hilda gave up her London flat and moved into Rocks Farm, an attractive house in the grounds of Penns in the Rocks.

There is little on record about their subsequent relationship, other than the fact that Dorothy came to depend on it more and more, and that Hilda was prepared to continue providing her with emotional support. As Dorothy became increasingly eccentric their friendship, along with all the other pressures on Hilda, must have imposed severe strain. Nigel Nicolson recalls Dorothy Wellesley's odd behaviour at Sissinghurst, including sleepwalking episodes which terrified the wits out of him and his brother. On one occasion Hilda gave a harrowing account of Dorothy to Leonard Woolf. But there were positive aspects.

As well as meeting Hilda's need to support other people, the friendship was based on shared interests other than Vita, in particular a love of poetry.

Their delight in literature was genuine and given free reign in Penns which became a centre for poets and other writers. Dorothy subsidised the Hogarth Press *Living Poets* series. While the veto which her money gave her was sometimes exercised with poor judgement – she refused to agree to the publication of poems by Louis MacNeice for example – her patronage encouraged many new poets. One of her anthologies, *New Signatures*, contained poems by W H Auden, C Day Lewis, William Empson, William Plomer and Stephen Spender. The poet and critic W J Turner was a frequent visitor and the triumvirate of Matheson, Turner and Wellesley was later to be responsible for producing a famous war-time series of books about Britain (see chapter six).

Ottoline Morrell brought W B Yeats to Penns in May 1935 and the ageing poet took to both Dorothy and Hilda, who later spent holidays with him and his wife and were present at his death in 1939. Yeats greatly admired Dorothy's poetry, a profusion of which he was later to include in his edition of *The Oxford Book of Modern Verse*, giving her more space than he allowed to others whose poetic reputation has survived rather better, including T S Eliot and Gerard Manley Hopkins. Hilda commented often on poetry and poets in her letters, particular favourites being Donne, Marvell and Eliot, but never on Dorothy Wellesley's own poetry.

Their relationship must have been in many ways an uneasy one. In addition to Dorothy's exaggerated sense of her poetic gift, which would have irritated Hilda's fastidious and critical sensibilities, there were often depressions and alarming tantrums. In Dorothy Wellesley's curious book, *Far Have I Travelled*, part autobiography, part travelogue, the many ghosts she describes seem more real and substantial than any of her family and friends who flit through its pages. References to Hilda Matheson are affectionate, but few, and give little indication of the importance or intensity of the friendship. Whatever its quality day-to-day, it survived for the rest of Hilda's short life.

No Proper Job

In 1932 and 1933 it must have seemed to her that she was trapped, with the prospect of spending the rest of her life looking after Dorothy Wellesley and writing in a small way. She asked Lady Astor to recommend her to J L Garvin as a regular contributor to *The Observer*, characteristically providing a draft letter which Lord Astor amended to make the rather more tentative suggestion of an article or two on BBC policy. It is possible that the letter was never sent. Another dead-end in May 1932 was a suggestion by John Lehmann, then manager of the Hogarth Press and complaining of being overworked, that she should be employed to assist him. Hilda was willing, but in the end negotiations broke down as the Woolfs shied away from such high power and opted for "competent underlings". In the same month she was appointed radio critic of *The Week-End Review* and began to expound the ideas she had tried to put into practice at the BBC.

Despite the history of battles within the BBC and the way in which she had been forced to resign, she never used her position as radio critic to attack the Corporation. Her broadcasting reviews, which were published each week from 14 May 1932 until January 1934, were not part of any revenge. She approached this latest task with intelligence and discrimination, avoiding the common weaknesses of reviewers; never self-indulgent, never spiteful or malicious, never one-sided, her judgements were calm, rational and fair. Sometimes she criticised, but always on matters of substance accompanied by practical suggestions for putting things right. Her weekly column did not merely list or summarise what listeners would have heard anyway. Instead she displayed a consistent philosophy of broadcasting with criteria for assessing the quality of broadcasts. Her readers were to be informed and educated by her comments, radio producers were to be helped and the BBC was to be kept up to the mark.

Most of her views about broadcasting will be apparent from the previous account of her work at the BBC so there is little point here in repeating them in a summary of her reviews. The range of the reviews was wide, from the need for audience research to the distressing influence of the art nouveau movement on radio design. The need for an international agency to control wavelenghs, pitfalls in political broadcasting, using radio to reach the rural parts of India, the way in which German broadcasting was becoming a political arm of the Nazis, all these and many more subjects were considered by her. At a time when most commentators ignored it, she regularly drew attention to the threat posed to democratic values by Nazi Germany. Some of her other forecasts of the future were also perceptive, such as developments in television and the survival of radio despite competition from visual media. Her prediction of technical changes, such as more portable radio receivers, reads very much like a description of the Walkman radio.

She combined this weekly journalism with other writing. Her book *Broadcasting* was published by the Home University Library in 1933, followed by three articles, two for the *Political Quarterly* and one for an international journal. None of these provided the sort of challenge she needed.

In the summer of 1932 the Nicolsons' secretary left and Hilda began to take over some of the secretarial duties of the household, helping in particular with arrangements for the visit Harold and Vita were to make to the USA at the turn of the year. For the remainder of 1932 she was in charge of everything at Sissinghurst and during the first months of 1933, when their parents were away, she acted as guardian to the two sons, Ben and Nigel. According to Nigel she was good with children and he remembers her with affection. Her delight in the boys is evident from her earlier letters to Vita in which she said she had lost her heart to this most attractive pair and challenged Vita's views on discipline:

Hairbrush or no hairbrush, I don't approve of beating ... I warn you if you ever get cross with me, harshness is a bad card to play. I respond unlimitedly to kindness.

Vita's mother, Lady Sackville, observed more bossiness than kindness in Hilda at this time, complaining to her diary of the way in which Hilda was organising Vita's life and of "instructions" she had received from Miss Matheson. A driving force such as Hilda Matheson was bound to discomfort other people at any time, but she must have been like a caged cat when confined to a weekly column on broadcasting, other pieces of writing such as her book, and the not very demanding task of running the Nicolson household. Then in July 1933 she was offered a job worthy of her great abilities.

Hailey's African Survey?

An African Survey, a study of problems arising in Africa south of the Sahara, was published by the Oxford University Press in November 1938 under the name of Lord Hailey. It was issued by the Committee of the African Survey under the auspices of the Royal Institute of International Affairs. A massive work of nearly 2,000 pages, which had been started more than five years earlier, the Survey described the physical nature of the continent and the histories, languages and social structures of its native peoples. It went on to assess their health and education, and the impact on them of colonisation and European settlement. The different approaches adopted by European powers in the territories they governed were described as were Africa's various economies, including consideration of agriculture, forestry, mineral workings, transport, labour, and its share of world trade. The Survey prescribed policies for the future and suggested how African Studies should be developed so as to put policy-making on a sound basis.

An African Survey was hugely influential, not only at the time of its publication when a second impression of the first edition had to be printed to meet public demand, but also after the Second World War when a second edition was published in 1945, and into the nineteen-fifties and sixties, being revised and reissued in 1957.

The committee which supervised work on the Survey consisted of eleven men headed by Hilda Matheson's friend Philip Kerr. (In 1930 he inherited the title Marquess of Lothian and from now on is referred to as Lord Lothian.) Others included the eminent Africanists Lord Lugard and Dr J H Oldham, and the scientists Julian Huxley and Sir Richard Gregory. Hilda Matheson was secretary to the committee and one other woman, the scholar Margery Perham, was also closely connected with the group although not listed as a committee member. In her biography of Lord Lugard, Margery Perham modestly described her own contribution as being "... drawn in on the fringe", but she contributed material for several chapters and attended meetings of the committee for most of the period. She recalled Lord Hailey's almost superhuman powers of absorption and synthesis and remembered her dear friend, Hilda Matheson, as an able and beautiful secretary. This is echoed in the Foreword to the Survey by Lord Lothian who paid tribute to Hailey's remarkable contribution as its director, "at a sacrifice of health, leisure and time", and added that a special obligation was owed to Hilda Matheson for the very important part she played in organizing the work.

Since then the Survey has always been linked with Hailey, never with Matheson. Her contribution was not ignored at the time, but the acknowledgement was muted. Yet she dominated the Survey, just as the Survey dominated her life from 1933 to 1938. Without her it would never have been published.

Her role in producing the Survey is one of the great stories of women in public administration: brilliant, selfless, tireless, anonymous, doing most of the work and much of the thinking, but taking the least of the credit. Working on the Survey nearly killed both its director and secretary, but whilst Hailey survived the ordeal, Matheson was dead within two years of its publication. *An African Survey* is one of her very great achievements in a life of achievement. It bears the name of Lord Hailey, but it is more a monument to Hilda Matheson.

Imperial Thoughts About Africa ...

The idea for a Survey has usually been traced back to the Rhodes House Conference on Africa held in November 1929. The chairman of the conference, H A L Fisher, then Warden of New College, Oxford, suggested in his opening address that the time had come to substitute fundamental thinking for aimlessness and drift in the management of the Empire. General Smuts, one of the leading speakers at the conference, urged that their purpose should be to get Africa's problems out of the political atmosphere and away from sentimentalists and to "... let science speak". He wanted a centre for thinking and co-ordination where African problems could be studied as a whole. The Conference went on to recommend the establishment of a Centre for African Studies in Oxford and requested Lord Lothian to draw up a general statement for circulation to Government, the Privy Council Committee for Industrial and Scientific Research and various Empire bodies.

Nothing came of the specific proposal. The Rockefeller Foundation refused a grant for a Centre, but the conference remit was used to promote support for a preliminary survey. Dr. Oldham, a great missionary who had travelled widely in China, India and Africa and done much to encourage research into Imperial problems, was very influential behind the scenes, while Lord Lothian more publicly drummed up support. In October 1931 the Carnegie Corporation confirmed a grant of $75,000 (£15,000 at the then rate of exchange and equivalent to about £500,000 today) over a two year period for a general study of equatorial and southern Africa.

Why was so much high-powered effort put into producing a Survey of Africa? Because there was a great need to resolve confusion in Imperial policies and disagreements about what should be done with the colonies, especially those in Africa where Britain was not the only colonial power. The first step had to be to establish the facts. About India there was an abundance of information, but on Africa very little.

The confusion and ignorance, which *An African Survey* was intended to sort out and clarify resulted from the many different interests competing in the colonies and the ideas about native peoples common at the time. British Government thinking was influenced by these various pressures and by a number of "old boy networks" in which most of the people connected with the Survey were involved; Lothian, Lugard, Oldham, Perham and others met and corresponded frequently as friends. Their ideas, which were better informed and more rational than most at that time, were developed and disseminated through such institutions as the "Round Table" of Milner's Kindergarten, Chatham House, and the Fabian Society, but they needed a wider audience.

British colonial policy had been mainly a matter of holding the ring between a hotchpotch of competing interests. The Christian mission to convert and humanist desires to civilise competed with economic imperatives to trade and settler determination to develop resources. There were even tentative suggestions, usually originating with missionaries or government officials working in the colonies, that colonial government should be primarily in the interests of the native peoples. There were also strong ideas about race, many of them based on little more than prejudice, that native peoples were somehow "different", indeed hardly belonged to the human race at all.

The spectrum of competing ideas available to policy makers was very wide. At the more liberal and practical end were those of people like Sir George Goldie whose Royal Niger Company laid the foundations for what was to become the British territory of Nigeria. He believed that the land belonged to the native peoples and that government should be through their existing institutions. His approach was developed by Lord Lugard with his dual mandate theory that the colonial powers had the right to develop the resources of their colonies, which would in turn benefit from that development and the free trade in goods which accompanied it. At the other end of the spectrum were ideas already developing in South Africa which were to end in apartheid. Meanwhile, British governments stumbled along, adopting something like the Goldie precepts of indirect rule. Native administrations were used as far as possible, guided by colonial office staff whose primary function was to keep the peace, enabling traders, colonists and missionaries to carry on with their own business.

... and Africans

There is a good example of the sort of debate taking place during the nineteen- thirties in correspondence between a colonial civil servant, Walter Crocker, and Dr Oldham. Crocker, whom Margery Perham described as one of the ablest of the younger men she had met in Africa, provided a bleak account of his experience in Northern Nigeria with one of the most truculent tribes in the country:

> *One does wonder whether there can be any future for them. Indeed more, whether there can be any future for the African in general ... The Negro in America, for all the persecution he has suffered, is a better man than the literate African living in Lagos or Abeokuta, or Accra or Freetown, for all the latter's having been encouraged and helped in every way. Is there any significance in this difference? It is a horrid thought, but might it be possible that the best way of raising the African from the jungle to the civilised life ... would be to subjugate him for a couple of hundred years and to tell him what is best for him? As with children you don't tell them to go and realise themselves; you "force them to be free".*

Oldham asked Margery Perham to comment and her response was more in tune with liberal and humane thinking today than with the currents of conventional thought in the thirties. Crocker had gone to one of the worst Districts in the country, she explained, and met "one of the most backwood (sic) tribes", but if he conducted further research he would find that their social organisation in the past would have been much better than now. She pointed out that the long, disintegrating drain of the slave trade had been followed by the appearance of white rulers who neglected or maladministered the territories they conquered and dissolved much of the old order, the good with the bad. The comparison with the American Negro she dismissed; they were a population of only twelve million, embedded in 100 million whites, and who had experienced a complete breach with their past. She rejected also the idea of two centuries of subjugation, which she did not feel colonisers were qualified to practice. The main problems for her were a lack of informed opinion in Britain, the ignorance, departmentalism and indifference of the Colonial Office, and short-term governors.

The great contribution of the Survey was to collect the informed researches of people like Margery Perham and provide a bedrock of facts about nearly the whole of Africa on which rational policies could be constructed. But this was all in the future. By the summer of 1933 all that was in place was a committee and the assurance of $75,000 from the Carnegie trustees.

Two Key Appointments

In June 1933 the Survey committee met with Sir Philip Antcliffe-Lister, Secretary of State for the Colonies, General Smuts, and Dr Keppel of the Carnegie Corporation to consider the appointment of a director. Dr Oldham had previously suggested Margery Perham, although even his progressive mind balked at the idea of the report being in her name because:

a certain number of people would discount its value if it were written by a woman.

However, Oldham thought that Margery Perham could act as its secretary; she declined the honour.

If women were not politically acceptable to direct this delicate task, neither were men who held rather too definite views on some of the issues to be studied. One was rejected because he would have alienated the Union Government of South Africa and all the settler elements in East Africa. Another would have forfeited the confidence of the missionary communities and those who took a liberal view of native rights. In the end the committee decided on Lord Hailey, at the time governor of the United Provinces in India and an outstanding member of the Indian Civil Service. Apart from his impressive record in India, knowing everything which any man could know about the attempt of a western people to govern the races of India, he had the supreme qualification of bringing an absolutely fresh mind to the problems of Africa. His sovereign merit was:

that neither he nor anyone else knows at this moment what attitude he will take on these burning questions and his views, when he forms and states them, will at any rate be entitled to be regarded as unprejudiced and judicial.

There was no doubt that Hailey had an outstanding record in India and was an impressive personality. Professor Cell in his biographical study describes a man born to rule; standing several inches above six feet, a hawk's nose above an austere face, his voice deep and commanding, he was socially adept and witty with a wealth of funny stories. He could be bold and decisive, patient and courteous, passionate and detached, with a quick mind able to go swiftly to the heart of complex problems while keeping in touch with massive amounts of detail. As a worker he was phenomenal and seemed an ideal choice. Unfortunately his health was poor and he was subject to periods of severe depression. An obsessive, compulsive personality, driven to dominate and control, he could be thrown off balance when he was unable personally to command the outcome. He was appointed nevertheless in July 1933 at a salary of £3,000 a year.

The choice of secretary fell on Hilda Matheson, another phenomenal worker, but one with a rather lower ego who was by now well used to working with dominant personalities. She confirmed her acceptance in July 1933 of a part-time appointment for two days a week at a salary of £400 a year. Writing to Lord Lothian to thank him for thinking of her for the work, she said that she had recently taken the view that she would never organise anything again or put a foot inside an office, but Africa had always interested her and it was difficult to resist working with people she knew and liked.

There was an early hiccup when she thought that she might have to withdraw. This was because she had intended to combine her work on the Survey with regular writing for *The Week-End Review*, but when that journal ceased publication as an independent magazine at the beginning of 1934 she was left with only the promise of very occasional articles for its new stable-mate, the *New Statesman*. The prospect of having to depend only on the Survey's salary was not inviting. At the same time she was being pressed to consider the post of secretary to the National Trust. For her that offer was tempting, partly because the job would be permanent and full-time, but mainly, as she explained to Lord Lothian, because it would provide her with a chance of helping to put through a decent survey of England and an agreement as to which areas should be preserved as national parks and which should be allowed to go. In the event she remained with the Survey of Africa, which was already consuming four days a week of her time and looked like continuing for rather longer than two years. Lothian and Hailey, both of whom were appalled at the prospect of losing her, agreed that she should be offered a three-year appointment.

Getting Started

The day to day work of the Survey was conducted from offices at Chatham House, while committee meetings were often held in Blickling Hall, Norfolk, one of Lord Lothian's houses. Margery Perham thought that it made the problems of Africa seem very far away as they ate out of gold plates while the lights around them were directed upon world-famous paintings, including some by Holbein and Van Dyck. Hilda Matheson enjoyed more the charm and beauty of Blickling's park and gardens and its peculiarly restoring atmosphere. Under the benign ownership of Lord Lothian she likened it to a vast convalescent home as well as an unofficial Chequers. She also worked from her new home, Rocks Farm. Progress was monitored by the main committee, which met three or four times a year, and by a smaller Executive Committee which met more often and whose prime movers were Lord Lothian, Dr Oldham, Lord Hailey and Hilda Matheson.

A number of problems made life difficult from the start. As the vast scale of the task gradually dawned on all those involved, they realised that the time-scale originally envisaged of two years was hopelessly optimistic and that the original funding of £15,000 from the Carnegie Corporation would be insufficient. In 1935 the Corporation provided another £3,000 and in 1937 a further £5,000. The Rhodes trustees chipped in with two payments of £1,000 each. At one stage Lothian himself had to pledge £1,000 to ensure that bills were paid, and Hailey offered to pay out of his own pocket for at least one researcher, although it is not clear whether his offer was taken up. In the end the necessary funding always appeared, but it was never wholly adequate. Staff salaries for their contracted hours were not generous and most of the staff, with Hilda Matheson as ever providing the example, worked many more hours than were paid for.

Lord Hailey detected an impression in some minds that the Survey was a cover for some mysterious purpose of the British Government. Such suspicions were understandable at a time of international tension; part of Hailey's tour of Africa took place during the Abyssinian crisis. Obtaining accurate information from other European governments was a perennial problem because they were anxious to show their colonial possessions in the best light. Lord Hailey thought that trying to get trustworthy information from the French Mandate territories was just a waste of time:

> The French representatives we examine just come here to hoodwink us; M Berson will never speak to me again because I accidentally revealed to him that I saw that his Togo budget was faked ... we spent all the afternoon discussing why there were not more than 300 half-castes in the French Cameroons; the discussion wavered between three alternatives:
> (a) the French had become moral (voted unlikely),
> (b) the Negroes practised birth control (voted possible),
> (c) the figures were as usual faked (voted most probable).

This sort of experience was not publicised at the time, but the introduction in a new 1945 edition of the *Survey* was frank about the fact that some administrations in Africa practised a noticeable economy in making information available to the public.

Two other problems persisted throughout the five years of work, right up to the time of publication. The first of these was, astonishing as it might seem, deciding exactly what the purpose of the Survey should be. The second was the absence much of the time of its director, Lord Hailey, when he was either engaged in completing Indian business or suffering a state of nervous collapse in a Swiss nursing home.

Objectives

How far the Survey should describe, and how far prescribe, was being debated even while the galley proofs were being corrected in 1938. Hailey identified two objectives: first to survey existing knowledge and say what was lacking; secondly to set out problems and indicate possible remedies. When it finally emerged in 1938 the Survey was the outcome of Hilda Matheson's planning in its early stages and her later efforts to guess at Hailey's thoughts. It had to be mainly factual and objective because the diversity of countries and political systems in Africa made generalisation more than usually dangerous; and any attempt to assess the merits of a policy or judge the manner of its application was liable to be treated as an attempt to satisfy one national outlook at the expense of another. Yet, underlying all the factual material was a definite stance and this was made clear in the introduction to the 1945 edition; the sole object for undertaking the Survey, it stated, was the hope that it might prove of some service to the Powers which had possession of territories in Africa and of some benefit to the African people. It was not to be an academic exercise, a mere record of the facts, but a basis for action. Indeed the whole of the Survey assesses everything from the point of view of its impact on the native Africans. It was easier to state this explicitly in 1945 than it had been in 1938. The 1945 opening statement on "The Approach to African Problems" drew out this underlying purpose, and suggested that history, looking back in retrospect on the part played by Imperial Powers in Africa, would be more concerned with the nature of the contribution which the European occupation made to the future of the African peoples, than with the profit or loss which the African connection may have brought to Europe. In short the underlying purpose, which Hilda Matheson was mainly responsible for articulating by means of her editorial skills, was to advance the interests of native Africans.

Lord Hailey's Absences

Lord Hailey's infirmity of purpose was made worse by frequent absences. From July 1933 until May 1935, he was almost wholly engaged on matters connected with his work in India, in particular advising the British Government on the India Bill. He did make some contribution during this early period: in 1933 he attended two of the Executive meetings and another five in 1935 just before he left for Africa, but there is little sign of any firm, directing hand. He intended to start work on the Survey with an extensive tour of Africa early in 1935, but as late as 25 July that year Lord Lothian expressed grave concern as to whether he was in a fit state of health to do so and urged him first to take a holiday.

His tour of Africa finally started in August 1935 and continued until June 1936. During his outward journey to Cape Town in August 1935 he would have had an opportunity to read the Survey material prepared in the previous two years. His visits to nearly all the Africa countries south of the Sahara added formidably to the research. Like Matheson in the two years before, he now began to work on the Survey "... long, hard, compulsively". In all he made a journey of more than 22,000 miles, mainly by car. Trunk-loads of data and memoranda were collected, but even at the start of the tour the signs of ill health and falling confidence showed. Hilda Matheson expressed her fears to Lord Lothian that the trip was turning out to be every bit as hard as the pessimists had prophesied and hoped that it wasn't "going to do Sir Malcolm in."

On his return in June 1936, Hailey began the difficult task of trying to assemble all the material that had been collected for him previously, together with what he had amassed on his tour, into some sort of coherent framework. Hilda Matheson thought that there were likely to be about 22 chapters which just might get drafted by Easter 1937. To do even that, she wrote to Dr Oldham, would require Hailey to trim his ambitions and Carnegie to provide more money:

> *I cannot really discuss these problems with Lord Hailey because they only aggravate his worry and perplexity. But as Lord Lothian and Mr Macadam are both away I felt I must explain the position to you before waiting any longer. I think Lord Hailey is definitely much less depressed than he was, and is beginning to think that progress is being made. But I hope very much that with your knowledge of the facts and with so much experience, you may be able to suggest ways of expediting the work which will commend themselves to Lord Hailey. I am of course sure that whatever he produces will be a remarkable production. It is only ways and means and timetables that bother me a bit.*

A month later she appeared to be more optimistic; as a result of discussion with Lord Hailey and further planning a shape was beginning to emerge. The report would analyse first principles and provide a factual description of all the fundamental issues. This could be done by the summer for publication in the autumn of 1937. Her optimism was premature as in the following month, November 1936, Hailey confessed that he had taken on a task much heavier than he had realised and had become doubtful of his ability to carry it through:

> *I cannot commit myself to hasty generalisations. I have not that gift of self-confidence which makes some people preach well of which they know nothing. In fact I am not really fit for work on this scale. If I could honestly give it up I should do so tomorrow.*

With his gift for making the best of things, Lord Lothian told the Carnegie Corporation that Hailey's despair about producing the Survey was because he wanted a work which would be much more than the original intention of a mere statement of problems. To realise this grander vision would require another £5,000. The money was obtained, but the depression continued. During the summer of 1937 Lord Hailey visited a clinic in Switzerland. When his wife was slightly injured in a car crash he came back to Britain a very jaded man. In October he suffered a complete collapse and had to return to the clinic where he stayed for the rest of the year and most of the next. It was not until June 1938 that he was able to look at the few remaining galley proofs, the others having gone to press in his absence.

What Hilda Matheson Did

Writing in her school magazine after the Survey had been published, Hilda Matheson gave this account of her work:

> *For the first year 1933-34 Lord Hailey was still in India; for the year 1935-36 he was in Africa and for nine months in the winter and spring of 1937-38 he was away ill. My own part has been to organise a central secretariat, which during his absences has had to shoulder considerable responsibility; to commission the collection by specialists in many fields of*

all available information and its preparation for Lord Hailey's consideration; to collect a staff of drafting assistants; to arrange with African governments for the supply of printed and other materials; to circulate preparatory drafts of the main chapters to experts at home and abroad and incorporate their comments; to supervise the final preparation for the press of Lord Hailey's volume of over 600,000 words together with two supplementary volumes; to arrange for their publication and to see them through the press.

One does not have to read too closely between the lines to recognise that she was effectively the director of the Survey. All the other evidence supports her account. From July 1933 until the autumn of 1935 the whole burden of the direction of the Survey as well as its administration fell on her. It was she who did most of the thinking about what work needed to be done. Dr Oldham provided helpful guidance day to day, and outside the committee there were many experts on Africa whose skills she could draw on, but it was left to her to develop a concept of the final report and to direct the collection of information. There is abundant evidence for this conclusion in the papers of Lords Lothian and Lugard, Dr Oldham and Margery Perham. Professor Cell acknowledges that executive manager would have been a better description of her role than secretary, but even he underestimates just how much the Survey owed to Hilda Matheson.

Hilda Matheson had the gift which all the best staff officers or secretaries of Royal Commissions and Public Enquiries need, which is to see from the start the shape of the final report and to identify the information needed to allow the chair or director to take an informed view on all the relevant issues. In his great historical novel *August 1914* Alexander Solzhenitsyn describes the exercise of this rare gift by Colonel Vorotyntsev when he arrives at the Russian-German front line and meets the Russian commander Samsonov. The colonel observes the chaotic administration and the need for effective staff work:

The job of a proper staff was to sift through the swirling mass of conjecture and lay down a solid roadbed on which sound decisions could march forward, to send out officers to check dubious reports on the spot, to be ruthlessly selective and to see that the really important information was not swamped by a flood of trivia. A staff's job was not to replace the commander's will, but to help it reveal itself ... Vorotyntsev soaked up all there was to know about the operational situation. It was as if he had not just arrived but had spent at least three weeks here absorbed in the problem- nay more, as though his whole life, his entire military career had been nothing but a period of training for this one operation ... The obsession which throbbed within him was to solve a riddle; *his destiny was to take a* decision; *and his tact must be used to make it seem to the Army Commander that it was Samsonov himself who had made it.*

Hilda Matheson acted as Vorotyntsev to Hailey's Samsonov, not only a bewildered, but an absentee, commander. Lord Lothian was able to reassure Hailey in July 1934:

> *Miss Matheson and our various experts ... are collecting a really valuable body of information, which will be ready for you by the end of the year. I have been in some doubt myself as to how much work could really usefully be done until your hand was upon it, but I feel satisfied now that the preliminary investigation will save you a great deal of time and give you a body of material to work on ... Miss Matheson will be sending you also a copy of her Memorandum. Dr Oldham and Henry Clay, whom Miss Matheson also consulted, and also Sir Arthur Salter, felt that Part I of the memorandum was a very comprehensive survey of the ground to be covered. Dr Oldham, indeed, felt it to be quite first class.*

In other words she was in total command of the situation despite the fact that her own health was beginning to give way and she had to take two weeks off to try and avert a stiffening process in her limbs with especially painful hands. By May 1937 ten of the chapters had gone to the printers and two more were complete, but this rosier picture was once again blighted, this time by Hailey's total collapse. Describing the breakdown to Lord Lothian, Hilda Matheson added that she too had been unwell and had lost a stone in the last few months and:

> *like Lord Hailey, had acquired a tired heart.*

She took a week off to replace the stone! Lord Lothian pointed out that even the fattening cure of the old German clinics would find it difficult to add a stone in a week.

In sight of the End

Five high-powered drafting assistants, mainly academics, were now recruited to work under her direction. In November further relief was provided when the Colonial Office agreed to the secondment of Frederick Pedler, secretary to Lord De La Warr, to help for three months. He was a lively, witty character, not at all over-awed by his task, and he enjoyed redrafting what he described as the dull writing of academics. He got on well with Hilda Matheson and admired her political skills, expressing the hope on one occasion that her "diabolical machinations" would get his draft through to the press without offending anybody. She remained confident even in Hailey's absence that the work could be published. The most important chapters had already been completed, she told Dr Oldham in November, and as they stood represented Lord Hailey's own work upon them. The remaining chapters were sufficiently far advanced for those who had been preparing them under Lord Hailey's instructions, to complete them "... with certain expert help", no doubt provided by Mr Pedler and herself. Lord Lothian reassured the Carnegie Corporation that the bulk of the report was already in print and the balance would be completed by people who had worked with Lord Hailey. In March 1938 he told Lord Hailey that:

> *Miss Matheson herself has unflinchingly taken on her own competent shoulders the responsibility for planning and organising the work and has done wonders.*

After six months of complete prostration Lord Hailey began slowly to recover and in June some of the galley proofs were sent to him, although as Hilda Matheson pointed out to Lord Lothian there was now little for him to do.

The Survey was published finally in November 1938 and copies were sold for a guinea each (one pound ten pence). After all the agonising about what the Survey should include it turned out to be a mixture not unlike the first outline proposed by Hilda Matheson in the summer of 1933; it described conditions in Africa as they were at the time of writing, it identified problems and areas for further research, and also made some suggestions for future policy.

The Public Reaction

The Survey was favourably received. The Government, through the Colonial Office, welcomed it. *The Times* gave it a preliminary notice of two full columns the day before publication, attributing its scope and form and the opinions expressed in it to Lord Hailey. After publication it offered a detailed critique and a leading article, again very favourable. All the London papers gave it considerable space, often using as reviewers ex-colonial civil servants. The *Daily Telegraph* had a notice by a former governor of Kenya. A previous governor of Nigeria and Tanganyika writing for the *Spectator* referred to "the riches" in the book which he described as "easy, indeed delightful reading". He expressed the hope that a smaller volume could be issued giving all the conclusions but less of the background material. Specialist journals such as the *Law Journal*, the *Medical Journal* and the *Bulletin of Hygiene* found little to quarrel with. The *Bulletin* approved its lucid exposition and lack of dogmatism, but was critical of its advocacy of a mass approach to medicine based on education about hygiene and sanitation rather than the transplantation of British Hospital medicine. (Thinking today would almost certainly favour the far-sighted approach of the Survey over the *Bulletin's* addiction to the high-tech medicine of the time.)

The BBC invited Lord Hailey to make two broadcasts. Perhaps most impressive of all was the special supplement published by the *Journal of the Royal African Society* which contained contributions by 14 authorities including two ex-Secretaries of State. That the Survey survived all this detailed attention and expert scrutiny seems miraculous. Even more surprising is that this massive volume sold out its first edition of 5,000 within a few months and a second impression had to be produced in 1939.

Importance of the Survey

How important was the Survey? One early practical result of its proposals was the "Colonial Development and Welfare Act" of 1940 and the allocation by the Government of £500,000 for colonial research and development. More important than its influence on such specific measures was its impact on colonial development policy. The thinking outlined in the Survey continued to be influential after the Second World War and in the judgement of one commentator became "the principal work of reference in development circles". Professor Cell in his later study of Hailey described the Survey as:

> *The pivotal project that culminated the discussion of African affairs by Britain's inter-war generation, helped set the agenda for the colonial reform movement of the war years, and indirectly pointed towards decolonization in the post-war era.*

A shift from the idea of primitive peoples being guided slowly towards civilisation to a concept of temporary stewardship leading to an early transfer of power, would have taken place anyway with the rise of nationalism in most colonial territories after the Second World War. The Survey anticipated that change and provided an intellectual framework within which the new thinking could grow, flourish and ultimately dominate. Although the Survey had to avoid favouring one model of development over another, its basic stance is clear. The key test for any policy or model was its impact on the future of the African peoples. Hitherto the main test of colonial policy had been the benefits which the African connection brought to Europe; in future it was the benefits to Africa, and in particular to native Africans, which would be the criterion against which all policies would be measured. Before the Survey there had been little evidence of any central direction of colonial policy beyond the mere establishment and maintenance of order. After the Survey, Governments had to take note of a body of informed non-official opinion which exerted its influence in the direction of systematic reviews of every aspect of policy from the point of view of native Africans. The social duty of the State to improve conditions began to be recognised.

The report noted two main obstacles to the development of such African-centred policies, namely the development of apartheid in southern Africa and the influence of European settlers elsewhere. It did not of course describe these as obstacles, but in its carefully balanced statements and its presentation of facts it made it clear that ultimately the focus of policy on benefits to Africans was both inevitable and right. Thus the sections of the Survey on health, education, employment, ownership of land, and the development of representative government, although expressed in cautious and measured language, all display the same liberal and humane approach. The idea of any innate inferiority of Africans was firmly rejected. Education should not be restricted to schooling Africans for subordinate positions. Land ownership rights of Africans should be protected and peasant agriculture should be encouraged. The political future of Africa had to be that of self-government based on representative institutions.

Running like a thread throughout the Survey is the contrast between developments in southern Africa with ideas of racial segregation and the position in most British colonies where, however feebly, the rights of Africans to full development were protected. The Survey did not comment adversely on the one or favourably on the other, but the constant juxtaposition of the two approaches and the descriptions of the problems and opportunities of each are sufficient to indicate which model of development was favoured by the authors.

Hilda Matheson's Contribution

All the papers relating to the Survey support Professor Cell's conclusion that Hailey personally wrote only a fraction of it and that he played a comparatively small role in its editing. The evidence does not support Professor Cell's further conclusions that Hailey planned and launched it, and that while he was sick during 1937-38 it was "... Pedler and his team" who were meeting the production schedule. This overstates the contributions of both Hailey and Pedler, and is less than just to Hilda Matheson.

Because most of the working papers have been destroyed it will never be possible precisely to demonstrate the relative contributions made by each of the principals and their helpers. But the indications that Hilda Matheson played the predominant part are clear. In April 1938 she wrote to Lord Lothian of the need:

> not only to de-Pedlerize, but also to Haileyize everything as far as possible.

One wonders whether even Hailey could recognise what was his and what was Matheson's; it was probably impossible for anyone to tell the difference. The fact is that Hailey's contribution was limited to one frantic year's work from the summer of 1935 to the autumn of 1936. Hilda Matheson was the person who planned the framework of the Survey, managed the systematic collection of information during the first two years from July 1933 to July 1935, guided Hailey through his depression to produce a synthesis not unlike her first framework documents of 1933, and ensured between 1937 and 1938 that the material was produced, edited and printed.

Of course there were vital contributions from many people, including those academics who wrote the specialist chapters, the drafters who edited, re-wrote and sometimes originated material, and people like Pedler who gave significant editorial help at a critical time. The great contribution made by all these people must be acknowledged. Similarly, one must be careful not to diminish unduly Hailey's contribution. He was a prodigious worker and even one year's effort was sufficient to ensure that he made an important contribution. Furthermore, as he was recovering from a breakdown that took him near to death he tried to keep a guiding hand on the work. In assessing whose Survey it was, however, the slight figure of Hilda Matheson towers above this giant of a man, as it does over all the others who had anything to do with it.

Recognition at the Time

Her contribution at the time was underplayed in public by both colleagues and herself. In March 1938 as the Survey was approaching publication, Lord Bledisloe wanted Lord Hailey to give evidence to a Commission he was chairing on the closer union of Rhodesia and Nyasaland. Lord Lothian explained that Hailey was sick and suggested either Hilda Matheson or Mr Keith who, he said, was in effect acting for Lord Hailey. Lord Bledisloe expressed regret that Lord Hailey would not be able to attend, but doubted:

> whether Miss Matheson would be altogether acceptable as a witness, as there is in the minds of many (including possibly some of my colleagues) an impression that women are apt to be influenced by strong prejudices, especially on native problems. Failing yourself, it might be as well if Mr Keith gave evidence.

Adept as ever at salvaging something from disaster, although it meant disparaging his friend, Lord Lothian replied that he would not suggest that Hilda Matheson should give evidence:

> Though she is a very sane and levelheaded person, I would agree with you in thinking that Mr Keith would be the more appropriate witness. What I meant to suggest was that you might care to have a talk to Miss Matheson ... who could tell you better than anybody else the information which was available and who could supply your Commission best with it.

So, as ever, the briefing would take place behind the arras, permitting the men to posture on stage.

The Survey Committee recognised her outstanding work by a payment of an extra year's salary of £400, which for once compared favourably with the additional sum of £250 paid to Lord Hailey. Writing to Dr Oldham to inform him of the payments, Lord Lothian said:

> As you know, if it had not been for her the Survey would have crashed altogether last autumn. She threw herself into the work in a manner never contemplated under her original contract and has succeeded in really doing the work of a quasi-director and as a result of her efforts and of the staff she has organised the Survey will, I think, be out in October after all.

Thanking the Committee for their reckless generosity, her modest response, in which she said that she didn't feel she deserved it, provides a generous assessment of the contributions made by others:

> The work rests on many shoulders. It could not have been completed but for my luck in finding such a fine group of people to see it through this last year, whose standards of scholarship and of work have made it possible to keep up the levels of judgement and accuracy set by Lord Hailey. Nor could it have been carried on at all without a Chairman and Committee so invariably encouraging and so accessible at any time. Indeed your own imperturbability in the face of recurring crises was what really made me believe the Report would one day appear. I can only say that I have never enjoyed any work more, and that I have never known such ideal conditions in which to work. This includes the whole atmosphere of Chatham House, with the friendliness and efficiency which run through the building from top to bottom. I really do thank you all for giving me a share in the work.

The Government recognised her contribution with the award of OBE which was announced in the New Year's Honours List of 1939. Lord Hailey was already so weighed down with honours that anything more would have been superfluous, so the embarrassment of an undeserved honour could be avoided without loss of face.

Later Recognition

Julian Huxley, another trustee, two years later referred to Hilda Matheson's rare combination of brains, character, charm and beauty and to the brilliant work she did on the Survey. Her many-sided gifts, he thought, enabled her to organise and facilitate the work in a way that would have been quite beyond most men's powers. But the final, generous, words should be left to Lord Hailey, written shortly after her death:

> I do not find it easy to express the full measure of the debt which I and those who collaborated in the work of the Survey owed to Hilda Matheson. Her connection with the enterprise was, indeed, larger than my own, for it fell to her to organise all the preliminary work of the Survey, from 1933 to the summer of 1935 ... but even when I was able to take charge of the work, the practical direction of the organisation remained largely in her hands. The field was a difficult one. We had to deal not only with our own Colonial Office, but with the Colonial Ministries in France, Belgium and Portugal, and with the Government of South Africa. It was necessary to commission a number of special studies not only on political and economic subjects, but on matters of a scientific nature. Here Hilda was never at a loss. She seemed to know at once the right quarters in which to look for assistance; but what is more – and this indeed was to me a matter of constant amazement – she invariably seemed able to ensure that it should be forthcoming. Colonial Ministers (and in one instance a crowned head

himself), scientists, economists and administrators all seemed equally ready to answer the call which she made on them. It was no doubt her previous experience in the BBC, which gave her a wide knowledge of those who moved in so many diverse walks of life; but it must have been some peculiar quality of her own that enabled her to secure so readily their interest on our behalf. There was a late stage in our work at which she had to take on even heavier responsibility. By the end of the summer of 1937 much of the material of the Survey was already in hand, and a number of the chapters of our book had been written. But in the autumn of that year I myself fell seriously ill in Switzerland and was forced to abandon all thought of work. In the early spring of 1938 Hilda came out to Bordighera where I was still in the stages of a slow and somewhat languid convalescence. I confess that my spirit was faltering ... But her own resolution never wavered. In my absence she found a means to secure the aid of new colleagues, who had already drafted most of the remaining chapters; little, indeed, was left to me but to edit and revise their work ... and the autumn of that year (1938) saw our book duly published ... but for her initiative and determination, it might never have seen the light ... An untiring energy was joined to a rare capacity for rapid decision; she had that direct approach to a problem which seemed to rob it at once of many of its difficulties. But these qualities alone would not have won for her the attachment, and indeed affection, which we felt for her ... We looked on her as one who had brought a fine spirit to our enterprise, and inspired us by her devotion to it and by her faith in its success.

It was at Bordighera that her father, too, had recovered from his breakdown thirty years before. There is no record of what she did to aid her father's recovery, but she does seem to have had a special skill in helping men to overcome their depressions, enabling them to resume those positions from which women were excluded.

A Postscript

In 1957 a new edition of the Survey was published, entitled rather confusingly *An African Survey Revised 1956*. (Referred to subsequently as the 1957 edition.) In his preface Lord Hailey said that because of the many changes in Africa and other countries since 1938 the original Survey had largely had to be rewritten. The present volume, he wrote:

though similar in its objectives and in the arrangement of its material to that published in 1938, is, in many respects, a new work.

After a careful reading of both editions it is difficult to support Lord Hailey's claim.

As well as preserving the basic arrangement of material, including the detailed organisation of sections within chapters, much of the original material remains as it was drafted in 1938. There is new material, of course, and figures have been updated, but there was no requirement for any change in the basic philosophy of the Survey. The new edition was not able to add much about the decolonisation of Africa. In British possessions the transfer of power to native governments was only beginning to gather pace in 1957, and in South Africa the only change was that the system of apartheid which the 1938 Survey had commented on was being reinforced.

About half the chapters were thoroughly revised, particularly those on systems of government, native administration, problems of labour, water supply, soil erosion, health, education, economic development, minerals, transport and the future of African studies. Even in these much of the original material and thinking survives. Other chapters contain much less new material and several are almost identical. To describe the 1957 edition as new is about as accurate as to call the 1938 edition "Hailey's African Survey".

There are so many ways in which the later edition echoes the earlier, even down to Hailey's acknowledgement in 1956 to a Professor Carrington who had generously dealt with the proofs of a number of chapters at a time when he himself was incapacitated from doing so. There is, however, one significant difference; Lord Hailey did not in 1957 acknowledge Hilda Matheson's work on the Survey.

Chapter Six

ANOTHER WAR
1939-40

A Short Respite

Lady Astor wrote to congratulate Hilda Matheson on the award of OBE and asked what work she would do now. Why not return to her, she suggested, but the invitation was too late. In November 1938, even before she was quite clear of the Survey, a mysterious man began telephoning her at her mother's house in London, but would give no name. Finally they met, and when she returned from the meeting she told her mother that the man knew all there was to know about her. This emissary from the Secret Intelligence Service (SIS), better known as MI6, agreed to wait for her reply until she returned from a much needed holiday in France. She spent six weeks on the French Riviera with Dorothy Wellesley, sometimes in the company of the dying Yeats who was staying nearby. In January Hilda instructed Vita by telegraph that she was to telephone Yeats' family in Dublin with the news that he was on his deathbed. Shortly afterwards she returned to London.

There was never any doubt about her decision, but she accepted the call from MI6 in the same way that she had accepted all her previous jobs, reluctantly. It was already likely that Chamberlain's settlement reached at Munich in September 1938 would not last, and that Britain would soon be at war with Germany again. Now she was being asked to act not as "a policeman", which had been her role with MI5 in the 1914-18 war, but as a propagandist within MI6, making particular use of her knowledge and experience of broadcasting. Her task would be to use the spoken word in furtherance of peace or, in the event of failure, to use the same skills in war. In order to understand her new work and the difficulties she encountered, some knowledge is necessary of the preparations for war made by government departments during 1938-39, and of the organisation of the security, propaganda and information services when war came.

Preparations for War 1931-38

Security matters were guided nominally by a committee of senior ministers, but this had not met since 1931 when it established the arrangements still in force on the outbreak of war. While roles were reasonably clear, there was no single authority recognised as such by all the various parts. There were three central groupings, each with its own sponsoring ministry. The Joint Intelligence Committee coordinated the intelligence work of the armed services departments and reported to the War Office. MI6 was responsible for the collection of intelligence abroad and counter-espionage outside the British Empire and, although a separate service, was required to inform the Foreign Office about, and to clear with it, many of its activities. MI5, which was responsible for the detection of espionage and subversion in Britain, related to the Home Office. In addition there was an intelligence section in each ministry which also worked with one or other of the central groupings, and there were other specialist services, for example the Special Branch of the Metropolitan Police which checked on subversion in the civilian population. There was a good deal of rivalry between these various parts and Hilda Matheson was to be caught up in the politicking which intensified as war approached.

War was not declared until September 1939, but international tension increased from January 1933 when Hitler became Reich Chancellor. Covert preparations for hostilities began to be made in Britain. As early as 1931 the Foreign Office had called for a meeting with the BBC about the possibility of transmitting British propaganda to certain countries, but nothing came of it because the BBC governors were hostile. From 1934, when Goebbels became the sole broadcasting authority in Germany and began feverishly to develop shortwave services to foreign countries, Foreign Office interest in broadcasting increased. It monitored Italian radio during the Italo-Abyssinian crisis of 1935 and, from the summer of 1937, German and Italian news broadcasts.

Reith, who worked secretly with the covert branches of government throughout the thirties advised the BBC governors that their Empire services should be extended and that serious consideration should now be given to broadcasting overseas. The governors were not impressed and he could not persuade them. It was not until 1938 that the BBC began foreign language broadcasts, with one service in Arabic and another in Spanish and Portuguese for Latin America. There was no European service and even at the outbreak of war the BBC had no regular foreign news service and no staff of foreign correspondents.

The reluctance of the BBC governors to do more earlier was partly due to suspicion of becoming involved in propaganda, but it reflected also the public mood. Most men and women had little idea that another war was imminent, or at least they preferred not to consider the prospect seriously. While David Low's cartoons in the *Evening Standard* depicted Hitler and Mussolini as war-mongers, the *Daily Express* with its much larger circulation asserted even as late as 1938 and during much of 1939 that there would be no war in Europe. The Abyssinian crisis, German rearmament, Hitler's re-occupation of the Rhineland and even his incorporation of Austria into Germany on 13 March 1938 did little to shake public complacency.

Crisis and Confusion 1938-40

Calm was succeeded by frantic activity, at least for a short time. The Czechoslovakian crisis in the summer and autumn of 1938 triggered feelings almost of panic as people woke up to the possibility of war. As Rose Macaulay put it, Britain became bomb conscious; trenches were dug and many Londoners went to earth in the country, warning sirens were tried over the radio, millions of gas masks were distributed and preparations made for evacuating children from London and other cities likely to be bombed. Chamberlain's return from Munich on 30 September 1938 encouraged most of the press and its readership to relax once again as he was hailed in Britain and throughout Europe as the man who had rescued the international community from war. The political classes, however, which had been increasingly aroused during 1937 and 1938, went into a complete spin.

The general confusion and lack of readiness was demonstrated in an absurd shambles at the height of the crisis in September 1938. The Cabinet was anxious that an important speech by Neville Chamberlain should be communicated in full to the German people. Yet by six o'clock on the evening of the Prime Minister's broadcast, neither the Foreign Office nor the BBC had been able to find suitable people to translate the speech into French and German for broadcasting. In the end the German born artist and cartoonist, Walter Goetz, together with a former London correspondent of a Viennese newspaper, Robert Ehrenzweig, were rushed to Broadcasting House at the last minute and had to do the best they could. Goetz found it difficult to read Ehrenzweig's handwritten German, which was given him in bits as soon as it was written down, and he kept running out of material. There were many long pauses. Adding to the confusion was the fact that to provide maximum sound quality in Germany the short wave transmitters were supplemented by medium wave transmitters, which usually broadcast regional programmes in Britain. Some British listeners tuning in as usual to the medium wave thought that the Nazis had taken over and a crowd of protestors stormed Broadcasting House.

From the Munich crisis of September 1938 until the end of the phoney war in May 1940 was a period of political turmoil. The military assessment of the Chiefs of Staff was bleak; they could not forsee a time when their defence forces would be sufficient to safeguard British interests against Germany, Italy and Japan at the same time. They supported Chamberlain's firm view that Britain could not and should not fight at the time of Munich. The new Foreign Secretary, Lord Halifax, who had been appointed when Anthony Eden resigned in 1938 after disagreements over policy towards Italy, did not agree entirely with his Prime

Minister, but was isolated in the cabinet. There were pressures to speed up rearmament and improve the condition of the fighting forces, together with a growing agitation for a propaganda war. At the same time other voices clamoured for peace. Officials and some influential individuals pressed for campaigns that would demonstrate to the Germans that Britain was hostile only to the Nazis, not to the German people. Vernon Bartlett, a broadcaster much used previously by Hilda Matheson and now a journalist and MP for Bridgwater, advised the Foreign Office that propaganda would be much more important than in the last war. He forecast economic difficulties within Germany and growing hostility towards the Nazis which Britain could exploit. Another broadcaster and friend of Hilda Matheson, Stephen King-Hall, developed similar themes.

Right up to the moment that war was declared on 3 September 1939 Chamberlain sought to avoid activities that might jeopardise his agreements with Hitler. At the same time he accepted that something had to be done to improve Britain's readiness for war and to keep Hitler guessing as to the real intentions of his government. After his Munich experience Chamberlain trusted Hitler to keep his word, but had to allow for the possibility that he wouldn't, so he was sympathetic towards proposals for improving the communication of government policies abroad. Hitler had to be persuaded that Britain might be prepared to go to war, and friendship with other countries had to be preserved or cultivated. The Munich crisis had demonstrated the lack of coordinated arrangements for the production of information and its conveyance into enemy countries, but neither the designate Ministry of Information nor the BBC was equipped for such a task. Contingency plans for that ministry were to be operated only in time of war and, as war had not yet been declared, the Foreign Office continued to cling to its peace time duties. The BBC was not able to help, even had it been thought appropriate for it to do so. Chamberlain was determined that something had to be done to get Britain's message across to friends as well as potential enemies.

Just before the Munich crisis the Prime Minister, guided by Foreign Office officials and senior intelligence officers, secretly requested Sir Campbell Stuart, who had been second in command of propaganda activities in the First World War, to set up a new department to be responsible for propaganda in enemy countries. This was to be under the supervision of the Political Intelligence Department of the Foreign Office. Stuart set up his new unit in Electra House, the headquarters of Cable and Wireless of which he was chairman. (Later on he moved his propaganda work to Woburn Abbey, but the original name stuck and "Electra House" was to become a great nuisance to Hilda Matheson.) It was at this time also, shortly after the post-Munich lull, that Hilda Matheson received her invitation to become director of yet another secret propaganda organisation which became known as the Joint Broadcasting Committee (JBC). The invitation came from Section D of MI6, a section which was soon to become one of the founding organisations of the Special Operations Executive but which during 1938-39 was charged with the duty of investigating every possibility of attacking potential enemies other than by military force. Its main weapons were to be sabotage and propaganda and the JBC was to be its propaganda arm.

While these preparations were being made the embryo Ministry of Information was effectively neutered, being put under the direction of civil servants many of whom at the same time held jobs in other ministries. The nominal responsibilities of this ministry-in-waiting were huge, with fourteen divisions covering the release of official news, censorship of films, press and radio, maintenance of morale, publicity campaigns for other departments and the whole field of propaganda to enemy, neutral, allied and Empire countries. Unfortunately all of these functions cut across the work of other departments, as well as that of the new secret groups, and the Foreign Office was determined to confine the ministry's activities to the home front. This rivalry between the Foreign Office and the new Ministry of Information was to affect Hilda Matheson profoundly. Each department regarded the JBC as part of its responsibilities, and for much of the time she had to work for and try to remain loyal to both.

When the Ministry of Information began seriously to operate under Lord Macmillan, once war had been declared, it had already acquired a poor reputation. On 4 January 1940 Chamberlain requested Reith to take it over. Had he been offered the job at the beginning of the war he felt he might have been able to make it do what it was meant to do. Now it was in notorious disrepute, the object of fierce running criticism in Parliament and press, and the subject of envy and obstruction throughout Whitehall. Its authority had been reduced when some of its responsibilites were hived off to other departments or to special groups such as Electra House and the JBC. Yet at the beginning of 1940 Chamberlain still would not agree to the parts being reassembled, and although Reith's post had cabinet rank he was refused a seat in the Cabinet.

By this time Chamberlain's leadership had been fatally compromised. During the last months of his premiership everything was up for grabs; existing departments fought to preserve their responsibilities, the central security groupings tried to retain their pre-war territories, Electra House and the JBC carved out their new roles, the Ministry of Information struggled to survive, the BBC and other quasi-government bodies such as the British Council twitched nervously at the likely impact of war on their well-established activities, and everyone fought for influence.

The German occupation of Denmark and Norway on 8 April, the subsequent invasion of the Low Countries on 10 May 1940, and the accession of Winston Churchill as prime minister that day marked the ending of the "phoney war" in the battlefields and the beginnings of a sort of peace in the domestic war of words. Reith was replaced at Information by Duff Cooper on 13 May. Soon afterwards Section D and Electra House and part of military intelligence came together in the Special Operations Executive (SOE) to be responsible for all covert propaganda work overseas. These changes together with the establishment of the Ministry of Economic Warfare and the Security Executive marked the long needed rationalisation of the security, intelligence, propaganda and information services. The JBC was left for a while to dangle between the Foreign Office and the Ministry of Information, but the latter finally succeeded in asserting its authority and got it transferred to the BBC, thus effectively keeping it under its own control.

It was in this political maelstrom, from the winter of 1938, during all of 1939 and up to October 1940, that Hilda Matheson made her last great contribution to public life. During this time the most vicious battles were fought not in the field, but in Whitehall, and much of her creative energy had to be spent fighting off opposition to the JBC as the Foreign Office, the Ministry of Information, the various parts of the security services and the BBC staked out their new war-time roles. It was not until 1941 that the various parties began properly to be coordinated, but by then Hilda Matheson was dead.

An Old Love Recaptured

Characteristically, the work she began in January 1939 was to be done out of the public gaze. Surviving behind the scenes as an official in these fierce political waters suited parts of her temperament, giving scope to her energy and powers of persuasion. The confusion, uncertainty and panic would have been a nightmare for some, but for her were a challenge to her sense of order and her gifts of clear thinking, analysis and organisation. An occasional taste for intrigue could also be satisfied, although her combative nature did not find Whitehall infighting congenial. To work confidently she needed strong, sympathetic support, and opponents and issues bigger than civil servants scrapping for survival. She was unwell for much of the time, but ironically her illness, Graves disease, synchronised with the urgency and desperation of the time, driving her on harder and faster than ever. Never had her fierce energy been more suited to the occasion, but never had it been more dangerous to her as she picked a way quickly through the mess when put in charge of the JBC.

The idea for a broadcasting organisation separate from the BBC had originated when the Munich experience was being digested. Major Lawrence Grand, who headed Section D, was instructed to devise ways of disseminating information to enemy and neutral countries using channels outside Britain. Whatever means were used had to appear to be independent of government or public bodies such as the BBC. He was the mysterious caller who so intrigued Meta, confirmation of which is contained in a report written by Hilda Matheson just before the outbreak of war. Papers prepared for a sub-committee of the Committee of Imperial Defence provide some of the details of what Major Grand and Section D had in mind for her. When the sub-committee met on 14 December 1938 to consider plans for activating the Ministry of Information, the Foreign Office pre-empted formal business. Officials announced beforehand that up to the outbreak of war the organisation of publicity and propaganda in foreign countries was to remain with them. Furthermore, on the Prime Minister's instructions the Foreign Secretary had put certain definite proposals to the Cabinet, the nature of which would be explained at the meeting.

The details given out on 14 December included plans for communicating the British point of view to the German public and to people in neutral countries by means of broadcasts, personal contacts and literature. The Foreign Office wanted to develop reciprocal broadcasting arrangements with other countries, but using an organisation other than the BBC. Time would be bought on foreign stations, for example Luxembourg, Strasbourg and Liechtenstein, by what would appear as a commercial firm, possibly a travel agency, which would broadcast a general news review and other items in the language of the country being addressed. While all programmes would be submitted to the Foreign Office in advance, any participation by the British Government would be concealed. The general aim was to spread information of a non-controversial character about Britain to produce a favourable impression of its strength and resources and the vehicle used turned out to be not a travel agency but the JBC. Whether the idea originated with Neville Chamberlain is not known, but the JBC was certainly one of the means he used to build a climate of opinion favourable to peace while promoting an awareness of Britain's ultimate readiness for war.

Hilda Matheson must have relished being offered her very own broadcasting company. She was probably not unduly upset by the fact that it was bound to bring her into conflict with the BBC. Although she did not know it at the time of her appointment, it was also soon to set her against her old antagonist, John Reith, when he was put in charge of the Ministry of Information for a short time in 1940. In his diary on 17 April 1939, recording a meeting with Lord Beaverbrook to discuss the latter's suggestion that he should become designate-minister of information, Reith noted that a good many observations were made during the meeting about broadcasting for propaganda purposes, including:

A weird and quite impracticable scheme for pirate transmissions by Jews and such like against Germany and Italy.

This bizarre scheme was of course the JBC, but Reith does not record whether he knew that the idea was already being put into practice by the talks director whom he had driven out of the BBC eight years before.

There were other potential sources of conflict from the start. Organisationally the JBC began as part of the Foreign Office, financed by their secret funds. Later, when it was also partly funded by the Ministry of Information, it retained its Foreign Office links. The position of the JBC in relation to the Ministry of Information was a constant source of irritation to civil servants:

It appears that we cannot regard them as on the staff of the Ministry and our payments to the JBC should be in the nature of a grant [because] they undertake activities of which we know little or nothing.

The JBC was in fact two organisations: one, covert, reporting to Section D within the Foreign Office and responsible for clandestine broadcasts to potentially hostile countries; the other, overt, broadcasting information about Britain to friendly and neutral countries. It discharged these roles in three distinct phases. The first was from January 1939 until war was declared in September of that year. During this time it worked almost exclusively for Section D, being deeply involved in efforts to avert war by means of propaganda or, when war became inevitable, to persuade friendly countries actively to help Britain or remain neutral. After war had been declared and Chamberlain was struggling for his own survival, the JBC never entirely lost its Foreign Office protection, but it was obliged to work more closely with the Ministry of Information, the BBC and Electra House. During this second phase, which lasted until the end of the phoney war in May 1940, it tried to maintain an independent role and promoted its own thinking on the sort of propaganda likely to be most effective. In the third phase from May to October 1940 it had at last to bow the knee to the Ministry of Information and even, when it lost the leadership of Hilda Matheson, to its arch-rival the BBC as well.

What the JBC Did

Working from commercial offices in Chester Square, until bombing forced its evacuation to Roger Eckersley's farmhouse and Hilda Matheson's cottage, the JBC presented itself as a goodwill organisation, ready to provide broadcast material of a cultural nature to radio companies abroad who expressed an interest. Its notepaper listed the Rt Hon The Earl of Rothes as chairman and Hilda Matheson as broadcasting director. Her friends Harold Nicolson and Sir Frederick Whyte were among the eight directors. From the beginning it had a fairly large establishment of about 40 posts, including seven agents abroad, which increased gradually to 50 posts. Hilda Matheson was paid £1,000 a year and specialist staff received between £6-800 a year. The usual civil service rules relating to the employment of married women or foreign nationals were waived, as were standard financial procedures; there was a JBC account for Ministry of Information funds at a bank in Tunbridge Wells, but funds from other sources:

are at another bank and will thus be kept apart and separate.

When difficulties over budgets arose they were overcome by charging amounts to the "other side". The size of the organisation at this early stage in the crisis and the way in which it could bend civil service rules indicate its sponsorship at the highest political and security levels and the importance that was attached to its work.

What did the JBC do? First of all it collected together people who were expert in the selection and rehearsing of speakers, the preparation of scripts and the production of records, and who had some knowledge of broadcasting and the specialised requirements of listeners abroad. These were the "Jews and suchlike" disparaged by Reith, and also bright young men like Guy Burgess, who had been a member of the BBC talks department since 1936, and Kenneth Matthews who had experience of educational and propaganda work in Greece and many years' experience in recording scripts. (Burgess had been recruited from the BBC and was at this time already a Comintern agent, but he deliberately hid his communist convictions and played the part of a broadcasting professional without raising suspicion. Indeed he was by now well versed in concealing his real self and it became impossible even for close friends to pin down his character and loyalties. His treachery was not discovered until several years after the end of the war.) Her old friend the journalist and critic W J Turner also helped, acting as music adviser, as did Elspeth Huxley with her wide experience of Africa and other countries, and her gift for popularising difficult subjects.

Their job was to prepare material in the form of radio scripts or recordings about Britain as seen through the eyes and ears of speakers native to the countries being targeted, to record the programmes and then to despatch them by various means. The underground side of the work was directed mainly at Germany and Austria and countries being threatened by Germany such as Poland and Czechoslovakia. This covert work concentrated on political and economic information to emphasise the strength of Britain and its Empire and the solidarity of British public opinion in resisting aggression.

Most of the recordings made as part of the JBC's overt activities were more cultural, intended as a supplement to BBC news by illustrating many sides of British life, its institutions, politics, social experiments, culture and war activities. The aim was to put British news in context, making it more readily understood, and generally to help foreign peoples become more aware of Britain. Great pains were taken to convince contacts abroad that the JBC was not part of official propaganda machinery. British censors were instructed that nothing should be done to hold up JBC correspondence or to do anything which would give their letters any appearance of an official communication. At this early stage of the JBC's work the main message propagated in all their material was not unlike that of the 1878 music hall song:

> We don't want to fight, But by jingo if we do, We've got the men, we've got the ships, We've got the money too.

This link to the previous century is not fanciful; in his first speech after the Munich agreement Chamberlain had re-used some of Disraeli's words about peace with honour which had been spoken after the latter's triumph at the Congress of Berlin in 1878. Disraeli never intended then to wage war on Russia, and Chamberlain never wanted to declare war on Germany, obviously hoping throughout most of 1939 that hostilities could be averted. Hence the need for propaganda, overt and covert, which demonstrated that Britain wanted peace, but had the will and resources for war. The JBC was thus very much a part of that double policy being pursued by Chamberlain with its combination of firmness and conciliation.

Hilda Matheson began working on this prime task with her usual ferocious energy. Recording equipment, both stationary and mobile, was designed and built especially for the JBC, and was an improvement on anything being used by the BBC. In addition JBC staff were authorised to use BBC studios and the recording facilities of commercial firms such as J Walter Thompson. The record discs used were the result of research and experimentation conducted especially for the JBC to secure ever more material onto ever smaller surfaces, to decrease weight, and to improve quality of reproduction. Recordings were despatched by the quickest possible means, sometimes by airmail or through the diplomatic bags of the countries concerned. The material was then transmitted through foreign broadcasting stations with their consent or, in the case of the covert work, dropped from aeroplanes or distributed by various subversive means for use in "pirate" stations or in listening groups. Use was made of nationals in "exile", who would play the recordings at meetings in their host country and contacts were made with embryo resistance groups once war had been declared.

In a jaunty report made in July 1940, by when communications had become very difficult, Hilda Matheson listed the ways in which recordings were still being despatched:

Iceland, Sweden, Spain and Portugal present few difficulties. The Balkans could be reached by cable, or from Cairo using diplomatic bags, and while it was difficult it would be extremely week-kneed not to try. New methods of approach are continually discovering themselves; only this week, for instance, an unexpected opportunity enabled us to despatch a lot of stuff to Malta, a place which most people had considered impossible to reach. Boats and aeroplanes to South America are irregular and slow, but they are still going ... we have also sent material by clipper to New York in a fortnight.

Nothing seemed to daunt her. Within a very short time of its being set up, the JBC was producing material for despatch to Germany, Austria, Czechoslovakia and Poland, and anti-fascist and anti-Nazi broadcasting services for the USA were being prepared. Broadcasting authorities in Denmark, Norway, Sweden, Finland, Belgium, Holland and Switzerland were offered programmes which included a regular "London Letter". Gradually the number of countries using JBC material widened to include Hungary, Romania, Yugoslavia, Greece, Bulgaria, the Middle East, and Latin and Central America. Programmes were made weekly in Chinese for Hong Kong and others were prepared for Ceylon, Burma, Kenya, Nigeria, Gold Coast, Malaya, the West

Indies and other parts of the Empire and Commonwealth. A check in one month showed that 142 discs had been processed and 3,760 pressings made. Monthly progress reports showed that on average each month, 200 recordings were made and several thousand pressings.

The material produced when the JBC was first established consisted of talks, plays, dialogues and songs, the exact approach being adapted to suit the requirements of each country. Romania, for example, wanted talks that would demonstrate the "might of Britain" and a series of twelve talks was commissioned with speakers such as Geoffrey Crowther of *The Economist* talking about the British Empire, Commander Stephen King-Hall on the British navy, and Professor J D Bernal on the British contribution to science. The Greek minister in London on the other hand preferred something less full-blooded, agreeing to talks about Eton and Harrow and their embodiment of classical Greek ideals. Scripts were prepared by JBC staff, but would always be read by a national of the country being targeted, sometimes an eminent exile who had fled persecution.

In August 1939 Thomas Mann was asked to record a message to the German people, pointing out that the Nazis had brought them to a position which would inevitably lead to war unless they got rid of the government. The script of his talk, it was suggested, should include hints about the subjects, including colonial problems, which the British Foreign Secretary would reconsider when faced with a government which did not always negotiate with a "pistol on the table". Clearly the JBC worked closely with policy makers at the Foreign Office.

As the prospects for peace diminished, and later when war had been declared, the JBC's focus shifted from Germany to friendly and neutral powers with programmes designed to reinforce the links with Britain. There was an extraordinary mixture of subjects which included programmes on Kew Gardens, George Eliot, the Spanish Falange, English Musical Comedy, Know thy Enemy, London's Mid-Season's Dress Collection, The New Order, Britain's Allies in the Air, The New Forest, Girls of the London Blitz, Post War Plans, Magna Carta, How Britain is Governed, Heroes and Heroines of the Blitz, even Soil Erosion. "Sound pictures" were a popular form, combining the sounds of machinery or war with voices and music; a Welsh choir singing folk songs might be combined with mining sounds, or voices of evacuees would be recorded with sounds of air raids and of the countryside. Some programmes were aimed at English and other exiles living in the United States or Commonwealth countries. One sound picture was made at an English public school using sound effects of the boys singing and cheering and the noise of a forge in their smithy and machine shop as they manufactured essential munitions. In another, British soldiers at Southampton sang sweetly and unselfconsciously, unaware that they were being recorded.

Less sentimental were programmes which capitalised on Arab hatred of Italians:

> Our plans include Palestine, Syria, Egypt, the Sudan, Transjordania, Iraq, Hedjaz, Bahrein, Saudi Arabia, Aden and also Iran. We are making gramophone records both in classical and in colloquial Arabic, and it is very much to the point that these records are not intended solely for broadcasting. There may not be many broadcasting stations, but there are a vast number of gramophones and we have been strongly urged to circulate our records for private use among the Arab population.

The production of cultural information inevitably provoked questions from the BBC and the British Council who felt that the JBC was entering territory they regarded as their own. To some extent these cultural programmes were a cover for the JBC's clandestine activities, but they were also regarded as necessary in their own right. Both the BBC and the British Council in 1939 were ill prepared for any wartime role and would in any case have regarded "propaganda" with disdain. As the JBC's activities began to grow, however, so the concern of these organisations increased. The British Council made an early take-over bid, but was soon brushed aside. In July 1939 Hilda Matheson dismissed a suggestion that the JBC should be incorporated into the Council, pointing out that the JBC's work at that time was mainly economic and political, not cultural, and that in the event of war when a more cultural approach would be needed the plan was to work with the Ministry of Information. The JBC's relationship with Section D, she argued, would also be an embarrassment to the Council. No transfer took place.

As peace gave way to war the JBC began to collaborate more closely with the Ministry of Information and the BBC. Broadcasting organisations in the Dominions and Colonies were provided with special programme material under the title of London Transcriptions, sometimes referred to as Empire Transcriptions, the role of the BBC and the JBC being to provide material specified by the Ministry. This co-operation began to reveal important differences in the approach to propaganda.

Views about propaganda in the Ministry of Information were at first rather crude, distinguishing between propaganda that would help win the war and educational and social values which were dismissed as "merely cultural", as though there was a necessary conflict between the two. The basic message of the Ministry of Information was one of assurance of victory coupled with the need for sacrifice and fortitude. This rather hectoring and bleak approach failed to recognise the persuasive power of carefully scripted understatement, sound pictures, and talks about literature. The JBC's approach was more subtle; not to supply news or arguments, which quickly got out of date anyway, and certainly not to rant, but to build up a picture of British life, British people, their ideals, and the ways in which they were trying to bring them into effect.

In a report of July 1940, produced when she was fighting for the survival of the JBC, Hilda Matheson defended vigorously the importance of cultural propaganda. Effective German propaganda during the years of peace, she pointed out, came from the branch offices of the German railway companies in all parts of the world:

> *It was there, among all the glossy pamphlets about the Rhine, castles, music, Heidleburg, Salzburg, and the rest that the true work of endangering the Peace began.*

The Germans still stressed the absence of British culture, she wrote, and in the past three weeks alleged British cultural weakness had occupied the highest percentage of time on German radio. During one week:

> *More than twice as much time was devoted to British cultural weakness than to German military strength.*

Surely what the enemy felt it so worthwhile to assert must be well worthwhile denying? Later, the value of such indirect propaganda began to be recognised, but in 1940, especially after the events of May when an invasion of Britain by the German army was feared, such approaches were dismissed by BBC and Ministry officials. They regarded the JBC as a nuisance, an outsider, a maverick organisation, and from January 1940, when Reith became Minister of Information, he tried to curb its independence. In a reorganisation of his department Reith made it clear that control over all propaganda activities would be tightened, and that he would become responsible for the JBC. Neither he nor his immediate successor succeeded entirely in controlling Hilda Matheson, but she began to resent what she saw as interference and bureaucratic rigidity.

At War With the BBC and Others

In developing propaganda by radio the JBC had far greater freedom than the BBC, and although the corporation was kept aware of its activities through a liaison officer it remained uneasy about another broadcasting organisation which could be mistaken by listeners for itself. Its anxiety about this woman buccaneer was not lessened by the fact that she was doing what the BBC could not do; overt propaganda on any significant scale would not have been sanctioned by the BBC governors who were still in charge of policy, having survived the original plans to ditch them on the outbreak of war. She was on the BBC's patch, and it wanted to kick her off. These jealous concerns would have been increased by nervousness about the capacity of the BBC itself to survive intact into 1940. Few commentators had anything good to say about its programmes on the outbreak of war and there would have been some sympathy for the view expressed in an anonymous article in the *Political Quarterly* at the beginning of 1940 that the BBC should be carved up.

The author, identified only as "A Listener", suggested in a tightly argued polemic that the present structure of broadcasting was, in time of war, unsatisfactory. Several months after war had been declared the BBC, according to "A Listener", continued in the timid way that characterised its peacetime operations. The worst defect of all monopolies, the tendency to lose elasticity and flexibility, was exhibiting itself at a time of national crisis. After six months of war listeners were still being given only a single Home Programme, recently supplemented by a programme for the forces. Without the BBC's monopoly of broadcasting it was doubtful if such a lamentable state of affairs would have happened. The "Listener" went on to argue that the right solution was to separate the question of monopoly from that of state control. In war time there could not be unrestricted freedom; some state control was essential, but not for all programmes. There had to be control of information and perhaps of talks, for example, but not of entertainment. The answer could be a plurality of authorities, some of them free of state control and others fully controlled.

Although there is no direct evidence, it seems likely that the author of this article was Hilda Matheson. She had contributed articles before on the subject of broadcasting to the *Political Quarterly*. The style of the piece is hers, for example frequent references to the characteristics of monopoly and the timidity of the BBC. Hiving off some BBC functions and placing them under tighter government control would have suited her ambitions for the JBC. Some parts of the article read like sections of her book *Broadcasting*. Whatever its authorship, this public attack on the BBC monopoly at a time when the future of the corporation was being questioned seriously, and challengers for some of its work such as the JBC and Electra House were up and running, must have affronted the governors. If Hilda Matheson was the author then it was a typically audacious piece of politics and it seems unlikely that she would have written it without official approval. Perhaps debates in government about the future of the BBC in wartime got closer to considering seriously its dismemberment than has been realised.

She tried to placate the BBC by drawing a distinction between its own role of broadcasting directly to foreign countries and the JBC role of indirect broadcasts by means of recordings for use in foreign countries. The BBC never accepted this as a valid distinction and remained jealous of a rival, especially one which never appeared to be short of money and had superior equipment. Ample funds were made available to the JBC from government sources, while the BBC was always short of money for feature programmes. BBC complaints increased in proportion to the increase in the JBC's work. Officials in the Corporation referred to increasing evidence which showed that the JBC's activities were bound to trespass on the BBC's monopoly:

A body which was formed in peacetime to do a small and well-defined piece of work has, in a very short space of time, created for itself, or solicited from government departments, a large volume of broadcasting work in a variety of different fields. Today that body is becoming a direct competitor with the Corporation in spite of the latter's monopoly status; moreover, it is to some extent recognised as an independent competitor by more than one government department ... obstruction is silly, but as things stand today we are bound to feel jealous of our rights as the sole broadcasting authority.

The overseas committee of the BBC directed that the JBC's activities should be investigated. These complaints probably say as much about the paranoia of the BBC as they do about the significance of the JBC, but the latter had a nuisance value out of all proportion to its size and the BBC was obviously frightened by the scale of its activities and the vigour with which they were pressed forward. Hilda Matheson must have enjoyed its discomfiture.

BBC staff were correct in suggesting that she had extended the role of the JBC. Once war had been declared its original purpose became redundant, but the Foreign Office obviously thought it worthwhile to keep the organisation in being. Some of that support perhaps derived from loyalty to a valued colleague, but there was more to it than that. The Foreign Office clearly found it convenient to have its own broadcasting organisation which was not subject to the same constraints as the BBC. From Section D's point of view it was also useful to be able to milk Ministry of Information funds ostensibly for the JBC's overt activities while applying a substantial proportion of them to the covert programmes of sabotage.

As the overt broadcasting work of the JBC required her to work more closely with the Ministry of Information, the BBC and Electra House, Hilda Matheson's resentment increased. Harold Nicolson had imagined her as a great under-secretary, but she was never a team worker. The civil service was far too restrictive for her. There were so many people to consult: Electra House had to be asked about programmes made for enemy countries, their staff had to be used in the distribution of the recordings, and programmes intended for neutral or friendly countries were subject to liaison with the foreign publicity division of the Ministry of Information. She did not object to cooperation as such and often volunteered ways in which the JBC could support the activities of other units. For example, she arranged for recordings to be made which publicised British Council exhibitions and Ministry of Information films, helping to stimulate attendance at these events. But when these organisations tried to exert control, she insisted on her independence.

As early as June 1939 she had expressed her anxiety to Harold Nicolson about the need to regularise the position of her committee, afraid that it would be absorbed into the Ministry of Information which was becoming more active. She visited him and other useful contacts often, usually to complain about how the JBC was being sidelined. David Astor recalls her calling on him in 1940 accompanied by Guy Burgess and Conrad Veidt, the German film actor. In September 1939 she complained to Harold Nicolson about Sir Campbell Stuart who was obstructing her plans for a scheme of enemy propaganda. She played some of the recordings she had made, including a speech by an ex-Nazi and a take-off of Hitler with passages from Mein Kampf, both of which Harold Nicolson thought excellent, but which had been coolly received by Stuart. She felt that too many highbrows were being used, especially by the BBC, and that people like Gracie Fields would do a better job in answering Lord Haw Haw. Two months later she expressed fears of rough political weather ahead for Section D and the JBC, as the Ministry of Information geared up with a new director-general to be followed soon afterwards by a new minister, her old adversary John Reith.

Officials in the BBC and the Ministry of Information continued to campaign systematically against her as political events turned decisively with the German invasions of Western Europe in May 1940 which led finally to the resignation of Chamberlain. The JBC, which had been created as part of his efforts to avoid war, immediately became vulnerable when he was swept from power. There was a widespread feeling that British propaganda on the home front was feeble, and Duff Cooper succeeded Reith at the Ministry of Information as part of Churchill's new drive to sort it out. The JBC had never worked "at home", but all propaganda bodies were now under review.

Internment

The pressures throughout 1939 and the first months of 1940 had been extreme as the JBC maintained its position in the teeth of opposition, but the advent of the Churchill government in May 1940 increased the strain in three ways. First there was the deepening emergency itself, with fears for the very survival of Britain. Accompanying this was the drive to rationalise the intelligence and information services. Campbell Stuart was forced to resign in August 1940. Would she be next? The third element which increased tension dramatically was the introduction of internment, because it threatened the refugees on whom the work of the JBC depended.

On the outbreak of war MI5 advised that only individuals considered dangerous should be interned, whereas the Home Office favoured general internment of aliens from enemy countries in order to satisfy and reassure the public. MI5 prevailed and only those enemy aliens on a list of people known to be active Nazis, the A list, were arrested and imprisoned. Others were placed on one or other of two other lists: the B list of aliens about whom there was some uncertainty and who would be dealt with later; and the C list of aliens who were obviously not a danger to Britain, indeed some of whom were engaged on work in support of the war effort. During 1940 British public opinion was becoming uneasy about the lack of any action against enemy aliens and potentially subversive groups such as Mosley's British Union and the Communist Party of Great Britain. With the invasions of Denmark, Norway and the Low Countries there was panic about the existence of a Fifth Column and the previous views of MI5 and the Home Office were reversed.

At a critical meeting in the early summer the Home Office representatives argued against general internment on grounds of democracy and the lack of any evidence of a Fifth Column. MI5 officers pointed out that if somebody didn't get a move on there would be no democracy, no England, and no Empire, and that this was a matter of days. Gradually the Home Office gave way. At first only men on List B were interned, but as panic grew with the fall of France and the entry of Italy into the war the new Prime Minister, supported by MI5, swept aside Home Office resistance and a policy of general internment was introduced. By the end of July a total of 27,000 people had been interned. This figure was never exceeded, despite the fact that there were about 64,000 people on the C list, because as soon as arrests began of people who were obviously harmless, public opinion swung round again.

This reaction was not swift enough to prevent the arrest of some of Hilda Matheson's staff. The JBC was full of enemy aliens without whom it could not do its job. Foreign nationals of the countries for which the information was intended made all the recordings. Many of the staff were German, Austrian or Italian and some were from eastern European countries which had active Nazi or Fascist political parties. Worse, this nest of potential spies was sponsored by MI6 and thus fair game in the rivalry between the various security services. So in the summer of 1940 she was obliged to rush around the country finding out who had been imprisoned where, and then to arrange their release. This was not an easy task. At the same time many other people were trying desperately to obtain the release of friends and colleagues they knew to be no threat to Britain. It took the redoubtable Tess Simpson, secretary of the Society for the Protection of Science and Learning, until March 1941 to secure the release of all those refugee scholars her Society had rescued from Germany and Austria during the thirties. Hilda Matheson, with her knowledge of the secret service and an impressive range of other contacts, was well placed to secure the release of her own people rather sooner, but the effort required a huge diversion of energy.

Furthermore, in the inflamed atmosphere of the time her protection of so many aliens made her vulnerable to charges of being complacent, possibly worse. The hysteria about enemy aliens provided the Ministry of Information with a convenient excuse to intensify its attacks on the JBC. On 5 August 1940 Sir Maurice Peterson, controller of overseas publicity, wrote to her in terms that would have destroyed most people. On grounds of security, and to conform to a general reorganisation, the JBC was to lose its name and its independence. Relations with all bodies other than the Ministry of Information and the British Council were to be discontinued immediately. Any further association with enemy aliens was forbidden. JBC staff in future were to work only from the Chester Square office, not from Rocks Farm, and for one month Mr Leigh Ashton of the Ministry was to be delegated to take charge, reporting directly to Sir Maurice. Meanwhile Sir Maurice thought that she might:

> *think it well, if only on grounds of ill health which we all deplore, to take leave of absence during that period.*

It is not clear just what precipitated this ultimatum. Did it reflect genuine security concerns about her as well as her staff? Or did internment policy simply provide a good opportunity for a final push against the JBC? Or was her illness making her impossible to work with? Fears about foreign spies were genuine, but Hilda Matheson's own loyalty could hardly have been in doubt. Whatever the reasons behind his letters, Sir Maurice did not succeed in ousting her.

Hilda Matheson responded with forceful dignity in a correspondence which went on until 10 August. She made it clear that she had no intention of taking sick leave, defended the use of Rocks Farm, denied insinuations that she had used public funds to entertain her friends there, and justified the work of the JBC and the need for it to continue. What must have infuriated Sir Maurice most was that she was able to use her connection with Lord Lothian, now a hugely influential ambassador to the USA, who had asked the JBC to resume its programmes in America to the extent of 500 a week. There is no record of what happened next, but the JBC carried on under her direction and did not change its name or function.

There is a rich irony in the fact that many of the "enemy aliens" about whom Sir Maurice was so concerned went on to play a distinguished part in British life. Some of the home-grown products of his own university, Oxford, and its sister cell, Cambridge, however, were able to continue their spying undisturbed. Guy Burgess's work for the JBC in the period up to the declaration of war made him privy to internal debates on one of the prime questions in international affairs – whether Britain had the will to fight Hitler. From his vantage point in the JBC Guy Burgess would have been aware of the intense discussions among politicians and officials, including the conflict of view between Chamberlain and Halifax, and even more severe conflicts between Chamberlain and (Lord) Vansittart, the aggressive head of the Foreign Office. He would have had first hand experience of the almost obsessive concern of Chamberlain for peace. The USSR, for whom Guy Burgess worked, would have been interested in judgements about the ultimate determination of Britain to resist Hitler. In August 1939, just a month before Britain declared war, the USSR concluded a non-aggression pact with Germany. There was no question, of course, of interning Guy Burgess.

It must have been especially galling to Hilda Matheson that she had to spend so much time defending her foreigners and herself, when all her energy and theirs was now needed for a completely new propaganda venture of her own.

Britain In Pictures

She asked me to write some damned book for some damned series, [recalled Virginia Woolf] it was to be patriotic; at the same time intellectual; also badly paid.

After she was told in July 1940 about Hilda Matheson's idea for a series of books about Britain, and invited to write an essay on fiction, Mrs Woolf confided to her diary that the whole thing was meritorious, meretricious, tidy-minded and detestable; and the fee of £50 was "poor pay". She decided not to contribute. By early October, as described in a letter from Hilda Matheson to Lady Astor, the project was well advanced. There were definite plans for the publication of eighteen volumes and tentative arrangements for many more to be published, eight or ten at a time every few months. The purpose of the letter was to explain to Lady Astor the thinking behind the proposal and to ask her advice about an American edition.

In the course of her propaganda work Hilda Matheson had discovered that the Germans had long ago distributed in the Balkans, Scandinavia, the Middle East and South America illustrated books in translation describing the glories of Germany, its soldiers, musicians, poets, museums, cities, mountains, everything. The Foreign Office, the British Council and the Ministry of Information had all confirmed the complaints of neutral and friendly countries that there was nothing comparable about Britain, but nobody was doing anything about it. So she and some of her friends stepped forward and set the whole thing up as a private enterprise. Keeping it in private hands was in any case desirable in order to overcome natural suspicions about official publications.

She acknowledged that there could hardly be a more frightful moment to begin to publish books when so many people were too busy to write them, and illustrated books would have particular difficulties when paintings in public galleries and private collections had been evacuated. Nevertheless she had found many people willing to help, including the royal household which put at her disposal everything not evacuated from Windsor. Lady Astor expressed herself appalled by some of the authors proposed, being especially rude about the idea of using Lady Tweedsmuir to write about Canada and Andre Maurois and other foreigners to write some of the volumes about Britain, but she offered to help. When the project for "Britain In Pictures" came to fruition, a Ministry of Information working party was still studying the possibility of a popular pictorial book about the Empire and had hardly got round to talking to authors and publishers.

"Britain In Pictures" (BIP) was the collective title for three series of illustrated books launched in March 1941. The individual series consisted of 113 volumes in "The British People In Pictures", seven volumes in "The British Commonwealth In Pictures" and six volumes in "The British Poets In Pictures". Most of the books were published during the war, although a few continued to appear up to 1950. Nearly three million copies were sold, many of them overseas in the United States, the countries of the British Commonwealth and Empire, and in Latin America. Some were translated and it has been claimed that eleven languages were used. There were also extensive sales in Britain, although the main purpose behind the books was to convince people in friendly countries that Britain and the British way of life were worth fighting for, or at least supporting.

Each book, illustrated with colour and black and white reproductions of British paintings, drawings, manuscripts, prints and photographs, described an important aspect of British life. (There is a list of authors and titles in the appendix.) The authors, of whom there were a hundred and seventeen, were eminent novelists, poets or journalists, or authorities on their subject who could also write well. The distinctive characteristic of the series was to provide a comprehensive view in words and pictures of British life in all its aspects at a time when the very survival of Britain was threatened. Within a strict limit of only 48 pages, the books were authoritative, well written and beautifully illustrated. They were also cheap; those in the Poets series sold for 2s 6d (12.5p) and the others for 3s 6d (17.5p). In some ways the title of the series is a misnomer, because while the pictures are a delight it is in the essays which accompany them that the British character and its achievements come to life. The result was a library which still instructs and pleases today. There is no doubt that the driving force behind the series was Hilda Matheson.

She was helped by Dorothy Wellesley, who edited the six volumes of poets, and W J Turner, who became general editor after her death. Turner was another remarkable character; poet, playwright, journalist and music critic, he had been born in Australia in 1889 and moved to England in 1907 with his mother after his father died. Following extensive travel in Europe, he served in the First World War and then became part of the literary and artistic life of London in the twenties and thirties. He was a friend of the Sitwells and the composer William Walton, a frequent guest of Lady Ottoline Morrell at Garsington and a close friend of both Yeats and Siegfried Sassoon. From 1916-40 he was music critic of the *New Statesman* and from 1942 literary editor of *The Spectator*. Turner stuck with the BIP project for more than six years until his death in 1946, helped by an outstanding assistant editor, Sheila Shannon. Dorothy Wellesley withdrew shortly after Hilda Matheson's death.

A group of Austrian refugees working for a firm called Adprint designed, produced and sometimes distributed the books. The owner and managing director of Adprint, Wolfgang Foges, had left a successful business in Austria in 1937 anticipating Hitler's invasion. Foges soon began to create in Britain an interest in high quality colour printing in books aimed at a popular market. One of his ideas was "King Penguins", the first five titles of which were produced by Adprint in 1939 on a sale or return basis for Allen Lane, who then continued the series. Foges was the ideal entrepreneur to take on Hilda Matheson's rather risky venture. Clever and excitable, a man who was not always easy to work with but easy to like, he managed to escape internment.

Not so some of the other refugee members of his gifted team. Walter Neurath, another bookman of genius, spent a short time in one or other of the camps. Neurath had had considerable experience of publishing fine books during his work for Frick Verlag in Vienna. He provided some of the expertise in design which Foges lacked and was responsible for all the various activities involved in designing and producing the BIP books when he received the final text from Turner. (Soon after the war ended Walter Neurath left Adprint and with his wife Eva founded Thames and Hudson, publishers of fine art books. At the time of writing it is still a family firm chaired by his widow.) His BIP work resulted in several innovations in book production, including the extended role of producer, at a time when the publisher usually did everything short of writing the book, and the close relationship of text to illustration in what became known as an "integrated" book. Except for the six volumes in the Poets series which had their own design, the format of the other 120 titles never changed. The simple, bold look of the last volume in 1950, *British Farm Stock* by the Earl of Portsmouth, was the same as that of the first in March 1941, *The English Poets* by Lord David Cecil.

The publisher, the long established firm of William Collins, had rather a subsidiary role compared with what was done by Turner, Sheila Shannon and the Adprint team. The venture was a private enterprise and became profitable, but it was launched with the aid of Hilda Matheson's secret fund. Her JBC budget for a time paid W J Turner's salary and also that of Sheila Shannon. There is no evidence of any government payments to Collins or Adprint – there were separate contractual arrangements between BIP (later W J Turner) and each of the other parties, namely authors, Adprint and Collins – but the project would not have got off the ground had it not been for the JBC connection. For behind it all was the urgent need for some systematic propaganda at the beginning of the war. The British Empire was often perceived in a negative way abroad, especially in the United States, and there were tensions within the Commonwealth. Support for Britain could not be taken for granted. The overtly propagandist objectives of BIP were set out on the dust-jackets of the first volumes as follows:

The English have never been good at describing themselves or their ways, either for their own benefit or for the benefit of others. It is, therefore, not surprising that no comprehensive series of books, at a popular price, illustrating, in print and picture, the life, art, institutions and achievements of the British People has ever been issued, either for British or for foreign readers. At this time, when it has become essential for citizens throughout the Empire to take stock of themselves and their ideas and to express them to others, it is desirable to fill this gap. The books in these three series will be of permanent interest and, in spite of the small cost, should appeal to the book collector for the excellence of their production. It is hoped that they will contribute to the better understanding of Great Britain and the British Commonwealth.

Although propagandist in intention, individual volumes were never "propaganda" in the sense of tendentious writing or the presentation of highly selective information. The aim was to present Britain in as many aspects as possible through the eyes of individual writers who would be free to interpret their subject constrained only by the limitation of space and the need for ample pictorial representation. Authors were not directed as to tone or content, although the basic propaganda purpose was clear – as Virginia Woolf had complained, she had been expected to be patriotic as well as intellectual, and all for £50. When the first books were published the reviewer for *The Listener* commented that the propaganda was of the oblique and detached kind which so often succeeds where barefaced trumpet blowing fails. Britain's best "case", after all, was her culture, her character and her democratic institutions, and it was on these elements that the series concentrated. In that respect they were not unlike JBC recordings.

The launch of the first eight volumes took place in March 1941, only three months after the night when the centre of the British book world had been devastated in a bombing raid. On 29 December 1940 nearly six million books were destroyed in London, almost four million in Stationers' Hall alone. When the chief editor of William Collins saw the first BIP books in a shop window on the deserted seafront of a battered south coast town, he described them as bright banners on the battlements of our island fortress, defiant cockades that a nation of shopkeepers could justifiably flaunt in the faces of their book-burning foes. His words sum up not only the desperate circumstances of the time, but also the striking appearance of the books. The paperboard cover used the same bright colour as the dust-jacket and repeated the clear white print and the simple but bold illustration at the centre of the jacket. These illustrations, which were appropriate to the subject of the volume, were drawn by Elisabeth Friedlander and Elisabeth Ullman of Adprint, both of them refugees from Austria.

The wide range of subjects covered by the 126 volumes can be seen from the appendix. Most successful in terms of sales were:

The Birds Of Britain	84,000	James Fisher
Life Among The English	62,000	Rose Macaulay
Wild Flowers In Britain	61,000	Geoffrey Grigson
The English Poets	60,000	Lord David Cecil
English Villages	57,000	Edmund Blunden
Wild Life In Britain	57,000	F Fraser Darling
The English Ballet	56,000	W J Turner
English Music	53,000	W J Turner
English Country Houses	52,000	V Sackville-West
The Story Of Scotland	51,000	F Fraser Darling

Least successful, selling less than ten thousand copies each, were those about the political parties, the trade unions and hymns and hymn writers. (It is not clear whether sales figures relate to United Kingdom or world wide sales, probably the former.)

Although Hilda Matheson had died before even the first of the books appeared in print, she placed her distinctive mark upon the whole series. The original concept of the books – authoritative but popular, comprehensive but short, beautiful to look at but cheap – was hers. She insisted on the highest standards of writing, illustration and production, despite all the difficulties of war, and as well as leaving behind a long list of possible authors, she selected the people who were to continue to produce the series until its end.

The novelist and critic Kate O'Brien, writing an introduction to one of the Omnibus volumes containing seven of the books on English literature which included her own BIP book *English Diaries And Journals*, refers to a harmony of feeling and conclusions in all the volumes which can only be accidental, but is all the more persuasive for that. She is right about the harmony, which consists of such very British elements as common sense, dislike of complication, a strong preference for the concrete over the abstract, a certain quietness of mind, an absence of triumphalism, a shrewd, tolerant judgement, and a greater interest in character and action than in ideas. These are also exactly the qualities which Hilda Matheson tried always to reflect in her work and it is fitting that they shine out of her last achievement. In some ways she realised what she had been seeking in BBC talks, a medium which challenged and instructed, but which at the same time entertained and was popular.

Nemesis

Meanwhile her continuing work with the JBC was being made more difficult by the opposition of BBC and Ministry of Information officials, the latter in particular more determined than ever to destroy her. JBC programmes intended for Latin America were attacked on the grounds that the BBC already had a Latin American service. Leigh Ashton, from his position in the finance department of the ministry and fresh from his failure in August, asked for an investigation. The result, following a close examination of JBC figures and reports from users of its recordings, showed that it was making real progress and did not overlap in any way with the BBC.

The Ministry tried once more, this time launching an attack upon the JBC's work in the United States. It was already battling to establish its authority within the Washington embassy as Foreign Office officials ignored its instructions and generally made life difficult for its information officers located alongside them. In this larger game of politics Hilda Matheson's broadcasting activities were hardly relevant, but her friendship with the ambassador, Lord Lothian, was itself a provocation. She was a convenient target for an attack, which, if successful, might at the same time establish the wider authority of the Ministry with the embassy.

In August 1940 Lord Lothian asked for JBC broadcasts to the USA to be resumed to supplement the BBC's overseas service, requesting in particular some of the actuality programmes which incorporated sounds of war. Hilda Matheson produced several suggestions immediately. One was that programmes made for Czech and Polish people living in exile in Britain could also be sent to America and distributed to the relevant national groups in their homes, clubs and churches. Another was to make use of British children who had been evacuated by their parents to America. Her idea of directing programmes at these children as a way actually of getting at Americans was ingenious. The programmes would be made especially for the children to remind them of home, and of how life was going on despite the war, but in the expectation that they would almost certainly be listened to by Americans as well. Thus American people would be provided with indirect but powerful evidence of high British morale and the ineffectiveness of German bombing. This message was especially important at a time when Joseph E Kennedy, who had in October 1940 given up his post of American Ambassador to the United Kingdom in order to get away from the bombing, was declaring to anyone who would listen to him that Britain was finished. With a presidential election due in November 1940 the need to buttress friends of Britain was obvious.

The American division of the Ministry of Information now became obstructive, asserting that her proposals went far beyond what Lord Lothian had requested. Lindsay Wellington, who had been one of her young men in the BBC and was now seconded to the ministry, doubted the wisdom of sending anything at all when the BBC was developing rapidly its own programmes for North America. He recorded his personal belief that it did little good to put amateurish programmes alongside American products. A cable was sent to Lord Lothian expressing doubts, but he responded by saying there would be no harm in experimenting with the JBC material. His view, although expressed in his usual diplomatic way, was perfectly clear: he wanted the JBC recordings to be made. This reply was misrepresented by civil servants in a memorandum of 25 October 1940 to Harold Nicolson, then parliamentary secretary to the Ministry of Information, and officials took the opportunity to make a full-blooded attack on the JBC:

> Only one or two JBC records are up to standard so far as modern competitive broadcasting is concerned. I understand that owing to war events many of the Committee's normal outlets have been closed down, and that they are now concentrating on the USA and South America ... the very countries in the whole world where commercial competition produces superlative programmes. Frankly I dont see where the JBC comes into the picture in present conditions, nor indeed do I see what way they can supplement the specialised work of the BBC, especially in North America. There would seem to be an unnecessary overlapping if the JBC and the BBC are both doing the same material for the same places. If however this is a private pigeon of the FO I suppose it is no business of ours, but as I see you are on the committee of the JBC I see this note for your reaction ... Lord Lothian when consulted recently by cable was not enthusiastic about the continuance of the JBC.

This time, Hilda Matheson, who was desperately ill in hospital waiting for an operation to remove part of her thyroid gland, was unable to defend her position. Harold Nicolson replied to the memo that as he was now working in the Ministry of Information he would be resigning from the JBC. Meanwhile, he commented, the JBC was a very mysterious body which had come in for much discussion and the person who knew most about it was Mr Leigh Ashton, who should now be consulted. Leigh Ashton's response in a manuscript note on the back of the memorandum was devastating:

> *I regard the position of the JBC as impossible; it is 95% cultural, therefore British Council, but BC won't touch it. It costs about £30,000 a year and has some good staff, a remarkable engineer and good equipment. Nothing else is of any importance and as regards America every child knows that American chains won't take recorded programmes. I propose to pack it up, take in the four necessary officers to M of I, attach plant and engineers to BBC, and save M of I £20,000 a year. FO are now sold on the JBC by persuasion on the part of Miss Matheson to R A Butler and wish to swallow the whole thing lock, stock and barrel ... I think it is a waste of public money, but it was sponsored by the FO and if they wish to reincorporate at great cost it is for Treasury to carry the expense.*

Mr Ashton had been seconded to the ministry from the Victoria and Albert Museum where he seems to have had a distinguished career as a curator in departments of architecture, sculpture, textiles and ceramics. After the war he returned to this museum to become its secretary and director. Neither before nor after the war did he have any experience of broadcasting.

Ashton's reference to R A Butler, then a Foreign Office minister and later a successful minister in several post-war governments who nearly became Prime Minister, is obscure, but indicates the high-level support Hilda Matheson enjoyed. On this occasion it did little good. Within a few days she was dead and the JBC without her was unable to survive as an independent body.

The attacks on her work were unfair. In the light of her previous record it seems unlikely that she would produce anything amateurish, and there is plenty of direct evidence that the JBC's work was much in demand. What was at issue was departmental politics, not the relevance or quality of JBC recordings. In January 1941 Clinton Baddeley, her deputy at the JBC, wrote to Lindsay Wellington to express his surprise that the American division of the ministry had such a poor opinion of their work. He pointed out that a recent Portuguese version of a sound magazine intended for parts of Latin America, and which they had never thought would be broadcast in Portugal itself, had been requested by Emission Nacional who now intended to broadcast them regularly. They received constant praise from Latin America for their Sound Pictures. Chile had asked for twelve a month. It seemed odd therefore that the American division should be the only people not impressed.

Clinton Baddeley's note had a weary ring to it. He must have been aware that no amount of evidence would save the JBC. There is plenty of paperwork on ministry files indicating its popularity and the demand for its work. A cable sent from the Washington embassy to the Ministry of Information in April 1941, just before the JBC was transferred to the BBC, seems particularly poignant in retrospect; it was from Columbia Broadcasting, in conjunction with Columbia Records, expressing great interest in JBC recordings. The cable was passed on to the BBC, now responsible for the JBC as part of the "London Transcription Service". JBC recordings remained in demand for the rest of the war as it continued its work uncontroversially within the confines of the BBC.

Hilda Matheson was at her worst when obliged to coordinate her activities with other people whom she saw as competitors. To her own staff she was a powerful and heroic figure, but to people in other departments she could have appeared rather frightening. Some of them found her difficult to work with. Yet this must have applied to many senior figures, especially at a time of war. The lethargy and bureaucratic obstruction of which she complained were not figments of her imagination. Her impatience for action was almost Churchillian in its energy and single-mindedness, but there was no room for even a mini-Churchill within the many divisions of the Ministry of Information, and certainly not for one wearing the equivalent then of a mini-skirt.

Her individual style of working did not fit easily into the paramount need for coordination and cooperation within an increasingly concentrated war machine. The struggles for power in Whitehall between 1938 and 1940 as that effective machine began to be constructed must have been awesome in their ferocity. Hilda Matheson was a fighter, but she needed the security of a single powerful figure to back her. Someone with whom she felt comfortable and for whom she could slave. Lady Astor, Lord Lothian, Lord Hailey had never felt threatened by her, and with them she flowered. Even Lord Reith for a time felt sufficiently secure to give her her head. Between 1938 and 1940, however, while she had many powerful friends there was not one single figure with whom she could relate and who would give her the continuing support she needed. With this sort of support she had been able to overcome the disadvantages of being a woman at work. Without it, she felt personally weakened and, simply as a woman, disabled for battle. The combination of some personal weakness and the prevailing male culture of the time was fatal.

In weighing up how far the anger of her peers was a righteous response to a presumptuous and difficult woman, and how far it was a jealous reaction of men not yet used to women in positions of power, one cannot avoid the conclusion that her main defect was not to know her place in a man's world. In the summer of 1940 she was desperately ill, and this no doubt made her more difficult than ever, but she still comes out of any objective assessment of the period 1938-40 better than do the officials of the BBC and the Ministry of Information.

Death

Her health had worsened during 1940, but she tried to ignore it. When Philip Noel-Baker MP saw her one afternoon in June 1940 as he was leaving the Ministry of Information he went over to speak to her because he knew she had been ill. As she talked about her work, and that "nine-day wonder" of a ministry from which he had just emerged, it became clear to him that she was still gravely ill. He urged her to rest, however important the work, because he feared she would kill herself by her efforts, but she replied that the job had to be done or "everything may smash". In a postscript to her letter of 14 October to Lady Astor about BIP she brushed off a recent operation for appendicitis as having gone beautifully, and said how maddening it was that now she had to have another, different, operation which the doctors had assured her would leave her a monument of strength for the rest of her life. Sheila Shannon recalls her at this time as "always in overdrive". Mary Bennett thought the speed at which she worked in the JBC towards the end, tossing out decisions at a frantic pace, seemed at times almost insane. Dame Ethel Smyth shared this impression when she saw Hilda towards the end of October in the Kettlewell nursing home near Woking; Hilda talked to her "at almost railway speed". Within two days, on 30 October 1940, she died during an operation to remove part of her thyroid gland. The death certificate recorded cause of death as toxic goitre (Graves disease) together with the operation.

The Times obituary gave a brief recital of her career but forgot about *An African Survey*, an omission put right the following day by Sir Julian Huxley who extolled the brilliant work he had observed at first hand. *The Star* concentrated on her time at the BBC when she had done her best between the rock and the whirlpool, and emphasised that there was not the slightest suggestion of the blue-stocking or the school-marm about her, being anything but a forbidding personality with her ready smile and sense of humour. The *New Statesman* regretted that her death had been too little noticed, and praised her achievement in building up the intellectual reputation of the BBC.

Vita got the news of her death during the same week-end that Long Barn was bombed and, with both disasters on her mind, had to dash off to Penns in the Rocks to comfort Dorothy Wellesley who was in a state of collapse. Despite her own distress Vita wrote the most complete obituary, which was published in *The Spectator*. She described tenderly her friend's personality and gifts, made a true record of her achievements, and lamented that Hilda had no stamina left to survive the operation because, in addition to her ordinary work, already more than enough for her tired strength, she had had to struggle throughout the summer to obtain the release of her staff from internment.

Vita also arranged, a little against her will, another memorial on which Hilda's mother was very keen, namely the publication by the Hogarth Press of a small book of short remembrances. Leonard Woolf had even more reservations: only two or three of the contributions by writers such as H G Wells were any good, he thought, whereas most of the rest by friends and colleagues were slightly silly. He pointed out to Vita that few people had any appreciation of how difficult it was to write obituaries without giving the reader goose flesh. Nevertheless he was persuaded, and the memoir was published in the winter of 1941. It is not nearly as bad as he described it; many of the memories are vivid and moving. The book included a tribute by Lady Astor, who had not heard of Hilda's death until after the funeral.

Lionel Fielden wrote in the same memoir how angry he felt that only a tiny group of people could muster to bid her farewell, particularly when he thought of all the grand and the great who owed her so much. Despite absences and the driving rain and the dismal short service, he felt sure that she would have been gay and gallant about it, and he would not have been surprised to see her slight, trim figure marshalling everyone to their cars and sending everyone off with a sense that each of their individual purposes was worthwhile.

Fixed into the floor of the temple to the muses and the gods of the countryside which was built for Dorothy Wellesley in the grounds of Penns in the Rocks, there is still a stone which records "Hilda Matheson Amica amicarum". The inscription has been partly erased, whether by Dorothy Wellesley or someone else is not known. There was talk at the time of an unseemly row between Dorothy Wellesley and Meta Matheson about what should be done with Hilda's ashes, but there are no details.

Virginia Woolf could call up no image when she first heard of Hilda's death and told Ethel Smyth that she was generally, but not personally, sorry. Hilda was so dried, so official, and she didn't get on with her, although she was grieved that their last encounter had been when she had refused to write that "damned book":

> *I thought her intolerably imperceptive of what I consider the irreconcilable differences. But publicly I admired: [adding outrageously] and I'm sorry she was driven to death by the poisoned arrows of Dorothy's egotism.*

In January 1941 Vita wrote that she had not realised how much Virginia had disliked Hilda, but Virginia responded that that was not true:

> *I only felt – what? Something opaque, pulverising; my fault, as much as hers. And one pang of wild jealousy.*

Lord Reith, an assiduous keeper of his diary in which she had figured prominently between 1926 and 1931, did not record her death or his feelings at the time. He had wiped her out of his own universe some years before her death.

In February 1941 the Ministry of Information policy committee agreed that the JBC,

> *which had originated in a small group under the inspiration of Miss Hilda Matheson,*

should be absorbed into the BBC, subject to the Treasury and the Foreign Office agreeing, which they did. As indicated earlier, it became part of the London Transcription Service and continued to produce its recordings throughout the war.

Hilda Matheson was 52 years old when she died on 30 October 1940. Her great friend Lord Lothian, who had been born in the same year as she was and was at the time of her death ambassador to the United States, died a few weeks later on 12 December 1940. Virginia Woolf drowned herself on 28 March 1941. Dorothy Wellesley died in 1956 aged 67, Vita Sackville-West in 1962 aged 70, Lady Astor in 1964 aged 85, Lord Hailey in 1969 aged 97 and Lord Reith in 1971 aged 82.

Main Sources

AB   Asa Briggs History *of British Broadcasting in the United Kingdom* pub OUP
       Vol 1 *The Birth of Broadcasting* 1961
       Vol 2 *The Golden Age of Broadcasting* 1965
       Vol 3 *The War of Words* 1970
CBM   BBC Control Board Minutes, BBC Written Archives Centre, Reading
GD   Victoria Glendinning *Vita: The Life of Victoria Sackville-West* pub Weidenfeld and Nicolson 1983.
HMM   *Hildai Matheson* a memoir pub The Hogarth Press 1941
HML   Hilda Matheson letters to Vita Sackville-West, loaned by Nigel Nicolson
HMB   Hilda Matheson *Broadcasting* pub Thornton Butterworth HUL 1933.
HND   Harold Nicolson Diaries, Balliol College Library Oxford
LP   Lothian Papers, National Archives of Scotland (NAS), Edinburgh.
OP   Oldham Papers, Rhodes House Library, Oxford.
RD   Reith Diaries, BBC Written Archives Centre
RT   *Radio Times*, BBC Written Archives Centre
S&L   Louise De Salvo & Mitchell A Leaska *The Letters of Vita Sackville-West to Virginia Woolf* pub Hutchinson 1984
VHL   *Vita and Harold: The Letters of Vita Sackville-West and Harold Nicolson 1910-1962* by Nigel Nicolson pub Weidenfeld and Nicolson 1992

VWD   *The Diaries of Virginia Woolf* Vols III & V, edit Anne Oliver Bell, pub The Hogarth Press 1980 & 1984
VWL   *The Letters of Virginia Woolf* Vols 4 & 6 edit Nigel Nicolson, pub The Hogarth Press 1978
WER   *The Week-End Review* 1930-34.

Page Notes

CHAPTER ONE

1 John Reith 1889-1971, administrator, knighted 1927, created first Baron Reith 1940, general manager British Broadcasting Company (BBCo) 1922-26, director-general British Broadcasting Corporation (BBC) 1927-38, chairman Imperial (later British Overseas) Airways 1938-40, Minister of Information 1940, after dismissal by Winston Churchill held many important public offices but never regained eminence he enjoyed as master of the BBC.

1 Virginia Woolf 1882-1941, novelist and critic, two of her novels, *Orlando* 1928 and *The Waves* 1931, were published at the beginning and the end of the period when her former lover Vita was conducting her affair with Hilda Matheson.

1 Victoria Mary Sackville-West (called Vita) 1892-1962, writer and gardener, her childhood, her writing, her marriage to Harold Nicolson, their restoration of Sissinghurst Castle and creation of its magnificent garden, and her love affairs, have all been exhaustively documented elsewhere and require no details here.

1 Woman who...HMM, p 32.

2 Nancy Astor 1879-1964, politician and hostess, born Danville, Virginia USA, settled in Britain, married Waldorf Astor 1906 (her second marriage, she divorced her first husband Robert Shaw in 1903), became Viscountess Astor in 1919 when her husband inherited the title, elected to Parliament November 1919 and retained her seat in the Sutton division of Plymouth for six subsequent elections, retired from Parliament just before the 1945 election.

2 See chapter five for *An African Survey*.

2 William Malcolm Hailey 1872-1969, civil servant, created baron 1936, Indian Civil Service 1896-1934 where he rose to be governor of the United Provinces, director of *An African Survey* 1933-38 which made him almost as great an authority on African as he undoubtedly was on Indian matters.

2 See chapters two and four for her BBC work.

2 Marmaduke Hussey in a conversation with Nigel Nicolson related to the author.

2 AB vol 1.

2   Ian McIntyre *The Expense of Glory: A Life of John Reith* pub Harper Collins 1993.

2   *Auntie: The Inside Story of the BBC* televised autumn 1997.

2   See chapter six for "Britain In Pictures"; also *Britain In Pictures: A History And Bibliography* by Michael Carney pub Werner Shaw 1995.

3   See chapter three for love affair with Vita.

3   The friend who commented, Marjorie Maxse 1891-1975, created Dame 1952, administrator then chief organisation officer Conservative Central Office 1921-39, vice-chair Women's Voluntary Service 1940-44, vice-chair Conservative party organisation 1944-51, writing in HMM p 46-8.

3   Family references, HML 25 December 1928, 4 January, 3, 10 February, 21 April and 13 May 1929.

4   Annual Reports of Putney Presbyterian Church 1880 to 1905, made available by J L F Buist, show stipend increased from £230 to £300.

4   Oxford stipend, Papers at St. Columba's Presbyterian church Oxford made available by the Minister and Mrs D K Green.

4   Probate of Donald Matheson's Will 1 November 1930; conversion figures and all subsequent conversions based on indices supplied by Central Statistical Office.

4   School information, The *Felician* supplied by Jayne Barnett, school secretary.

5   Programme of Granard Society for 1934.

5   Putney Church reports for 1899-1906.

5   Article by Rev Donald Matheson in *Monthly Leaflet* of Putney Presbyterian Church February 1899.

5   Centenary booklet of same church 1979 containing extracts from an earlier jubilee booklet of 1929.

5   Letter of 17 January from Mrs Jean Furley-Smith to author provided information about the church and the Mathesons. (The Granard, later Putney, Presbyterian Church became the Putney United Reformed Church in 1972 and ceased to exist in 1996.)

6   Oxford details, *The Fritillary*, a magazine produced by the Women's Societies at Oxford, *The Ship*, the magazine of the Society of Home Students (later St. Anne's College magazine), and other papers in the St. Anne's archives including the History of the College published in 1930 referred to in the text.

7   HMM recollections of friends and tutors.

7   Papers in St. Columba's Presbyterian Church, Oxford

8   Gilbert Murray 1886-1957, classical scholar and internationalist, regius professor of Greek, Oxford 1903-36, founder of League of Nations Union.

8   Meta told Mrs Mary Bennett, daughter of Warden and Mrs H A L Fisher, Hilda's great friends and respectively her employer and tutor, that Hilda had many suitors.

8   For H G Wells incident see chapter two p 45

8   The vamp is referred to in HML 30 January, 4, 5, February 1929.

9 Herbert Alan Laurens Fisher 1865-1940, historian and statesman, MP for Hallam division of Sheffield 1916-18 and for combined English universities 1918-1926, president of Board of Education 1916-1922, introduced the Education Act of 1918 and established state scholarships at universities, Warden of New College Oxford 1925-40.

9 Her treachery, RD 4 December 1928.

10 Her First World War work, The *Ship* 1911-1919, HMM pp10-11.

10 The organisation of security during the First World War and the success of MI5 is recorded in chapter one of F H Hinsley's and C A G Simkins' official history *British Intelligence in the Second World War* vol 4 pub HMSO 1979.

10 Maj-Gen Sir Vernon Kell 1873-1942, soldier 1894-1904, staff captain war office 1904-07, Imperial Defence Committee 1907-09, re-employed by war office 1909-14, directorate of military intelligence 1914-24, re-employed by war office 1924-40.

11 Account of the MI5 registry is based on papers KV 1 43/49/50-56/59/63 in the Public Records Office and the following papers in the Imperial War Museum – memoir by the wife of Vernon Kell PP/MCR/120, history by Mrs D G B Line 92/22/1, a surviving programme of revue "Hush-Hush" p 391, and a letter of 8 August 1919 from Major Kell published in *The Nameless Magazine*, the house paper of "The Nameless Club" formed by the women who worked for MI5.

12 The trials and executions of German spies are described by Leonard Sellers in *Shot In The Tower* pub Leo Cooper 1997.

12 Astonishment, HMM p 11.

13 The section on her years with Lady Astor is based on the Astor papers at the University of Reading Library; Christopher Sykes *Nancy: The Life of Lady Astor* pub Collins 1972 particularly pp 106, 125, 129, 149, 226, 228, 233/4, 278, 284, 316, 354, 506; John Grigg *Nancy Astor: Portrait of a Pioneer* pub Sidgwick and Jackson 1980; Derek Wilson *The Astors 1763-1992* pub Weidenfeld and Nicolson 1993; *The Clarion* 19 May 1934; The *Daily Herald 19 April 1950*.

14 Philip Henry Kerr 1888-1940, inherited title of Marquis of Lothian in 1930, becoming the eleventh marquis.

14 Their friendship, HMM p 15.

14 Miss Benningfield's letter, Astor papers.

16 Harold Laski 1893-1950, political theorist and university teacher, professor of political science at the London School of Economics 1926-50, an influential chairman of the Labour Party.

17 Final days with Lady Astor, correspondence in Astor Papers University of Reading.

18 Public *Faces* pub Constable 1932 (reprinted 1968), by Harold Nicolson 1886-1968, diplomat, politician, author, gardener, diplomatic service 1909-29, journalist 1930-32, National Labour MP 1935-45, parliamentary secretary Ministry of Information 1940-41, governor BBC 1941-46.

18 Oxford tutor was Ruth Butler, senior tutor of the Society of Home Students, writing in HMM p 31, 33, 35, 74.

18 Marjorie Maxse in HMM p 46-48.
19 The battle-axe, Glendinning p 208.
19 Superiority, HMM p 74.
19 Lionel Fielden 1896-1974, joined BBC 1927, head of general talks 1930-35, controller of broadcasting India 1935-40, civil servant in Second World War, writing with others in HMM pp 32-8,46-7,69-70,74.
19 Jeremy Wilson *Lawrence of Arabia* p 577-8 pub Heinemann 1989.
20 Perceptions of self, HML 28 December 1928, 1, 2, 12, 17, 21 January 1929.
20 Unattractive appearance, S&L 24 July 1929. See chapter two and chapter six for Virginia Woolf's comments.
20 Jane Campbell's liking for order, *Public Faces pp 31-34, 310*.
20 The snow pudding, V Sackville-West to Harold Nicolson quoted by James Lees-Milne in *Harold Nicolson – A Biography* p 375 pub Chatto and Windus 1981.
20 Negatives needing order, HML 23, 29 December 1928.
21 Controlled and ardent, Philip Noel Baker MP 1889-1982, Labour politician awarded Nobel Peace Prize 1959, writing in HMM p 17-21.

CHAPTER TWO

23 Stuart Hibberd *This Is London* p3 pub 1950 Macdonald and Evans. Vernon Bartlett writing in HMM.
23 Vernon Bartlett 1894-1983, journalist, author and broadcaster, director of London Office of League of Nations 1922-32, one of HM's most brilliant finds, his radio series "The Way of the World" ran from 1928-34 when he resigned following public criticism of a talk on the walk-out of the Nazis from the Geneva disarmament conference of 1933, diplomatic correspondent of the *News Chronicle* 1934-54, opposed appeasment, during 1939-45 war broadcast three times a week to America.
23 Proportion of young people, HML 12 January 1929.
23 Salaries, *The Times* January 1926.
23 Role model, Janet Adam Smith writing to the author in March 1995 about what she could remember of HM. (Janet Buchanan Adam Smith OBE [Mrs John Carleton], author, journalist, literary editor of *The Listener*, started work at the BBC shortly after HM became talks director, later wrote two of the books in the "Britain In Pictures" series initiated by HM.)
24 The other woman was Dorothy Violet Wellesley 1889-1956, poet, edited "Hogarth Living Poets" series and published several books of her own poetry, one of them, *Selections from the Poems of Dorothy Wellesley*, with an introduction by Yeats who was a great friend, married Lord Gerald Wellesley in 1914, two children, later lived apart from her husband, became duchess of Wellington when he succeeded his nephew as seventh duke of Wellington in 1943, see chapter five for her relationship with HM.

24 Rose Macaulay *Life Among the English* pub Collins 1942, another of the BIP books originated by HM.

25 News and talks Amateur, based on undated article *History of Education and Talks Organisation* in BBC archives by R Wade who arranged talks up to 1924.

25 Lady Astor writing in HMM p 16.

26 Development of radio, AB Vols I and II, various sections.

27 R S Lambert 1894-1981, head adult education BBC 1927, editor *The Listener* 1928-43, Canadian Broadcasting Corporation 1940-43.

27 J R (Joe) Ackerley 1896-1967, writer and literary editor of *The Listener* 1935-1959, wrote *The Prisoners of War* a play, *Hindoo Holiday* a fictionalised account of a brief working life with the Maharaja of Chatarpur, two accounts of life with his alsatian dog *My Dog Tulip* and *We Think the World of You*, and an autobiography *My Father and Myself*

27 Critical comments, *Daily Telegraph* 23 October 1926.

27 Roger Eckersley *The BBC And All That* p 58 pub Samson Low, Marston & Co Ltd 1946/47 – there is no publication date given but various references place it after 1945 and before end 1947 (subsequently in notes as Eckersley).

28 Accounts of rows, *The Times* 28 July, 31 December 1926, 4 January, 2 February 1928, 5 January 1929.

28 George Clarendon, sixth earl, 1877-1955, a junior minister for dominion affairs 1925-27, chief whip in Lords 1922-27, chairman BBC 1927-30, governor general South Africa 1931-37.

28 Ethel Snowden, viscountess from 1931, prominent position in Women's Suffrage Movement, lecturer, wife of Philip Snowden minister in Labour and National Governments.

28 Vice-Admiral Sir Charles Douglas Carpendale 1874-1968, Royal Navy 1887-1923, controller administrative services BBC 1923-35, deputy director-general 1935-38.

28 The Red woman, RD 21, 22 March 1927 and 6 March 1928.

28 *The Times* 19 November 1926.

28 Oh no John, CBM 14 July & 16 November 1926.

28 Plus fours, Hibberd p2.

29 Standards of conduct RD 19 November 1926.

29 Reith's own conduct, his passion for another man, which continued during his marriage, is described in his diaries and was dramatised on Radio 3 in August 1998.

29 Eckersley p 100. (The dog was a spaniel named Torquil.)

29 RD 28 October, 13, 17 and 20 December 1926, 28 January, 22 February 1927, 13 February, 1 March, 13 April 1928.

29 Relations with colleagues, Eckersley p 76, 156.

29 Sydney A Moseley *Who's Who In Broadcasting* pub Pitman's 1933.

30 R S Lambert *Ariel and All His Quality* p25 pub Gollancz 1940.

30 HND 7 February 1930.

30 Glendinning p 208.
30 Standoffishness, HML 17 October 1928.
30 Mary Bennett thought her incapable of mimicry – "she just wasn't interested enough in individual people".
31 Charm and overstatement, Eckersley p 100.
31 Peter Parker *Ackerley: A Life of J R Ackerley* pub Constable 1989 (subsequently Parker).
31 Organisation CBM 18 January 1927.
31 General Strike, *The Times* 6 January 1926.
31 Broadcasting Developments, Briggs Vol I p 71 and 285-6.
32 Drummond quotation, Humphrey Carpenter *The Envy of the World: Fifty Years of the BBC Third Programme and Radio 3 1946-1996* p 327 pub Weidenfeld and Nicolson 1996.
32 What she looked for, HM *Listener Research in Broadcasting* Sociological Review Vol xxii 1935.
32 BBC News File R 28/177/1 18 and 25 October 1927.
32 Macer report *Suggestions for the Improvement of the BBC News Service*.
33 See chapter four for her radio reviews.
33 Monitors and spies, R S Lambert p 57.
33 Crawford Committee, Briggs Vol I p 257. (The BBCo's licence was due for renewal in 1927 and the Government set up the Committee in the summer of 1925 under Lord Crawford to advise on the future development of broadcasting.)
34 References to controversy, BBC File R 34/317/1&2 on controversial broadcasting, BBC Handbook 1929, BBC Talks Files R 51/118/1 February 1927, April and October 1928.
34 William Ralph Inge 1860-1954, dean of St Paul's 1911-34, known as "the gloomy dean" for his weekly diaries in the *Evening Standard* 1921-46 which criticised popular illusions.
34 Lady Astor to HM 10 April 1928. Josephine Butler 1828-1906, social reformer, campaigner against white-slave traffic and for measures to control spread of venereal diseases by prostitutes.
35 *The Times* 20 January 1928. Philip Guedella 1889-1944, historian and essayist.
35 Developing controversy, *The Times* 11, 13, 16 February, 3 March 1928, CBM 6 March 1928, The *Times* 6 March, 2 April 1928.
35 Political broadcasting, A J P Taylor *English History 1914-1945* pub OUP 1965.
36 Negotiations with Government, HML 4, 5, 6, 8, 10, 16, 22, 25 January 1929, CBM 10 January 1929.
37 Relations with establishment figures, Lord Reith *Into the Wind* p131 pub Hodder and Stoughton 1949 (subsequently R-ITW).
38 Too much education, W Burnham 7 December 1925 quoted by Briggs Vol I; *The Times* January 1926, 13 July 1928.
38 The MP who liked things light, Mr Macpherson MP to PMG 13 July 1928.

38 Cartoons in, *Evening Standard* 8 January 1929.
38 Rosita Forbes 1893-1967 traveller, explorer, journalist.
38 HML 20, 21 December 1928 and 2 July 1929.
38 Leonard Woolf 1880-1969, author, publisher, political worker, married Virginia Stephen 1912, writing in RT 11 December 1931.
39 Aldous Huxley in RT 12 October 1928.
39 FY in RT 22 March 1929.
39 Social importance of broadcasting, HM article in *Women's Leader and Common Cause* 2 January 1931.
39 Anon article RT 14 January 1927.
40 Retrospects in, RT 18 October 1929.
40 Letter from A B Longbottom on the crisis.
40 Ellen Wilkinson MP *The Times* 15 January 1929.
41 RT 17 June 1927 letter from librarian E B Camp.
41 Surprised by response, Eckersley p 159.
41 RT 4 January 1929, *The Listener* 30 January 1929.
42 The pudding lady, HML 6 February 1929.
42 Poetry criticism, Eckersley p 76.
42 Fabia Drake audition, HML 12-25 December 1928, January, February, May and June 1929.
43 Articles on poetry, RT 30 November 1928 and 5 April 1929.
43 Keep things simple, Lionel Fielden in HMM p 32-8.
43 BBC *Suggestions for Speakers* MS 1416/1/1/60.
43 Castrating Brummell, VWD vol III p 267.
43 "The Waste Land" first pub 1922.
43 Tawdry magazine, was Martin Hoyle's description in a radio review in the *Financial Times* 14 February 1998.
43 Anthology, HM correspondence with Leonard Woolf 17 August and 17 October 1930.
44 Persuading Vita, HML January and February 1929.
44 FY was of course Filson Young, Desmond was the author and literary critic Desmond Mac Carthy 1877-1952, knighted 1951, Garvin was James Garvin then editor of *The Observer*, Henderson was Arthur Henderson MP then foreign secretary.
44 Most of the details about talks taken from RT and *The Times*.
44 Guardian report, Glendinning p 233.
45 Rebecca West and others, HM letters January, February, June 1929.
45 H G Wells thoughts and actions, HMM p 56-7 and HML 18 June 1929.
46 Article by Laski in WER 17 January 1931. (The WER was a radical weekly magazine which started on 15 March 1930 and published its last issue in January 1934 when it merged with the *New Statesman*.
46 Article in *Wireless Commentator* January 1929.
46 RT 30 September, 13 May 1927, A *Rural University in the Making* by Prof Eric Patterson.

46 Hadow Report, *New Ventures In Broadcasting: A Study In Adult Education* pub BBC 1928.
46 *The Times* 3 February 1927, 7, 9 April, 26 May 1928, 25 February 1929.
46 RT 24 August, 14 September 1928.
47 Meets Vita, Glendinning p193.
47 HML 31 December 1928.
47 VHL letter of 24 June 1928.
48 Vita's broadcast, James Lees Milne *Biography of Harold Nicolson* p 343 pub Rupert Hart-Davis 1952.
48 HML 17 October, 18 December 1928, Glendinning p 208, VHL p 209.
48 Virginia Woolf to Vita Sackville-West 14 December 1928 quoted in Lees Milne p343, Mary was either Mary Campbell wife of Roy Campbell the poet, or Mary Hutchinson, with both of whom Vita had had affairs just before she met HM.

CHAPTER THREE

49 Darling, HML 12 December 1928 and 2 January 1929.
49 Fiftieth letter, HML 24 January 1929.
49 I keep them in a bundle, HML 9 January 1929.
50 Will of the Revd. Donald Matheson made 4 June 1915; he died 20 September 1930.
50 Pompous oak-panelled, HML 10 January.
50 By Jove, 7 February 1929; Marcel Proust *Remembrance of Things Past: Swann's Way* first pub in English by Chatto and Windus 1922.
51 I must try, HML 30 December 1928.
51 Yet here we are, HM Letters 27 December 1928 and 15 January and 4 February 1929.
52 It is so odd, HM Letters 25 January 1929; *Orlando* by Virginia Woolf, pub 1928 Hogarth Press, a tribute and tease to her lover Vita Sackville-West in the form of a fictionalised biography stretching over several hundred years; HML 31 January 1929.
52 It is a pity, VHL p 210 13 December 1928
52 VHL p 215 25 June 1929.
53 Of course I understand, HML 23 February 1929
53 What I thought, HML 25, 27 December 1928.
53 Glendinning p 47.
53 HML 13 December 1928.
53 S & L 24 July 1929.
53 Harold consults Hilda, VHL p 218-220 22 July 1929.
53 Honorary aunt, conversation with Nigel Nicolson 1995.
53 Counting the seconds, S & L 12, 25, 29, 31 January 1929.

53 Oh my dearest, HML 25 December 1928.
53 My God what friends, VWL Vol 4 p 5.
54 She never told me, VWD Vol III p 239.
54 I feel also, HML 16, 19, 31 December 1928 (Dottie was Dorothy Wellesley).
54 Falsity of relationships, S & L 22 August 1929.
54 Letter from Evelyn Irons to author June 1997.
54 If you were to tell me, HML 25 December 1928.
55 Whatever happens, HML 1 February 1929.
55 HML 6 February 1929. The red-haired photographer was a Frau Riess introduced to Vita by the playwright Pirandello
55 People of your complexity, HML 14 January 1929.
56 Who picked me up, HML 30 January and 4,5 February 1929.
56 Our love for each other, HML 7 January and 15 May 1929.
56 I shall say the musician one, HML 5 February 1929. The reference to dragon's tongues and reversing calendars is to a gift from Vita of a calendar on which the days were consumed by extending the dragon's tongues.
57 Virginia Woolf is right, HML 7 January 1929, 5,15 January and 6 February 1929.
57 And then I want, HML 5, 21 January 1929.
57 Sadistic games, Glendinning p 14.
58 It is a queer thing, HML 28 January 1929.
58 Lesbian novel and poems, VHL 4 August 1928 and 11 August 1929.
58 I told Vanessa, S & L 5 April 1929.
59 Look here, HML 28 December 1928. Sumner Place was the house in Kensington which HM shared with Marjorie Maxse and Dorothy Spencer; others named are BBC staff, most of them noted previously.
59 I suppose there, HML 23, 29 December 1928, 3, 30 January and 4 February 1929.
59 Rosita Forbes see note to p 38 chapter two.
59 Tallulah Bankhead 1903-68, American actress with an uninhibited and louche public persona expressed in a rich laugh and throaty drawl, after film and stage appearances in America had many stage successes in Britain 1923-30 before returning to America.
60 Dame Rachel Crowdy 1884-1964, created dame 1919, social reformer, principal commandant of the VADs in France and Belgium 1914-18, later joined secretariat of the League of Nations, adviser Ministry of Information 1939-46.
60 Katharine Furse 1875-1952, pioneer of women's services in the armed forces.
60 Dame Janet Vaughan 1899-1993, medical practitioner to 1945, director northwest London Blood Supply Depot 1939-45, principal Somerville College Oxford 1945-67.
61 I have been having, HML 7, 8 January 1929.

61 Mary Somerville 1897-1963, began in BBC schools broadcasting 1924 and became director 1929-47, assistant controller talks 1947-50, controller talks 1950-55.
61 Lionel was Lionel Fielden and Roger was Roger Eckersley.

CHAPTER FOUR

63 RD 3 December 1929.
63 Wells writing in HMM pp 56-57.
63 Editorial in *The Listener* 16 January 1929.
63 So I accepted, HML 31 January 1929.
64 When one is, HML 27 January 1929.
64 Perennial tensions, HML 20 and 30 December 1928, 11 January and 9 February 1929.
65 A meeting of, HML 20 December 1928, 1,3,14,15,26,28,30 January and 11 June 1929.
67 The wartime acquaintance, HML 16 January 1929, 23 January 1928.
67 I adore, HML 12 February 1929.
68 Most of the difficulties were recorded in three letters from HM to Vita dated 20 February 1929.
69 Awfully difficult, HML 22, 24 April, 12 June 1929.
69 RD 14 and 20 June 1929.
70 HML 21, 26 June 1929. Charles Siepmann 1899-1985, housemaster HM Borstal Institutions Feltham and Rochester 1922-24, talks department BBC 1927-32, director of talks 1932-35, director regional relations 1935-36, director programme planning 1936-39 then moved to academic jobs in USA.
70 Arguments and a present, RD 25 July, 9, 22 November, 13, 17, 23 December 1929.
71 HND 10 February 1930.
71 CBM 2 December 1930.
71 Memo from Siepmann to DG 19 December 1929.
71 RD 1, 28 January 1931.
71 CBM 10 and 25 February and 3 March 1931.
71 Two views, RD and HND 29 June 1931.
72 Reith's book orders, RD July 1931.
72 John Henry Whitley 1866-1935, Liberal MP 1908-28, originator of Whitley Councils, speaker of the House of Commons 1921-28, chairman governors BBC 1930-35.
73 HND 20 July, 12 August, 8 November 1931.
73 WER 28 November 1931.
74 HND 18 November 1931.

74 HND and letter to Reith 23 November 1931.
74 HND 9, 10 December 1931.
74 James Joyce 1882-1941, author; *Ulysses* pub in 1922 had been received immediately as a work of genius by many eminent writers, but the first UK edition did not appear until 1936.
74 Eckersley p 100, *News Chronicle, Evening News,* 3 December, *Manchester Guardian* 4 December, *Daily Telegraph* 6 December, Daily *Herald* 9 December 1931.
75 The draft letter is in the Astor papers at the University of Reading, but there is no record in these or BBC archives to show if it was sent.
76 Memo from Roger Eckersley 15 December 1931.
76 Brief on talks file dated 23 December 1931.
76 Carpenter p 4-5.
76 RD 29 January and February 1931.
77 Carpenter quoting P H Newby then on staff of Mary Somerville, p 126 & n 6.
77 End of love affair, Glendinning p 238.
77 Being there, HML 18 June 1929.
77 I get into awful states, HML 26 January 1929.
78 Information on Graves disease from Mr K A Steer, consultant physician.
79 A nerve wracking time, Eckersley p 159.
79 Fielden writing in HMM and his own book *The Natural Bent* p 116 pub 1960 Andre Deutsch.
80 Briggs Vol II p 62.
81 The new Controller of Output was a Colonel Alan Dawnay.
82 Sally Feldman's views were reported in an interview with Sue Summers in *The Times* 30 January 1998.
82 The BBC renaissance of the sixties was described in *Auntie: The Inside Story of the BBC: Making Waves 1960-70* shown on BBC 1 11 November 1997.
83 Siepmann the firebrand, Eckersley p 129.
83 Review Committee, Briggs Vol II.
83 Carpenter p 5.
84 I am puzzled, Glendinning p 297.

CHAPTER FIVE

85 HML 30 December 1928, 12 January, 24 April 1929, 15 January 1934.
86 HND 11 April 1932. William Joynson Hicks, later Lord Brentford, 1865-1932, Home Secretary 1924-29. For earlier reference to *Public Faces* see chapter one.
86 The section on Dorothy Wellesley is based on HML 31 December 1928, 20, 24, January, 18, 21, 23 February, 30 April, 13 May, 1929, Dorothy

Wellesley to HM 16 February 1929, VW to Ethel Smyth 13 December 1937 in VWL p 190, DW *Far Have I Travelled*, pub James Barrie 1952 p 49, 52, 75-76, 162-3, 167, 170, 216,

87 Dictionary of National Biography article on DW.

87 Sir George Goldie 1846-1925 founder of Royal Niger Company, deputy governor Nigeria, campaigner against slave trade.

87 Lord Gerald Wellesley succeeded his nephew as seventh Duke of Wellington in 1943.

87 Conversation with Nigel Nicolson 1995.

88 For W J Turner and the series of wartime books "Britain in Pictures" see chapter six.

88 For some of DW's poems see the Yeats' edition of The *Oxford Book of Modern Verse 1892-1935*, pub 1936.

88 Astor papers 21 January, 17 October 1932.

88 VWD Vol IV pp 101-104.

88 John Lehmann *Thrown to the Woolfs* p 34 pub Weidenfeld and Nicolson 1978. John Lehmann 1907-1987, journalist and publisher, later became Leonard Woolf's business partner and general manager of The Hogarth Press 1938-46, produced a successful magazine *New Writing* which became *Penguin New Writing* edited by him and Roy Fuller 1940-50.

89 The articles were "Politics and Broadcasting" and "The Record of the BBC", Vol V No 1-4 1934 and Vol VI No 4 1935 of the *Political Quarterly*, and "The Educational Role of Broadcasting" pub International Institute of Intellectual Cooperation.

89 HN Diaries 28 July, 19 August, 19 November 1932.

89 Conversation with Nigel Nicolson 1995.

90 HML 1, 2, January 1929.

90 Vita's mother, Glendinning p 263.

90 Lord Hailey see notes to chapter one.

90 Lord Lothian see chapter one and notes.

90 Frederick John Dealtry Lugard 1858-1945, created baron 1928, soldier, administrator, author, governor general of Nigeria 1914-19, governor of Hong Kong 1907-12, an acknowledged authority on colonial administration who was chairman of the International Institute of African Languages and cultures which he founded jointly with Dr Oldham.

90 Dr Joseph Houldsworth Oldham 1874–1969, organizing secretary for Edinburgh World Missionary Society 1908, editor *International Review of Missions* 1912–1927, co-founder and administrative director of International Institute of African Languages and Culture 1931–38, a constant advocate and promoter of systematic research into the problems of the colonies.

90 Sir Julian Huxley 1887–1975, knighted 1958, zoologist, philosopher and public servant, secretary Zoological Society of London 1935-42, became a national figure as a result of his broadcasts in BBC Radio's Brains Trust 1939-45, along with H G Wells and Sir Richard Gregory one of the most influential popularisers of science in the country.

90 Sir Richard Arman Gregory 1864-1952, knighted 1931, author and journalist, left school at the age of twelve, worked in a shoe factory, later took a first class degree in astronomy and physics, editor of *Nature* 1919-38, became the greatest scientific journalist of his day and a noted scientific policy maker.

90 Dame Margery Perham 1895-1982, writer and lecturer on African affairs, tutor and research fellow at St Hugh's College Oxford, a confirmed tom-boy who loved riding, shooting and golfing, among her papers at Rhodes House are holiday photographs of her and friends which include some of Hilda Matheson together with a copy of the Howard Coster photo of Matheson reproduced here.

91 Background to *Survey*, LP, OP and Margery Perham *Lugard: The Years of Authority 1898-1945* pub Collins 1960 p 698-9.

92 Lord Milner 1854-1825, statesman, great public servant with profound conviction of need for Imperial unity, after journalism on *Pall Mall Gazette*, philanthropy in helping found Toynbee Hall in Whitechapel, and work in Inland Revenue, became High Commissioner for South Africa 1897-1905, hugely influential in determining British policy towards Boers, secretary of state for war 1918, for the colonies 1918-21, inspired young men to work in Empire, hence his "kindergarten" of young men who produced the magazine *Round Table*.

92 J M Lee *Colonial Development and Good Government: A study of the ideas expressed by the British official classes in planning decolonization 1939-64*, pub Clarendon Press, Oxford, 1967 pp 9, 21, 23, 43, 45, 63 (subsequently Lee)

93 Crocker and Perham, OP Ms 1/3 f 65-70.

94 LP, NAS, GD40/17/21 May to July 1933.

94 R W Cell, *Hailey: A Study in British Imperialism 1872-1969*, pub Cambridge University Press 1992 (subsequently Cell); and his article "Lord Hailey and the Making of the African Survey" pub in *African Affairs* October 1989.

94 Cell's Preface to his study of Hailey.

95 LP, NAS, GD40/17/122,123,124.

95 OP Ms 1/3 f 41, Ms 2/4 f 95.

95 HMM p12-13.

95 Chatham House, headquarters of the Royal Institution for International Affairs in St James's Square, London, provided office space for staff working on the Survey and acted as trustee for the Carnegie funds. (The papers in Chatham House relating to the Survey are less comprehensive than LP and although read were not used.)

96 LP, NAS, GD40/17/126 and 127.

96 HM to Lord Lothian 13 March. 26 July 1935.

96 Perham *Lugard* p 698-9.

96 LP, NAS, GD40/17/122,12711 July 1933, 4 October, 8 November 1935.

96 Perham Ms 691/1 ff 16/17.

96 LP, NAS, GD40/17/127, Lord L to HM 21 October 1935, Lord H to

Lord L October 1935, Lord L to Lord H 12 March 1936, Lord H to HM November 1936.
97 1945 edition of Survey p xxii.
97 The sections on the Survey's objectives and Hailey's absences are based on LP GD 40/17/122,123,126,127, OP Ms 1/3 f 6, and Cell.
98 Quoted in Bernard Keeling's proposed *History of St Felix School*.
99 LP, NAS, GD 40/17/123, OP Ms 1/3 ff 88/89, GD 40/17/123 25 January 1934.
99 Alexander Soltzhenitsyn *August 1914*, pp 190,114, trans Michael Glenny, pub The Bodley Head 1971.
100 LP, NAS, GD40/17/125 26 July 1934.
100 Work on the Survey during 1937-38 is based on LP, NAS, GD40/17/127, 128, 129, 130, OP Ms 1/3 ff 96-118, Lugard Ms 149/3 and Pedler Ms 9/63 both in library of Rhodes House, and Cell chapter 15.
100 Sir Frederick Johnson Pedler b 1908, after the *Survey* worked in the Colonial Office and then for the United Africa and other companies, knighted 1969.
101 Minutes and journals on dates recorded; minutes of the African Research Society, 2 June 1939 (HM was secretary of the Society).
102 Principal work of reference, Lee.
102 Pivotal project, Cell pp xi, xii, 217, 235.
103 Hailey's preface to the 1957 edition of *An African Survey*.
103 1945 edition of the Survey.
104 LP, NAS, GD 40/17/129 13 April 1938, OP Ms 1/3 f 123 15 July 1938.
104 LP, NAS, GD 40/17/129 25 March 1938.
104 Charles Bathurst, first Viscount Bledisloe 1867-1958, agriculturalist and public servant, Conservative MP for South Wilts 1910-18, parliamentary secretary to Ministry of Food 1916-17, chairman Royal Commission on Sugar Supplies 1917-19.
104 Northern Rhodesia, Southern Rhodesia and Nyasaland are now known as, respectively, Zambia, Zimbabwe, and Malawi.
105 LP, NAS, GD 40/17/130 30 June 1938.
106 Huxley's comments were made to *The Times* in November 1940. 190-192 Hailey's are taken from HMM 1941.
106 *An African Survey* and An *African Survey Revised 1956* pub Oxford University Press 1938 and 1957 respectively.

CHAPTER SIX

109 Letter in Astor papers 6 January 1939.
109 HMM (her mother's recollection in the Memoir of the date of the agent's call as November 1939 is wrong by exactly a year).
109 Yeats, Glendinning p 299.

109 FO 898/1.
110 CBM 8 September 1931.
110 Briggs vol II p 625-6, 652.
110 R-ITW.
111 Briggs vol III p 82-7
111–114 Charles Cruikshank *The Fourth Arm: Psychological Warfare 1938-1945* p 9 pub Davis-Poynter 1977 (subsequently Cruikshank).

Michael Balfour *Propaganda in War 1939-45* pub Routledge and Kegan Paul 1979.

A J P Taylor *English History 1914-1945*, pub OUP 1965.

Rose Macaulay *Life Among The English* pub William Collins 1942.

Obituary of Walter Goetz in *The Times* September 1995.

History of the Second World War: British Intelligence in the Second World War pub HMSO 1979 vol I, F H Hinsley and others, vol IV, F H Hinsley and C A G Simkins, vol V, Michael Howard.

Ian Mc Laine *Ministry of Morale* pub George Allen and Unwin 1979 (subsequently Mc Laine).

R-ITW.

HND 18 June, 17 and 28 September 1939.

FO 898/1.

Peter Neville *Neville Chamberlain: A Study in Failure?* pub Hodder and Stoughton 1992.

112 Vernon Bartlett see chapter two and notes.
112 Sir Campbell Arthur Stuart 1885-1972, born and raised Canada, deputy director propaganda in enemy countries 1918, director of *The Times*.
113 Hugh Pattison Macmillan 1873-1952, Baron Macmillan, judge, lord advocate in Labour government 1924, lord of appeal in ordinary 1930-39, minister of information 1939-40, member BBC advisory council 1936-46.
113 Alfred Duff Cooper 1890-1954, first Viscount Norwich, diplomat, politician, author, Foreign Office 1913-24, Conservative MP Oldham 1924-29, financial secretary War Office 1928-29, 1931-34, to Treasury 1934-35, secretary for war 1935-37, first lord admiralty 1937, resigned over Munich, minister of information 1940-41, chancellor Duchy of Lancaster 1941-43.
114 FO 898/1.
114 HM report 24 August 1939 PRO T162 1858.
114 HM note on work of JBC 18 November 1940.
114 Cruikshank p24.
115 RD 17 April 1939.
115 Lord Beaverbrook (Max Aitken) 1879-1964, newspaper proprietor, owned *Daily Express* (from 1916), *Sunday Express* (which he founded 1918) and *Evening Standard* (from 1923), ministerial office in First and Second World Wars.
115 R-ITW p 350 onwards.

115 Memo from Mr Woodburn to Mr Leigh Ashton, Ministry of Information 1 January 1940.

116 The Eckersley farmhouse, used no doubt because Roger's son Tim was an engineer with the JBC, is referred to in a letter to me of 20 May 1996 from Mrs Cora Blyth de Portillo who worked for the JBC.

116 Sir Frederick Whyte 1883-1970 Liberal MP for Perth City 1910-18, worked in India and China then director-general English Speaking Union from 1938, head of American division Ministry of Information 1939.

117 Details of JBC staff from PRO papers.

117 Guy Francis de Moncy Burgess 1911-63, worked for BBC 1936-39, served with MI6 1939-41, worked for Foreign Office after war including a short period in the Washington embassy before his recall in 1951 for serious misconduct, in same year fled Britain and resurfaced in the Soviet Union in 1956 having worked for that country secretly since his recruitment by the Russian secret service, the KGB, in the nineteen thirties.

117 Kenneth Matthews 1908-94, writer and broadcaster, after JBC was absorbed by BBC became latter's Middle East and Balkan correspondent and later worked in Latin America, a chess expert who reported graphically in 1972 on contest between Boris Spassky and Bobby Fischer.

117 W J Turner 1889-1946 see p 127 for career details.

117 Jenny Rees *Looking for Mr Nobody* pub Weidenfeld and Nicolson 1994.

117 Andrew Boyle *The Climate of Treason* pub Hutchinson 1979.

117 FO 898/1, INF 1/165, INF 1/169, INF 1/41B.

118 Monthly reports on JBC work made by HM to Section D.

119 HM report of July 1940.

120 Briggs vol III p 31-5, 169-78, 185-7, 344.

121 *Political Quarterly* vol IX Nos 1-4 1940, the PQ papers of Professor W A Robson at the London School of Economics do not contain any details about the article or its author.

123 HM report of July 1940 and other JBC reports.

123 HND 15,18 June, 17, 28 September 1939, 6 January, 6, 29 February, 4 April. 1, 15 June, 3 August 1940.

123 David Astor to author 17 January 1995.

124 Lord Haw Haw was the nickname given to William Joyce, an Irishman who broadcast from Germany and despite his nationality was later executed as a traitor to Britain.

124 Gracie Fields 1898-1979, created Dame 1979, actress, singer and comedienne who in films, musical comedy and radio combined an exceptional soprano voice with a vivacious and down to earth personality.

124 Michael Howard vol V.

125 R M Cooper *Refugee Scholars – Conversations with Tess Simpson* pub Moorland Books 1992.

125 Correspondence between HM and Sir Maurice Peterson 5-10 August 1940.

125 Sir Maurice Drummond Peterson 1889-1952, Foreign Office 1913-1940, ambassador to Spain 1939-40, controller of overseas publicity Ministry

of Information 1940-41, an under-secretary at Foreign Office 1942, ambassador to Ankara 1944-46, Moscow 1946-49.

126 VWL vol 6 letter of 14 November 1940.

126 VWD vol V 1936-41, entry for 5, 12 July 1940 p 300-302 (Bell suggests in note 5 that the "proposed anthology" was never published, but in fact it was, as the series "Britain In Pictures").

127 HM to Lady Astor 14 October 1940 and Lady Astor to HM 23 October 1940 in Astor papers University of Reading library.

127 Lady Tweedsmuir 1883-1977 spent four and a half years in Canada as wife to its Governor General, John Buchan.

127 INF/1/170 "Progress Report on Publicity About the Empire" 17 February 1940.

127 Most of the material about BIP is taken from the present author's book *Britain In Pictures; A History andBibliography* pub by Werner Shaw 1995 which provides a full history, references, and a comprehensive catalogue.

130 BIP sales figures have been rounded.

131 INF 1/170, INF 1/171, FO 895/5.

132 HM letter of 29 August 1939.

133 Leigh Ashton, knighted 1948, V&A museum curator to 1939, finance and other divisions Ministry of Information 1939-45, director and secretary V&A 1945-55.

135 Everything may smash, HMM p 17-21, 50-55.

135 Sheila Shannon, now Mrs Dickinson, widow of the poet and broadcaster Patric Dickinson.

135 Dame Ethel Smyth 1858-1944, composer, author, worker for women's rights, fought hard for her own career as a musician, for recognition as a composer, and for women's suffrage, a woman of high spirits and serious purpose.

135 Obituaries *The Times* 1, 2 November, *The Star* 1 November, *New Statesman* 16 November, *The Spectator* 22 November 1940.

135 Vita gets news, Glendinning p 305, HND 1, 2 November 1941.

135 Memorial volume, correspondence between V S-W, Leonard Woolf and John Lehmann 22 April-11 September in Hogarth Press papers at Reading University.

136 Lionel Fielden in HMM p 32-38.

136 Unseemly row, conversation with Mary Bennett.

136 VWD vol V 1 November 1940 p 335.

136 VWL vol VI 14 November 1940, 14 January 1941.

136 Letters V-SW to VW 14 & 19 January 1941.

Appendix

AUTHORS AND TITLES OF BOOKS IN "BRITAIN IN PICTURES" SERIES

(Names and titles are given as they appeared on the books. Numbers refer to catalogue entry in *Britain In Pictures: A History And Bibliography*)

ADAM SMITH, Janet
Life Among The Scots, 101
Children's Illustrated Books, 126

ANSON, Peter F.
British Sea Fishermen, 69

ARBERRY, A. J.
British Orientalists, 37

AYRTON, Michael
British Drawings, 105

BARKER, Sir Ernest
British Statesmen, 13

BATCHELOR, Denzil
British Boxing, 130

BEATON, Cecil
British Photographers, 71

BELL, G.K.A. The Bishop of Chichester,
The English Church, 28

BETJEMAN, John
English Cities And Small Towns, 48

BICKNELL, Peter
British Hills And Mountains, 116

BIRCH, Nigel
The Conservative Party, 122

BLAKE, George
British Ships And Shipbuilders, 104

BLUNDEN, Edmund
English Villages, 11

BONE, Stephen
British Weather, 97

BOULENGER, E.G.
British Anglers' Natural History, 109

BOWEN, Elizabeth
English Novelists, 23

BURDON, Randal
New Zealand, 26
Jointly with Ngaio Marsh

BURKE, Thomas
English Inns, 67

CARDUS, Neville
English Cricket, 93

CECIL, Lord David
The English Poets, 1

CHAPPELL, Metius
British Engineers, 47

CITRINE, Sir Walter
British Trade Unions, 45

COLLIS, Maurice
British Merchant Adventurers, 27

CRUIKSHANK, R. J.
The Liberal Party, 123

DARWIN, Bernard
British Clubs, 63
British Golf, 107

DAVIES, Rhys
The Story Of Wales, 62

DISHER, M. Willson
Fairs, Circuses And Music Halls, 46

DOBRÉE, Professor Bonamy
English Essayists, 106

ELTON, Arthur
British Railways, 83

EVANS, Admiral Sir Edward
British Polar Explorers, 53

EYRE, Frank
English Rivers And Canals, 84
Jointly with Charles Hadfield

FISHER, James
The Birds Of Britain, 36

FOX, Adam
English Hymns and Hymn Writers, 98

FRASER DARLING, F.
The Story of Scotland, 21
Wild Life of Britain, 52

GILMOUR, John
British Botanists, 79

GLOAG, JOHN
British Furniture Makers, 89

GREENE, Graham
British Dramatists, 32

GREGORY, Sir Richard
British Scientists, 14

GRIERSON, Sir Herbert
The English Bible, 66

GRIGSON, Geoffrey
Wild Flowers In Britain, 65

HADFIELD, Charles
English Rivers And Canals, 84
Jointly with Frank Eyre

HALL, William Glenvill
The Labour Party, 124

HAMPSON, John
The English At Table, 51

HASKELL, Arnold
Australia, 5

HAWKES, Jacquetta
Early Britain, 92

HENNELL, Thomas
British Craftsmen, 38

HERBERT, John
The Port Of London, 115

HISLOP, John
The Turf, 129

HONEY, W.B.
English Glass, 99

HOWARD, Alexander L.
Trees In Britain, 91

HUDSON, Derek
British Journalists And Newspapers, 86

HUXLEY, Elspeth
East Africa, 6

IVES, A.G.L.
British Hospitals, 131

JOHNSON, S.C.
British Postage Stamps, 72

JOHNSTON, S.H.F.
British Soldiers, 50

LAMBERT, Margaret
English Popular And Traditional Art, 102
Jointly with Enid Marx

LINDSAY, Kenneth
English Education 17

LINDSAY, Martin
The House Of Commons, 117

LOCKLEY, R.M.
Islands Round Britain, 85

LOW, David
British Cartoonists, Caricaturists and Comic Artists, 25

LYNAM, Edward
British Maps And Mapmakers, 73

LYND, Sylvia
English Children, 30

MACAULAY, Rose
Life Among The English, 31

Mc CALL, Cicely
Women's Institutes, 61

MARSDEN, Christopher
The English At The Seaside, 112

MARSH, Ngaio
New Zealand, 26
Jointly with Randal Burdon

MARX, Enid
English Popular And Traditional Art, 102
Jointly with Margaret Lambert

MATHEW, David
British Seamen, 58

MATTHEWS, Kenneth
British Philosophers, 60
British Chess, 127

MEYNELL, Francis
English Printed Books, 95

MILES, Bernard
The British Theatre, 119

MILLIN, Sarah Gertrude
South Africa, 18

MORRAH, Dermot
The British Red Cross, 74

NEWMAN, Sir George
English Social Services, 24

NICHOLSON, Lady Dorothy
The Londoner, 64

NOON, Sir Firozkhan
India, 10

O'BRIEN, Kate
English Diaries And Journals, 55

O'FAOLAIN, Sean
The Story Of Ireland, 39

ORWELL, George
The English People, 100

PAGET, Guy
Sporting Pictures Of England, 87

PARIS, HJ
English Watercolour Painters, 88

PARKER, Eric
British Sport, 2

PIPER, John
British Romantic Artists, 34

POOLEY, Sir Ernest
The Guilds Of The City Of London, 82

PORTSMOUTH, The Earl of
British Farm Stock, 132

REYNOLDS, EE
Boy Scouts, 75

RICHMOND, Ian
Roman Britain, 113

ROBERTS, Harry
British Rebels And Reformers, 33
English Gardens, 59

ROBERTS, S.C.
British Universities, 110

RUSSELL John
British Portrait Painters, 76

RUSSELL Sir John
English Farming, 16

SABINE, Noel
The British Colonial Empire, 40

SACKVILLE-WEST, V.
English Country Houses, 15

SEMPILL, Cecilia
English Pottery And China, 77

SETTLE, Alison
English Fashion, 121

SITWELL, Edith
English Women, 29

SKILTON, C. P.
British Windmills And Watermills, 120

SMITH, A. Croxton
British Dogs, 96

SMYTHE, F.S.
British Mountaineers, 22

TANGYE, Nigel
Britain In The Air, 68

TAYLOR, Geoffrey
Insect Life In Britain, 94

TAYLOR, George M.
British Garden Flowers, 103
British Herbs And Vegetables, 108

TEMPLE, Vere
British Butterflies, 125

TURNER, W. J.
English Music, 3
The English Ballet, 80

The British Commonwealth And Empire, Omnibus Volume (OV) 133
Impressions Of English Literature, OV 134
The Englishman's Country, OV 135
Nature In Britain, OV 136
Aspects Of British Art, OV 137
British Adventure, OV 138
British Craftsmanship, OV 139

TWEEDSMUIR, Lady
Canada, 9

ULYETT, Kenneth
British Clocks And Clockmakers, 111

VULLIAMY, C.E.
English Letter Writers, 81

WALMSLEY, Leo
British Ports And Harbours, 35

WARNER, Rex
English Public Schools, 90

WARREN, C. Henry
English Cottages And Farmhouses, 128

WEDGWOOD, C. V.
Battlefields In Britain, 78

WELLESLEY, Dorothy
Shelley, 7
Byron, 8
Tennyson, 19
Keats, 20
Coleridge, 43
Wordsworth, 44

WENTWORTH, Lady
British Horses And Ponies, 57

WILSON, R Mc Nair
British Medicine, 12

WOODWARD, E.L.
British Historians, 49

YONGE, C.M.
British Marine Life, 70

YOUNG, G.M.
The Government Of Britain

Index

A
Ackerley, JR, 27, 31, 59, 79
Adam Smith, Janet, 27
Adprint, 128
Alan, AJ, 32
An African Survey, 2, 14, 79, 90-107, 135
   Appointments to, 94
   Government reaction, 102
   Importance of, 102
   Hailey's illnesses, 97-98
   HM's role, 98-101, 103,104
   Objectives, 96
   Omission in *The Times* obituary, 136
   Origin, 90, 91, 95
   Press reaction, 101
   Publication, 101
   Specialist journal reaction, 101
   1957 Edition, 107
Astor, David, 123
Astor, Nancy, 2, 3, 13-17, 19, 25, 28, 29, 30, 34, 50, 62, 67, 68, 70, 78, 88, 109, 127, 135, 136, 137
Astor, Sir John, ix
Astor, Waldorf, 13, 15, 62, 88
Ashmolean Museum, 10
Ashton, Leigh, 125, 131, 132
August 1914, 99

B
Baddeley, Clinton, 134
Baldwin, Stanley, 13, 20, 26, 35
Balliol College, vii
Bankhead, Tallulah, 59
Bartlett, Vernon, 23, 41, 112
Beecham, Sir Thomas, 38
Beaverbrook, Lord, 115
Bennett, Mary, ix, 29n, 135
Benningfield, Miss, 14
Bernal, Prof J D, 119

Birt, John, 83
Bledisloe, Lord, 104
Bott, Michael, vii
Boyle, James, 83
Briggs, Asa, 2, 80
Bright, John, 5
"Britain In Pictures", (BIP) 2 127-131
   Adprint, 128
   Best sellers, 129
   BIP Books, 2, 127
   Collins, William, 129, 130
   Foges, Wolfgang, 129
   Internment of staff, 124-127
   Objectives, 128
   Origins, 10,126
   Launch, 129
   MI6 links, 128
   Neurath, Walter 129
   Turner, WJ, 116, 127
British Broadcasting Corporation (BBC), 22-48, 63-84,
   African Survey broadcast, 102
   Conflict with JBC, 120-123, 130-134,
   Controversy policy, 25, 33-35
   Early years, 19, 23
   Education policy, 37-40
   Foreign services, 31, 109
   HM resignation, 72, 74-81
   News, development of, 30-32
   Poetry readings, 41-43
   Talks innovations, 40-44
British Council, 120, 123
Brown, Clare, ix
Buchan, John, 18
Buist, J L F, ix
Burgess, Guy, 117,126, 127
Butler, Josephine, 34
Butler, RA (Rab), 134
Byron, Lord, 9, 54

C

Campbell, Jane, 18, 20, 26, 86
Campbell, Mary, 48
(See also Hutchinson, Mary)
Campbell Stuart, Sir, 112, 124
Carleton, Janet, See Adam Smith, Janet
Carnegie Corporation, 92, 96, 98, 101
Carpendale, Charles, 27, 36
Carpenter, Humphrey, 75, 84
Cecil, Lord David, 129
Cell, Prof, 94, 99, 102, 103
Chamberlain, Neville, 35, 109, 111, 112, 113, 114, 115, 118, 124, 126
Chatham House, 92, 95
Churchill, Winston, 35, 112, 123
Citrine, Walter, 33
Clarendon, Lord, 28, 29, 67
Collins, William, 129, 130
Crawford Committee, 33
Crocker, Walter, 93
Crofts, Professor, 40
Crowdy, Rachel, 60, 61
Crowther, Geoffrey, 119

D

Daily Express, 110
Daily Herald, 75
Daily Mail, 38, 76
Daily News, 40
Daily Telegraph, 75, 101
Dane, Clemence, 44
De La Mare, Walter, 42
De-rating Bill, 36-37
Donne, John, 57, 88
Drake, Fabia, 42
Drummond, John, 31

E

Eckersley, Peter, 27, 31, 60, 66
Eckersley, Roger, 23-48, 63-84, 115
Economist, The, 119
Eden, Anthony, 110
Ehrenzweig, Robert, 111
Electra House, 112, 116, 122, 123
Eliot, TS, 9, 43, 88
Empire Transcriptions, 120
Epstein, Sir Jacob, 67
Evening News, 75
Evening Standard, 38, 68, 110

F

Fabian Society, 92
Feldman, Sally, 83
Fielden, Lionel, 19, 31, 59, 61, 65, 79, 80, 136

Fields, Gracie, 124
Fisher, HAL, ix, 9, 14, 19, 91
Fisher, Lettice, ix, 9
Fisher, Mary, (See Bennett, Mary)
Foges, Wolfgang, 129
Forbes, Rosita 38, 60
Ford, Sir Edward, ix
Friedlander, Elisabeth, 130
Fry, Roger, 28
Furley-Smith, Mrs Jean, ix
Furse, Katherine, 60

G

Garvin, James, 43, 63, 64, 88
General Strike, 24, 31
Glendinning, Victoria, 29, 53
Goebbels, 75, 109
Goetz, Walter, 111
Goldie, Sir George, 87, 92
Goldsmith, Cmndr VH, 61, 64, 65
Granard Society, 5
Grand, Major, 114
Graves disease, 78, 114, 135
Green, Mrs D K, ix
Greene, Sir Hugh, 83
Gregory, Sir Richard, 90
Grossmith, George, 43, 65
Grosvenor, Rosamund, 52
Guardian, see *Manchester*
Guedella, Philip, 34

H

Hadow, Sir Henry, 46
Hailey, Malcolm, 2
   African Survey, 90-108
   Acknowledgment of HM's contribution, 105
   Director of *AS*, 94
   His death, 137
   His Survey? 90
   His view of French officials, 96
   Illnesses, 97, 98
   Personality and appearance, 94
   Tour of Africa, 97
Hailsham, Lord, 5
Halifax, Lord, 111, 126
Hall, Radclyffe, 59
Hamilton, Mary, 43
HarperCollins, vii
Haw Haw, "Lord", 124
Hibberd, Stuart, 22
Hill, T, vii
Hitler, 110, 123, 124, 126
Hogarth, David, 20

Hogarth Press, 43, 88, 94, 136
Homosexuality, v, 51, 58-61
Hussey, Marmaduke, 2
Hutchinson, Mary, 48 (See also
 Campbell, Mary)
Huxley, Aldous, 38, 44
Huxley, Elspeth, 117
Huxley, Julian, 27, 90, 105, 136

I
Information, see Ministry of
Inge, Dean, 34, 44
Internment, impact on HM's work,
 124-127
Irons, Evelyn, 55

J
Johnson, Mrs BH, 6
Joint Broadcasting Committee (JBC)
 112-133
 Aims of, 114
 Broadcasts to USA, 131
 Covert role, 115
 Establishment and origins 113
 Propaganda, 119
 Rivalry with BBC, 114, 116, 119,
  120-123, 130
 Rivalry with Ministry of
  Information, 112, 113, 115, 119,
  122, 125, 130-134
 Transfer to BBC, 136
 Work of, 115-120
 Wound up, 136
Joyce, James, 23, 72, 73

K
Keats, John, 47
Kavanagh, Jacqueline, ix
Kell, Captain, (K), 10, 11, 12
Keeling, Bernard, ix, 98n
Kennedy, Joseph E, 132
Kennedy, Margaret, 44
Kerr, Philip (Marquess of Lothian)
 African Survey, 90-108
 Ambassador USA, 126, 131, 132,
  136
 Death, 137
 Friendship with HM, 14, 16, 19
Keynes, JM, 44
King-Hall, Stephen, 112, 119

L
Lambert, L H, see Alan, A J
Lambert, RS, 25, 29

Laski, Harold, 17, 46
Lawrence, DH, 72
Lawrence, TE, 20
Layland, Mrs A, ix
League of Nations, 24, 41, 50
Lehmann, John, 89
Line, Mrs H, 11
Listener, The, 26, 29, 38, 62, 63, 64, 66,
 122
Lloyd George, David, 20, 35
London Transcription Service, 120,
 134, 136, 137
Lothian, Marquess of, current Lord, vii
Lothian, Marquess of, See Kerr, Philip
Low, David, 110
Lugard, Lord, 90, 92

M
Macaulay, Rose, 24, 111
Mac Carthy, Desmond, 44
MacDonald, Ramsay, 5, 20, 70
Macmillan, Lord, 113
Macer-Wright, Philip, 32
Manchester Guardian, The, 44, 74
Mann, Thomas, 119
Matheson, Donald Macleod, 3, 50, 85
Matheson, The Rev Donald, 3, 4, 5, 6,
 49, 76, 85
Matheson Hilda –
 Analogy with Vorotyntsev of *August
  1914*, 99
 Astor, Nancy, Secretary to 13-17
 Award of OBE, 105
 Birth and Family, 3-5
 "Britain In Pictures", 127-131
 BBC talks director, 22-48, 62-84
 BBC resignation from, 72, 74-81
 Extravagance, 85
 Death and obituaries, 1, 134-137
 Father, relations with, 5
 Health, 3, 77, 125, 134
 Hogarth Press, relations with, 43, 88,
  94
 Homosexual love, v, 3, 58-61
 HUL, 9
 Journalism, 89, 122
 Mother, relations with, 4,
 MI5, work for, 1, 9-13, 109
 MI6, work for, 1, 10, 109, 111, 113,
  see all chapter six
 National Trust, job possibility, 95
 Oxford, 6-9, 17
 Personality, 1, 3, 7, 9, 18-21, 29, 36,
  85

Sackville-West, Vita, letters to, vii, 2, 49-61
School, 4
Stoker, 3, 52
Slave, 1
Vita's children, 55, 89, 90
Week-End Review, 89
Writing and journalism, 38, 46, 89, 122
Wellesley, Dorothy, relations with, 47, 54, 55, 76, 86-88, 108, 127, 135, 136
Matheson, Meta, 3, 5, 6, 8, 49, 85, 108, 113
Matthews, Kenneth, 117
Maxse, Marjorie, 18, 56
MI5, MI6, see Matheson, Hilda
Milner's Kindergarten, 92
Ministry of Information, 112, 114, 116, 119, 120, 123, 127, 131, 133
-Conflict with JBC, 122, 123, 125, 127, 130-34
Morning Post, 73
Morrell, Lady Ottoline, 88, 127
Mosley, Oswald, 24, 125
Moule, Lady Christian, 5
Munich crisis, 111
Murray, Gilbert, 8, 9

N
National Trust, 95
Neurath, Walter, 128,
New Statesman, 95, 128, 135
News Chronicle, 74, 78
Newspaper Proprietors Association, 25
Newman, Sydney, 83
Nicolson, Nigel, ix, 53, 87, 90
Nicolson, Harold, 18, 44, 47, 49, 52, 53, 58, 71, 72, 73, 85, 116, 133
Nineteen-Thirties, 23, 72, 85
Nineteen-Twenties, 23
Noel-Baker, Philip, 135

O
O'Brien, Kate, 131
Observer, The, 63, 88
Oldham, Dr JH, 90, 91, 92, 93, 94, 95, 98, 99, 101
Osborne, Dorothy, 51
Oxford Presbyterian Church, 7

P
Pedler, Frederick, 100, 104
Penns in the Rocks, 47, 87, 136

Perham, Margery, 90, 92, 93, 94, 95
Peterson, Sir Maurice, 125, 126
Poetry andPoets, 9, 41, 43, 47, 88
Political Quartely, The, 89, 121
Portsmouth, The Earl of, 129
Proust, Marcel, 23, 50,
Public Faces, 18, 85
Putney Presbyterian Church, 3, 5

R
Radio Times, 26, 36, 38, 40, 41, 42, 45, 46
Reith, John, 1, 2, 9, 16, 23-48, 63-84, 110, 112, 115, 124, 137
Republic, Plato's, 40
Reuters, 31
Rhodes trustees, 96
Richards, Anthony, ix
Rockefeller Foundation, 91
Rothes, The Earl of, 116
Royal Niger Company, 92
Russell, Bertrand, 34

S
Sackville, Lady, 90
Sackville-West, Vita, 1
  Broadcasts by, 42, 43, 46, 75,
  HM, first meeting with, 22, 47
  HM, letters to, vii, 2, 49
  HM, letters from, 49-62
  HM, obituary of, 136
  HM, memorial volume to, 136
  Relations with Dorothy Wellesley, 87
  Vita's children, 55, 89, 90
  Vita's death, 137
  Vita's poetry, 64, 57
St Anne's College, vii, 6
St Felix School, 4, 99
Secret Services, see under Matheson, Hilda
Shannon, Sheila, ix, 129, 135
Shaw, George Bernard, 44
Shelley, Percy Bysshe, 47
Siepmann, Charles, 70, 71, 79, 83, 84, 86
Simpson, Tess, 125
Sitwells, The, 67, 69, 128
Smuts, General, 91, 94
Smyth, Dame Ethel, 135
Snowden, Ethel, 27, 69, 70
Society of Home Students, ix, 6-9
Solzhenitsyn, Alexander, 99
Somerville, Mary, 59, 62, 71, 76, 77, 79, 80

Spectator, The 101, 128
Star, The, 135
Stobart, JC, 33, 44
Stoker, 3, 51
Sunday Express, 59
Sykes, Christopher, 17

T
Tennant, David, 36, 67
Times, The, 20, 28, 31, 35, 38, 42, 46, 101, 135
Trevelyan, Charles, 46
Turner, W J, 88, 116, 128
Tweedsmuir, Lady, 127

U
Ulysses, 72, 74
Ullman, Elisabeth, 130
Universities, 44, 45

V
Vamp, The, 8
Vaughan, Janet, 60
Veidt, Conrad, 123
Vinteuil, Mlle, 50

W
Walpole, Hugh, 47
Walsh, Kate, 56, 65
War, 1914-18, 9-13, 108
War, 1939-45, 108-136
Wasteland, The, 42
Waugh, Evelyn, 72
Webb, Sydney, 40
Week-End Review, 73, 81, 89, 95
Wellesley, Dorothy, 47, 54, 55, 77, 86–88, 109, 128, 136, 137
Wellesley, Lord Gerald, 87
Wellington, Lindsay, 133
Wells, HG, 8, 34, 46, 45, 63, 136
Werner Shaw, ix
West, Rebecca, 45
Westminster Gazette, 31
Whitley, John, 72, 73, 78
Whyte, Sir Frederick, 116
Wild, Pat, 8
Wilkinson, Ellen, 40
Women's Institutes, 39
Wood, Sir Kingsley, 36
Woolf, Leonard, 38, 88, 136
Woolf, Virginia, 1, 20, 43, 47, 48, 52, 53, 54, 55, 57, 59, 86, 126, 137

Y
Yeats, W B, 88, 109, 128
Young, Filson, 28, 36, 38, 44, 60, 64, 79